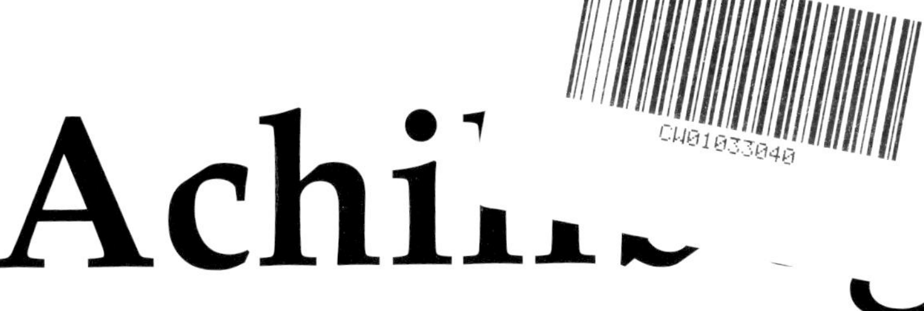

Achillbeg

The Life of an Island

by

Jonathan Beaumont

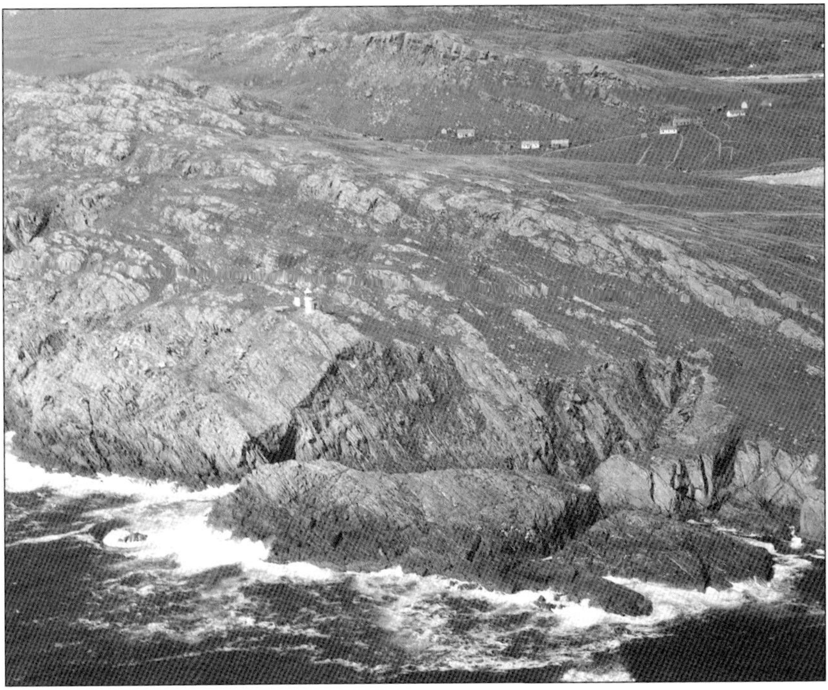

THE OAKWOOD PRESS

British Library Cataloguing in Publication Data
A Record for this book is available from the British Library
ISBN 0 85361 631 0

Typeset by Oakwood Graphics.
Repro by Ford Graphics, Ringwood, Hants.
Printed by Cambrian Printers, Aberystwyth, Dyfed.

Dedicated to the people of Achillbeg

A study of an abandoned Irish island carried out with the assistance of the Millennium Commission, through a Millennium Award made by the Community Foundation Northern Ireland.

Réamhrá

D'fhéadfaí Oileán an Acaill Beag a fheiceáil ó Cheann Iardheiscirt Corrán in Iarthar Chondae Mhaigheo nó ó Bhinn dheisceart an Acaill Mhóir taobh leis an Chloch Mhór. Oileán beag gaelach is ea an tAcaill Beag atá scartha ón bheirt acu le caolas fealltach farraige.

Níl an t-Acaill Beag níos mó ná seasca heachtair ina bhfuil dhá chnoc agus gleann eatarthu le trá gaineamhach álainn ar an taobh amháin. Saol eile ar fad atá ann.

Cé chomh álainn agus atá an t-Oileán chaith muintir na haíte saol crua ann. Níor athraigh daonra an Oileáin sa 19ú haois ach le teacht an 20ú haois d'imigh sé in íseal brí go dtígur tréigeadh an t-Oileán faoi dheireadh trí scór is cúig bliana ina dhiaidh sin.

Spreagann an talamh treígthe samhlaíocht an duine le bóithre ar a bhfuil féar ag fás agus claíocha teorann le feiceáil on Chloch Mhór. Is tithe samhraidh anois cuid de na botháin ar leo na hoileánaigh fadó ach seasann an chuid eile go cúin agus na cinn tuí tite isteach acu le blianta fada anuas gan gíog astu faoi spéir leathan Iarthair Mhaigheo.

Seo Sceál an Acaill Beag ó chian, cur síos ar an Oileán ar a fhásra ar a hainmithe, ar a chloch-eolaocht agus ar mhuintir na háite. Insítear dúinn faoi Phobal an Oileáin agus iad i mbarr a réime. Cuirtear ar fáil fosta stáidéar cruinn faoi bheatha ar an Oileán faoina chultur agus faoina logainmneacha - agus seo an chéad uair a fhoilsítear eolas faoina logainmneacha. Breactar síos titim daonra ó bhlianta tosaigh an 20ú haois go dtí lár na seascaidí le caibidil faoi caidé atá i ndán don Oileán ó d'imigh an Pobal buan faoi dheireadh.

Ní mór don té a bhfuil suim aige/aici in Eirinn, sna hoileáin agus i saol iargúlta bánaithe - an leabhar seo a cheannach.

Seo an darna leabhar de chuid an údair ar Sheanchas Aitiúl Mhaigheo. Foilsíodh *Rails to Achill* sa bhliain 2002. Scéal an Bhóthair Iarainn idir Cathair na Mart agus Acaill sna blianta 1895 go dti 1937 atá ann.

Síolraíonn an t-Udar ó Bhaile Atha Cliath agus Chill Dara ó dhdchais ach chaith sé an chuid is mó dá shaol i gContae an Dúin agus i gContae Aontroma ar an taobh eile den tír ar fad. O bhí siad óg ba ghnách leis an Chlann a teacht go Corrán agus go hAcaill acha'n bhliain i rith an tSamhraidh. Ba é an darna baile é Oileán Acaill, dá thuismitheoirí, dheirfiúracha, bhean chéile agus ar ndóigh dá chlann uilig.

Title page: Jagged coastline, shaped by the raw forces of nature. This picture was taken from the air just off the south-western tip of the island. The lighthouse is visible above the coastline, and the houses shelter in between the two hills which make up the island's bulk. The area above the lighthouse is Oileán an Sciorta. *Liam Lyons Photography*

Published by The Oakwood Press (Usk), P.O. Box 13, Usk, Mon., NP15 1YS.
E-mail: sales@oakwoodpress.co.uk
Website: www.oakwood-press.co.uk

Contents

View from the front window of the *Paorach's* house. From here, he and his successors could admire the beach, and distant Corraun. Periodically, the beach would burst into life as a turf boat pulled in and was unloaded. *Author*

Aerial view looking south, showing the mainland Corraun peninsula (*left*), Achill Island (*right*), and in the left distance Achillbeg Island and Clare Island (further out to sea). This view dates from the 1970s. Achillbeg shows as the two small hills at the southern end of Achill, separated by the narrow stretch of water at Belnaglea. It is clear from this photograph that Achillbeg would have been joined to Achill, or Corraun, at one time. In the bottom right-hand corner of the picture, the modern road bridge connecting the mainland with Achill may be seen. Achill Sound village is just on the island side of the bridge. The district of Saula is just out of the picture to the right of the bridge. It is from here that Achillbeg islanders brought their boatloads of turf, under the bridge, and along the narrow stretch of sea in the centre of the picture, all the way down to Achillbeg. The considerable physical effort involved in this may be guessed from a look at this view, though what it does not show is the extent to which the currents could be treacherous.

Simmons Aerofilms

Introduction

One of Ireland's most scenic roads skirts the southern side of the Corraun Peninsula in County Mayo, giving breathtaking views of Clew Bay and Clare Island. Travelling towards Darby's Point from the Mulrany direction, a view of the southern end of Achill Island will launch into view as you near the point. Just to the left of this, two low hills may be seen with a small secluded beach in between - at first glance it is another part of Achill Island to the uninitiated, but a closer look reveals that these two hills are separated from the rest of Achill by a narrow channel, the Blind Sound.

These two hills, with the narrow valley between them, make up Achillbeg Island, a small piece of Ireland some 60 hectares in area, and an individual little world in itself. The name Achillbeg comes from *Acaill Beag*, or 'Little Achill'.

Achill itself is Ireland's largest island. Successive years of famine, hard weather and economic underdevelopment have failed to bow the spirit of its inhabitants, who still number several thousand at the start of the 21st century. Since 1887 it has been connected to the mainland by a causeway and swing bridge across the Sound, doubtless contributing to its well being and helping prevent depopulation.

Alas, Achillbeg was not so fortunate. Before the ravages of the Great Famine, in the mid to late 1800s, the island boasted a population of almost 200, but by the early 1960s barely a sixth of that number remained and the school enrolment was down to single figures. Despite the recent introduction of electricity and a phone line, the end was in sight. With the Government of the day having little interest in helping remote communities sustain their traditional life, and better job opportunities available elsewhere, the remaining inhabitants decided to move out in 1965.

Much of the land is still owned by the families of those who left, and many surviving islanders live on Achill within sight of their old island home, but Achillbeg is now host to grazing sheep and birds, and is a haven of peaceful solitude. In recent years, several of the old cottages have been renovated as holiday homes, and the electricity link remains to service both these and the automated lighthouse. But the rest stand silently, abandoned under the wide western Mayo sky.

Jonathan Beaumont

By the same author
Rails to Achill : A West of Ireland Branch Line (Oakwood Press, 2002).

Front cover: Aerial view of Achillbeg, taken from the west side of the island overlooking the Iron Age remains at Dún Chill Mhór. The circular fort enclosure can be clearly seen. Some of the island's cultivated area may be seen at the top of the picture - this area was called Gort Breac - the 'speckled field'. *Mick Gibbons*

Rear cover: A view looking down from Creig an Lomáin towards An Baile Amuigh (or Baileamuigh), the central village. This view dates from the 1970s, a few years after abandonment. The small stony beach on the island's west side can be seen on the right. *Nick Pollard*

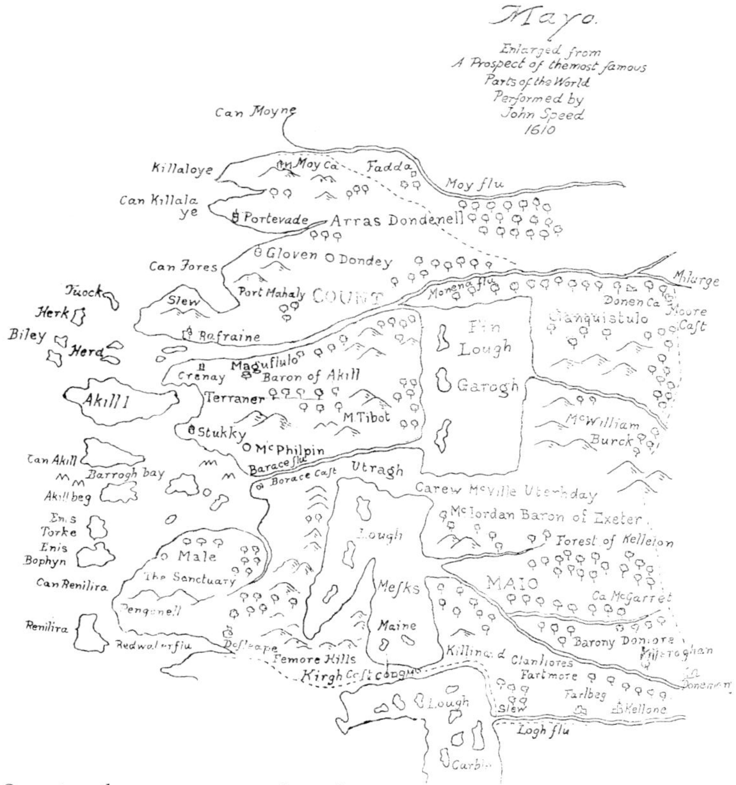

Seventeenth century map maker John Speed prepared two maps of the area in 1610 and 1620. In this one (1610) his map is said to show 'A Prospect of the most famous Parts of the World'. He appears to have shown Achill itself in two parts; 'Akill beg' is to the south. This map was reproduced in John O'Donovan's *Letters containing Information relative to the Antiquities of the County of Mayo* in 1838.
Author's Collection

From Petty's Map of Mayo, 1683. Achillbeg is here described as 'Kill-danat', indicating some early relationship with Kildownet Castle on nearby Achill. It will be noted that Achill Island and the neighbouring mainland district of Corraun are described as the 'Islands of Achill'. Ballycroy is also incorrectly placed. The Corraun district was denoted in this way on several maps of this period - it is likely that one map maker would refer to the work of others who had previously covered the area.
Author's Collection

Chapter One

The Island and Surrounds

Achillbeg lies off the southern tip of Achill Island, and to the south-west of the (mainland) Corraun peninsula in Co. Mayo. Achill Island is Ireland's largest island, and one of its most westerly. The origin of the name of Achill is uncertain, due in part to the fact that early maps and records of the area show the name spelt in a variety of different ways, thus making an accurate translation difficult. Until the 19th century, eagles were common throughout this part of Ireland, and the Latin name of the white tailed sea eagle (*Aquila albicilla*) may give a clue to the origin of the name. Certainly, a prevailing view at one time was that the name 'Achill' had its origins in one or other of the various recorded spellings of Irish names for the bird. Irish place names will often include '. . . mór' or '. . . beg'; 'mór' means great, big or large, while 'beg/beag' means small. Thus, Achillbeg is 'Little Achill'.

The surrounding mainland area is a mixture of farmland, blanket bog and mountain. In common with other areas of the West of Ireland the weather is temperate, due to the maritime surrounds, leading to an abundance of plants which may seem out of place to the visitor due to their almost tropical character - ferns, fuchsia, rhododendron and orchids may be found, as severe frosts are rare. In addition, plants of this nature thrive due to the acidic nature of the ground. However, high and constant wind is another feature of the area, so much so that even these plants grow only in sheltered locations, and for the same reason there is an almost complete absence of naturally growing trees. Achillbeg itself has no native trees at all, though two or three small ones were planted in recent times in the shelter of a wall in Garraí na Loinge. Had the wall not been there, even these could never have grown. The scenery is wild and beautiful, but much of the land is of poor quality for farming. For many years, sheep have been the main focus of the farming industry, though local people have become very adept at draining and cultivating what small patches of good farmland they can gain crops from, and as in many coastal areas, fishing is a feature of the local economy.

There are a number of offshore islands in the area. Some, like Achillbeg, are now abandoned, others were never inhabited, but several are still inhabited by small but thriving communities. Among this latter group are Inishturk, Inishbofin and Clare Island. All of these are to the south of Achillbeg. Nearby Inishark was abandoned in 1948, while the Inishkea islands north of Achill island finally lost their population in 1934 following a disastrous drowning tragedy a few years earlier. Just to the north-east of Achill, Inishbiggle Island is also still inhabited - separated from Achill to its west, and the mainland to its east, by narrow sea channels.

Strong sea currents, exposed rocky coastline and the wind combine to outwit all but the most strong, experienced and skilful boatman - though many who may be described thus have also fallen victim to the Atlantic, as it pounds the western coastline. To the north and south of Achillbeg, tales of misfortune

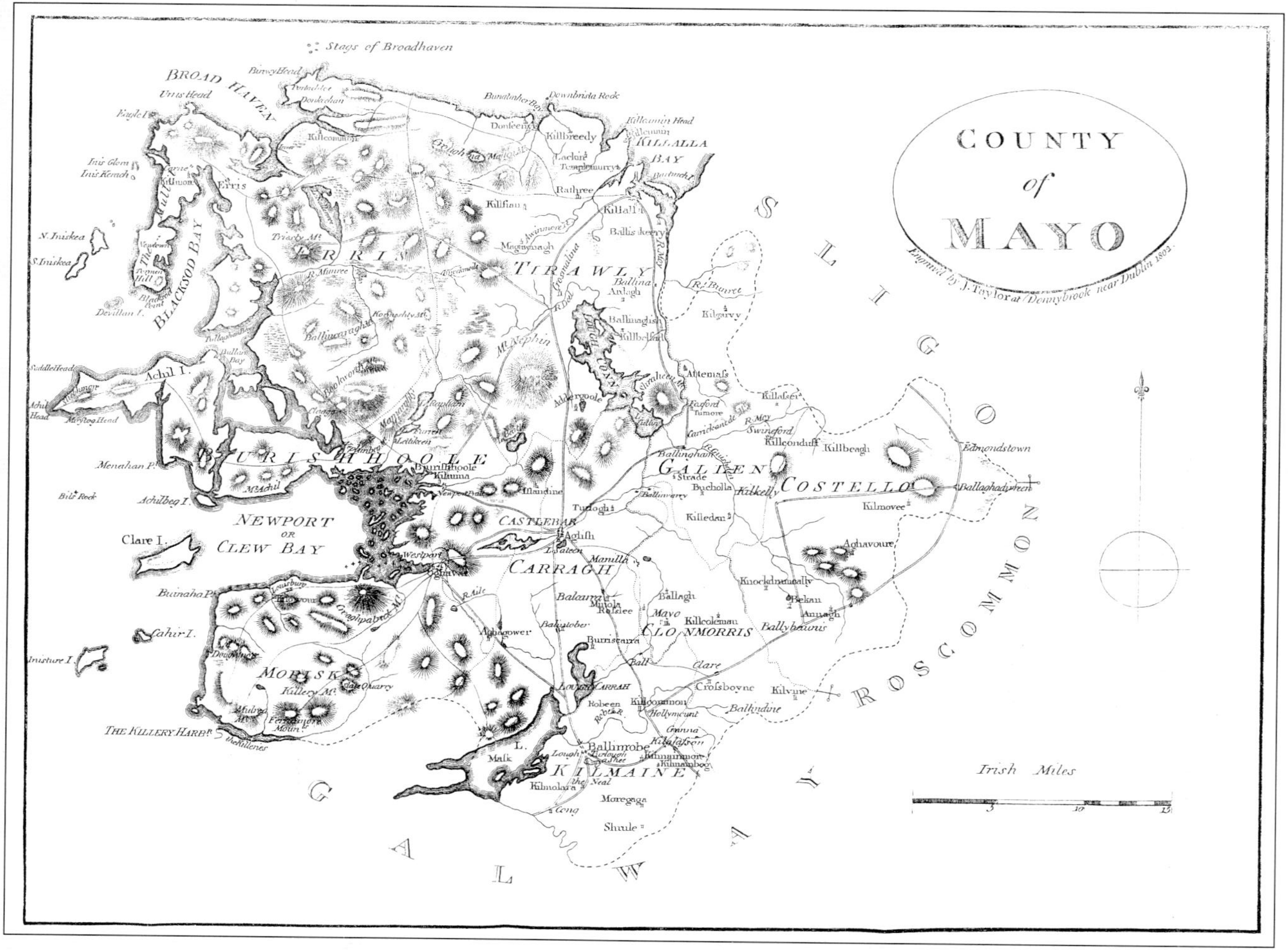

COUNTY
of
MAYO

Engraved by J. Taylor at Donnybrook near Dublin 1802.

Irish Miles

From the *Statistical Survey of the County of Mayo*, by James McParlan, MD, 1802. Achillbeg Island is shown here, and although its shape is inaccurate, the overall quality of the cartographic standard is much more accurate than previously seen.

Author's Collection

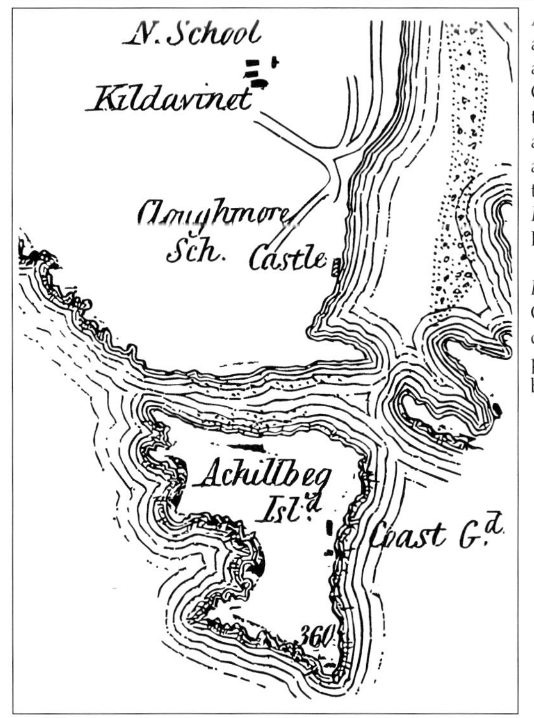

Above: One of the earlier maps showing the area with some degree of geographical accuracy (apart from one major error - the Corraun peninsula is shown as an island; together with Achill, the two seem to labelled as the Achill Islands). Achillbeg is named here as Kildanat Island, and Clare as Clara. This is taken from *An Account of Ireland Statistical and Political*, published by Edward Wakefield in London, 1812. *Author's Collection*

Left: From a map produced for the Irish Church Missions, July 1852. Achillbeg is shown complete with Coast Guard presence. It is probable that this consisted of a building or buildings rented from islanders at this stage. *Michael Patten*

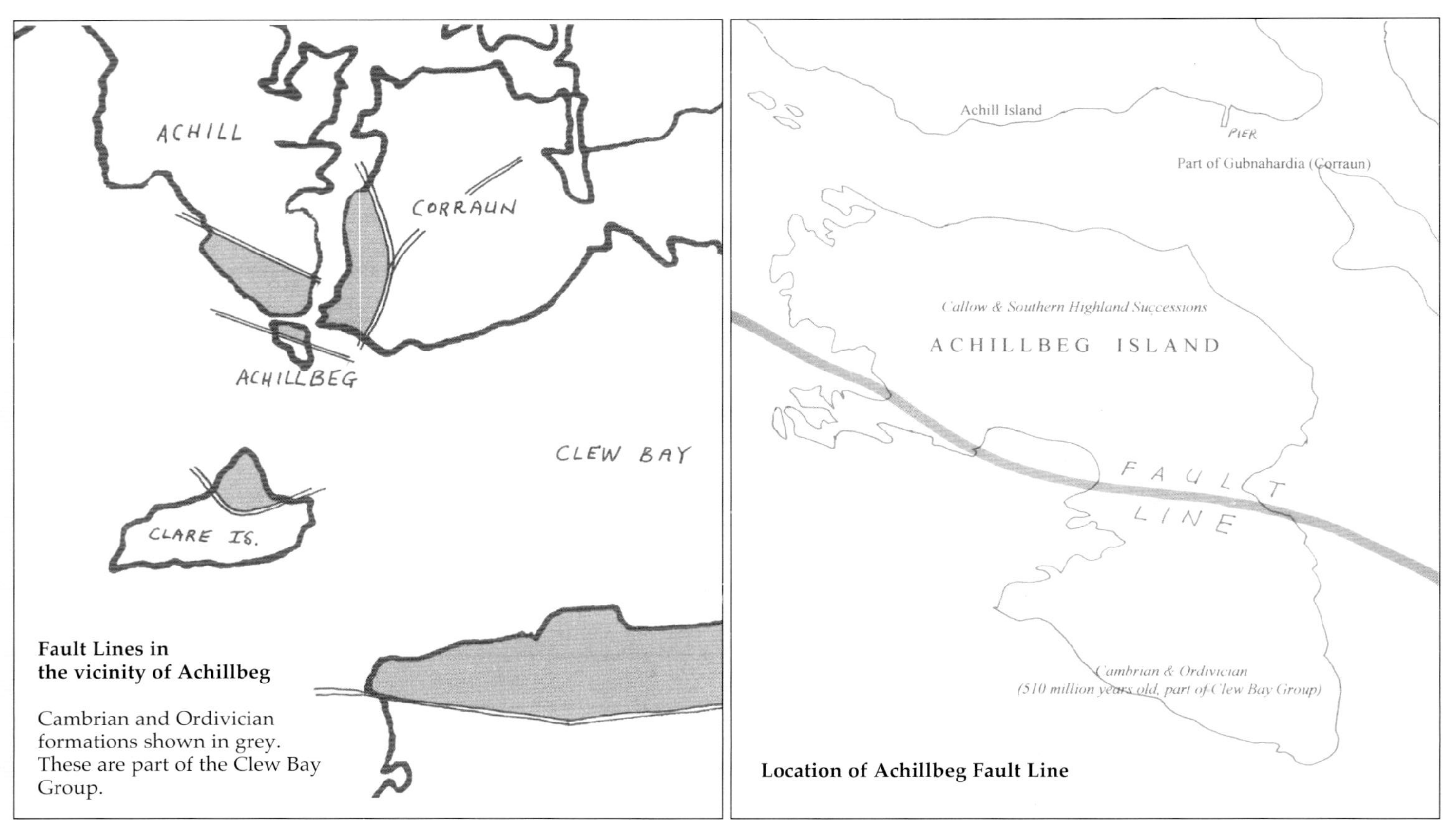

Fault Lines in the vicinity of Achillbeg

Cambrian and Ordivician formations shown in grey. These are part of the Clew Bay Group.

Location of Achillbeg Fault Line

abound - on the day Inishark was abandoned by its last inhabitants in 1948, a reporter asked an elderly man if he would carry fond memories of his island home, and if he would miss it. 'Not at all', came the answer, 'for that stretch of sea (between the island and Inishbofin) claimed my son . . .' Between Achill and Inishbiggle, vicious currents have caused many a death over the years, and off Achillbeg itself similar incidents have occurred. An account published in 1906* describes the sea channel running from Achillbeg, between Achill and Corraun, to the Bull's Mouth on the north side of Achill, thus:

> The turbulence of the tide, that twice daily rushes through this narrow channel, is easily understood, for the two large bays of Blacksod and Clew have to balance their waters by means of it. In fact, it is a miniature Straits of Dover, where the North Sea and the Atlantic similarly daily strike a water-balance. The Admiralty chart shows that the depth varies from six fathoms to one-quarter of a fathom, and the smaller numbers and fractions predominate, indicating that the straits are by no means easy to navigate. Skill, and a thorough knowledge of the tides, are required to navigate the straits; but fishing-boats and hookers naturally prefer the passage of the Sound, which in a favourable wind may mean an hour to an entire day spent in rounding Achill Head. The two entrances are, in short, most dangerous, and the list of deaths from small boats and large sailing vessels, which have attempted the passage and foundered, would be a long one. On the other hand, Bull's Mouth and the quiet waters within have saved many a vessel from shipwreck in a strong westerly gale. There are two sides to every picture.

Achillbeg covers approximately 326 acres in area, and consists of two low hills, the higher of which is some 120 metres above sea level. In the Ordnance Survey's Field Name books of 1838, it was stated that only some 80 acres were arable. According to islanders, there were about 200 acres of commonage for grazing animals. The island consists of schist, with sandstone to be found on the southern hill. This is significant. While at first glance the two hills that make up the bulk of the island are broadly similar, they have different geological characteristics, as a fault line runs across the narrow middle of the island.

Islanders have long known of the different characteristics of the north and south of the island. The local tradition that the north hill is 'part of Mayo' and the south hill 'part of Connemara' is therefore not without substance. Scattered along the north shore facing Achill traces of pyrites ('fool's gold') have been found, while slate is to be found in the south of the island - indeed, small amounts of slate were quarried just above the school, along the fault line.

Underlying the northern hill are rocks that are a continuation of the southernmost part of Achill Island. This forms part of the South Carrowgarve Formation, the southern boundary of which is the Achillbeg Fault which runs right across the middle of the island from east to west, dipping north at 60 degrees.

South of the fault line, the southern hill of the island is known as the South Achillbeg Formation, part of the Clew Bay Complex, and composed of somewhat younger rocks.

In common with Bills Rock to the west of Achillbeg, and south of Achill, the rocks in the area are mostly conglomerates, greywackes and slates (deformed mudstone). Some slates are of a dark colour, being rich in carbon, and have

* *Connemara and the Neighbouring Spots of Beauty and Interest* (J. Harris Stone, London, 1906).

The small rocky islet of Dunnaglass, between Achillbeg and Achill, is thought to be the remains of a land connection between the two which was severed by the relentless battering of the Atlantic several thousand years ago. The remains of an Iron Age fortification on the rocks is thought to be related to the Iron Age remains on Achillbeg. *Author*

Achillbeg as seen from the southern tip of Achill. The two hills of the smaller island are clearly seen. The rocks in the sea between the two islands are the islet of Dunnaglass. The old field patterns of Achillbeg's sheltered north side are still clear. The narrow rock on the extreme right, just off the western extremity of Achillbeg is Oileán na nÉan, the 'island of the birds'. Many seabirds may be seen in this area. *Author*

Looking towards Clare Island from across Uaich a Dún, the 'cove of the fort'. In front is the area where the Iron Age settlement of Dún Chill Mhór stood, and where two giants are reputed to be buried. The roughly triangular area in the right foreground is the Dún, and beyond it is the Daingean. On the extreme right is a small rocky islet called Oileán na nÉan, the 'island of the birds'. The area on the left is Cill Mhór, the 'big church', giving a clue to the location of the church which is believed to have stood here in medieval times. Clare Island's 'big mountain' (Cnoc Mór) is visible in the distance on a good day such as this. In poor weather, Clare Island would not be visible at all. *Author*

Cove, Garrí an Dúna. *Author*

The north-western extremity of the island, An Rioball (the 'rubble'), looking back towards Leárgan. *Author*

One of a small number of beaches to be found at the bottom of sheltered coves in the ragged western coastline. This one is beyond Garraí an Dúna. *Author*

associated quartzites. These rocks were probably deposited on an unstable undersea slope, subsequently sliding into a trench after disturbances by earthquakes.

The fault line separates the Carrowgarve Formation (Dalriadan) from a series of lower grade pelitic schists and pebbly greywackes which constitute the Achillbeg formation. The Achillbeg Fault is an extension of the Ox Mountains shear zone which extends under Clew Bay into the North Ox Mountains fault, and follows a sub-surface magnetic line which stretches via Clew Bay and Fair Head into Scotland. It is the southern boundary of the Dalriadan rocks of North Mayo.

The two hills are connected in the middle by a narrow valley named Baileamuigh. On the eastern side of the valley is a small sandy beach, onto which boats were drawn up in the past. This beach is called 'Trá Bó Deirge' - the 'Strand of the Red Cow'. The arable land is mostly on the northern side opposite Achill, and in the central valley, Baileamuigh. That being the case, it comes as no surprise to find that little variety exists in naturally occurring flora and fauna compared with mainland districts or the neighbouring larger island. Plant wise, heather is ever present, with small heathland plants to be found as on Achill. However, Achillbeg had almost no turf*, and fuel had to be taken into the island from the mainland or Achill. Settlement in recent centuries was therefore concentrated in the areas mentioned above where not only was land better, but so was the level of shelter. Having stated that, earlier settlement in medieval times was to be found in the very area mentioned by Lewis as being wild and 'unapproachable' in the form of the Iron Age promontory fort at Dún Chill Mhór. Therein lies the clue: while in later times agricultural usefulness was of paramount importance, in earlier times fortification was more so. The remaining evidence of these early settlements will be dealt with in a later chapter.

Animal life on the island was also limited to a lesser number of species than in neighbouring areas. Former residents had no recollection of seeing rabbits or mice†, though hares and foxes were plentiful - two residents with memories as far back as the 1920s recall foxes stealing chickens regularly. Rats were not often seen - though one resident stated that in his lifetime on the island (of some 50 years) rats came over twice, but were caught by the islanders in traps and did not manage to form a population - to the great relief of the islanders, of course! Badgers were rare visitors, though a colony of them became established a few years before the island was abandoned, giving substance to the old folk tale that when badgers arrived, people would go. Stoats and hedgehogs were also seen very occasionally.

Today, sheep owned by former islanders graze freely, tended by their owners who travel in to Achillbeg by day for the purpose when necessary. When inhabited, the island had its complement of sheep dogs, as most households owned a few sheep as well as cattle and pigs. A local superstition at one time claimed that it was bad luck to see a hare (or, for that matter, a red haired girl),

* In recent times no turf was available, but at one time a small amount of very poor turf was to be found on the north-west side of the island.

† However, it seems mice had arrived by the 1950s if not before - (one resident remembered them running up her leg as she tossed hay at that time!).

Rock surface on Achillbeg showing some of the small rock-based plants which thrive in the area. *Author*

Uaich Dhilisc Mhilis (the 'cove of the sweet dilsk'). Dilsk, or dulse, is an edible seaweed. The cove on the other side of the headland is Tonn Scardeoige. *Author*

The sun tries to sneak a glimpse of Achillbeg through dark winter clouds, January 2004.
Author

Approaching Athoire from Dún Chill Mhór. The island's southern hill, Oileán an Sciorta, is clearly seen here. It is connected to the hill the photographer is on by the narrow strip of land behind the beach in the valley. On the left, the high ground is Ardán Leathan, the 'broad height'. The rock to the left is Creigh na Cille, the 'rock of the church', near the Mass Rock. *Author*

Evening sun over the sea at one of the coves west of Uaich na Sionnach. Here, older island children and teenagers used to gather on summer evenings, according to a former esident who remembered sitting here with her friends in the late 1920s. Clare Island looms in the distance. Tonight at least the sea is calm. *Author*

Spectacular rock outcrop, Uaich Bhuí. *Author*

Adjacent to the area known as Duirling (flat stony beach area) is the narrow cove, Uaich Dhoirlinge, the 'cove of the flat stony beach'. In this photograph the tide is out, but it will soon fill up again. *Author*

The 'Tail' of Achillbeg, looking across from Achill, with the islet of Dunnaglass in between. The area is known as Beal na Glaise - the 'mouth of the plain'. *Author*

The severe coastal erosion continues . . . This area, known as 'the gravel', is beyond Uaich na Sionnach. The southern hill, Oileán na Sciorta, looks like a separate island from here, as the land connection is not visible at this point. *Author*

when leaving in a boat to go out fishing - if you did see either, you would catch no fish . . . In recent years, and certainly since the permanent population left, foxes are no longer to be seen. Golden Eagles were to be seen on adjacent parts of Achill and Corraun until the turn of the 20th century.

The island's surrounding sea contains pollack, wrasse, lobsters and crabs in areas up to 22 metres deep. Various varieties of flat fish and eels are also to be found - one former resident spoke of seeing a neighbour's son bringing an eel home from the strand - it was the biggest he had ever seen, so long that as the boy carried it, its head was trailing along the ground behind him. Just off the strand, squid and dogfish have also been caught.

There is evidence to suggest that Achillbeg was not always an island. Between the island and Corraun, underwater sandbanks suggest that the sea broke through a land barrier in prehistoric times. To the north of Achillbeg there is a small cluster of rocks with the remains of a fortified settlement on them - this is believed to be related to, or part of, Dún Chill Mhór, the ancient fort which has all the appearance of having been built to guard a narrow strip of land which probably connected Achill with Achillbeg. Thousands of years of attack by the Atlantic would have severed this connection. This division of Achillbeg from its neighbouring land masses would appear to have occurred since the first people came to the area, as local place names also give a clue to a common origin of mainland with island. Old maps refer to Achillbeg as 'Kildownet' or 'Kil-da-mat' island. The name 'Kildownet' is nowadays, and for some time has been, given to a nearby townland on Achill, while the townland name of Gubnahardia is shared on mainland Corraun and Achill Island sides of the water.

A view of the narrow piece of land still connecting the 'Tail' with Garraí an Dúna. Erosion is taking place even within the comparatively sheltered small cove on the right. There is a drop of some two metres to the sand and rocks on the left. This stony beach is known as Cladach an Rioball, the shore area of the 'Tail'. *Author*

The wind skims across the water's surface on an autumn day in 2002. Achillbeg, seen here from Cloghmore, basks silently beyond. *Author*

Centuries of relentless battering by the Altantic Ocean have created this jagged rocky coastline near Carraig a Choiscéim, which was known as a good place to fish. The headland beyond is Gob Leice Buí - the 'point of the yellow flat stone'. *Author*

Chapter Two

Early History and Settlement

The first inhabitants of Achill Island and neighbouring Corraun came to the area between 5,000 and 7,000 years ago. They hunted and fished in the dense forests which covered the area at the time. By some 5,000 years ago, farming people had arrived - it is possible that Achillbeg may have been home to some of them, as it was almost certainly still attached to Achill or Corraun by land. Around 2000 BC, Iron Age settlers had brought tools like knives and spears. By 1000 BC, Achillbeg was certainly inhabited, as it is from around this era that the spectacular promontory fort at Dún Chill Mhór may be dated. In the Journal of the Royal Society of Antiquaries of Ireland, a Mr T.J. Westropp reported in 1914 that this fort was one of a type found in Cornwall and Brittany, and one of the most complex of its kind. In the same journal some 15 years earlier, it was suggested that the fort may have contained a tower at one time, as local folklore at the time stated that in recent times the sea had reclaimed a section of the coastline where this had been situated. Subsequent examination has suggested it dates from between 1000 BC and 400 AD. It is believed to have been abandoned by the 12th century. Recent archaeological expeditions to the island suggest Bronze Age remains of a field system above the school, and a round house near the northern village.

Dún Chill Mhór is located on the west side of the island, some quarter of a mile from Cill Mhór. It consists of a fragmented headland containing the remains of a ring fort which stretches across the width of the headland. To the west of this the headland divides in two, the northern part (The Daingean) being now cut off from the rest of the island by a narrow sea channel. The southern part (the Dún) was protected from the rest by a wall, the site of which may be seen, and in the middle of this area the remains of what may have been a tower or guard-room was recorded by T.J. Westropp. It is worth looking at Westropp's description of this site, which he described as 'the most complex of the Irish Promontory Forts, save Doon-Eask fort near Dingle . . .', this may be read in full in *Appendix One*.

There are the remains of two other small fortified enclosures on Achillbeg. One is Dungurrough (Dún na gCurrach) - some short distance north of Dún Chill Mhór, and with a good strategic view of the southern tip of Achill Island. The other is Dún Beag. Between Achillbeg and Achill in the same area is Dún na Glaise, a small rocky islet, on top of which are the remains of what may have been a related fortification at a time when Achillbeg was joined to Achill here. At low tide it is possible to walk across the rocky sea bed from Cloughmore (Achill) to Dún na Glaise.

From about the 5th century AD, Christianity came to the general area. From these earliest times, there is evidence of the Christian message finding its way to Achillbeg. The early name of the island, Kil-da-mat, or Kildavnet, may possibly refer to a 7th century saint named Davnet, though the translation is somewhat loose. The place was, and is, also known as Kildownet. However,

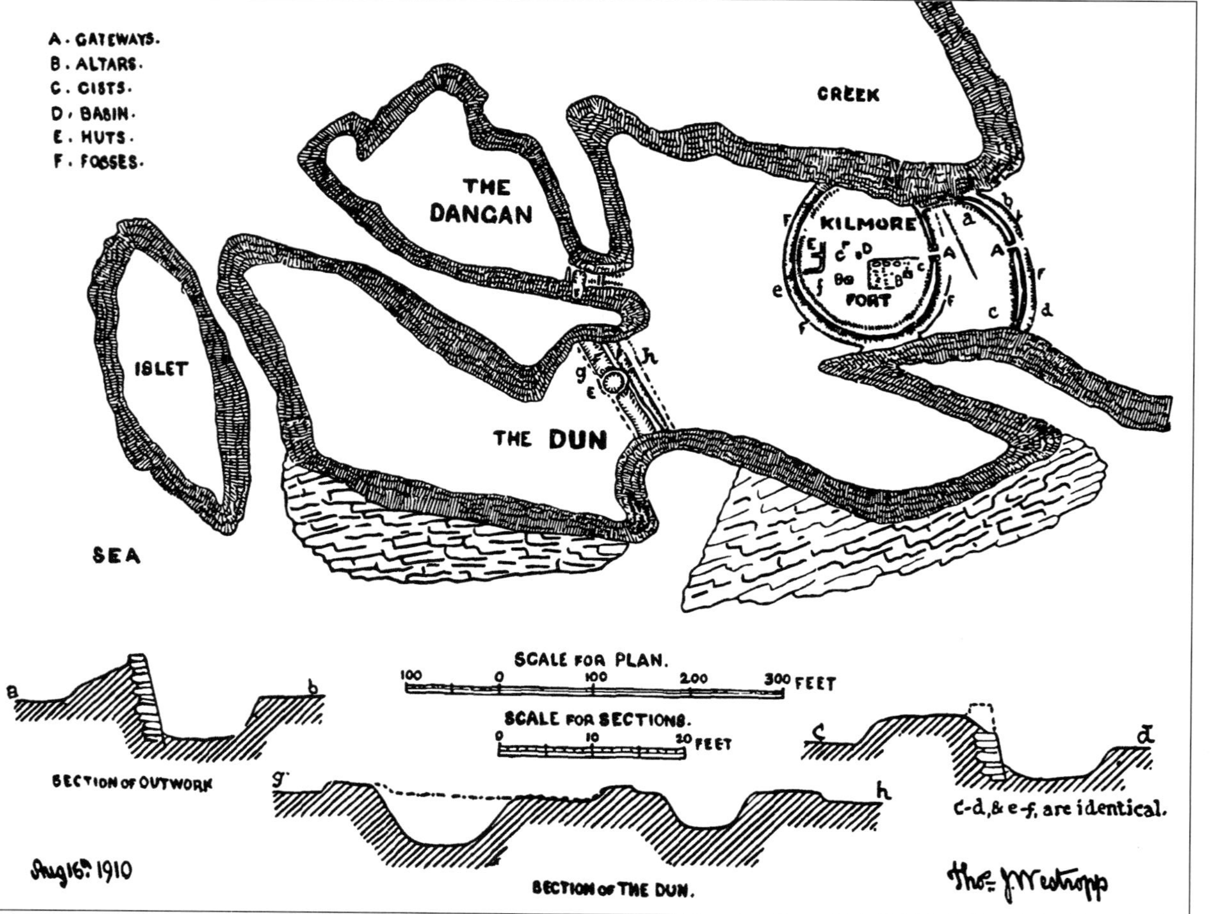

Thomas J. Westropp's map of the Iron Age fortifications at Dún Chill Mhór.

Iron Age fort, Dún Chill Mhór. In the foreground a deep trench below the wall has become filled with stones and overgrowth over the years. The wall is still some two metres high in places. The 'Giant's grave' is on the far right. The coastal erosion so prevalent on this side of the island is very evident at the bottom of the picture, despite this place being inside a cove. *Author*

Ramparts, Dún Chill Mhór. The difference in height between the author's plastic bag in the bottom of the trench, and camera bag on top of the ridge, is about 2.5 metres. Incidentally, Achillbeg is entirely litter free, a point to be borne in mind by casual visitors. This rampart acted as a line of defence on the eastern side of the fort - see diagram opposite. *Author*

Coastal erosion near the Tail. The wall is part of the remains of the Iron Age fortifications on the western end of the island. *Author*

In penal times, the island had its own Mass Rock, Creig An Aifrinn. This is in the distance above the Iron Age remains of Dún Chill Mhór on the left. *Author*

Iron Age remains at Dún Beag, the 'small fort'. Achill Island is on the left in the distance.
Author

Looking towards Cúl an Garraí, the back of the garden' or 'last garden'. In the foreground was a patch of land known as 'Bernaglasha' where hay was made. The circular structure in the foreground appears to be Iron Age remains related to Dún Beag. Achill Island's southernmost district, Carrow garve, is across the short width of sea to the right. *Author*

sounder evidence exists in the form of an old stone cross within the promontory fort at Dún Chill Mhór. According to a folk tradition there may have been a wooden-built church near here at one time. This is believed to have existed from about the 6th to the 10th centuries. The remains of a *leacht* (stone altar), a *bullaun* (stone basin) and a *cillín* complete the picture of an area used for early worship. A *cillín* was a graveyard for children who died before being baptised, and examples are to be found in many parts of Ireland. Since an unbaptised child could not be buried on consecrated ground, *cillíní* were outside normal church graveyards. Small rocks and boulders were used to denote individual graves, without other markings. By the end of the 19th century, the Church succeeded in gradually outlawing this practice throughout Ireland. Achillbeg also had a holy well; this was situated between Dún Chill Mhór and Baileamuigh and was the subject of many local beliefs until recent times - former residents still speak of its characteristics, as will be seen later.

Achillbeg, and Achill, were part of the ancient territory called Umhall, whose inhabitants were supposedly descended from a nephew of Niall, the King of Ireland at the time St Patrick was kidnapped in the 5th century AD. Among the families associated with Umhall was the famous O'Malley clan - from which came Gráinne Ní Mháille, or Grace O'Malley, the 16th century Pirate Queen. Gráinne at one time exercised great power in the West of Ireland, and Achillbeg was within her sphere of influence. On Achill Island, one of her castles still stands at Kildownet, not far from Achillbeg.

In 1235 the Anglo-Normans arrived and plundered the area, but nothing specific to Achillbeg is recorded in relevant historical records save that which relates to the area as a whole - Achill, Corraun, and Mayo in general. At the start of the 17th century the Tudors conquered much of Ireland, and local chieftains had to swear allegiance to the British Crown. Locally, life would have continued as normal. Farming was practised according to the old methods in the area, known as 'booleying'. This system involved common ownership of land*, and the practice of moving animals seasonally to better pastures. In summer, the cattle were taken up to mountain pasture generally accompanied by teenage herdsmen who remained with them until the onset of bad weather in the winter, whereupon they came back down to the main village. In some cases a 'booley village' would be built for varying periods of years. This would be a permanent or semi-permanent settlement inhabited in the summer seasons only. Achill Island contains the remains of one such in the form of the remains of small oval shaped houses of rough stones, in the valley high above Keem Bay. At the other end of the scale, the practice of booleying might only last a season or two in the same place, or might simply involve following the herds up a mountain wherever they chose to go, with those looking after them setting up simple temporary shelters from the elements. Achillbeg itself was too small to sustain a 'booley' village as well as the general settlement of houses in the island centre, though the islanders traditionally brought their animals over to Bolingleanna (on neighbouring Corraun) in summer months for this purpose.

* Known as 'commonage' to this day. In Achillbeg, the number of collective owners of the 'commonage' there was recorded as 19 in the 1901 census, 21 in the 1911 census, and 22 were referred to in files relating to the construction of the lighthouse in the early 1960s. In many areas of Ireland, including the uninhabited Achillbeg of today, and neighbouring Achill and Corraun, there is still a considerable amount of land which is owned in commonage.

Once people became more mobile, Achillbeg islanders continued to move locations seasonally - but not only to local hilltops; they emigrated to England, Scotland or elsewhere in Ireland for agricultural work in spring, returning home in autumn.

By 1636, many of the old Gaelic landlords who had their land confiscated by the British had received them back as grants. The Earl of Ormond came into possession of Achill and Achillbeg, which was now situated in the Barony of Burrishoole, which extended onto the mainland as far as Newport. A descendant of the powerful O'Donnell clan of Ulster came to the area in the early 1700s and eventually converted to the Protestant faith, later buying a tract of Burrishoole which included Achillbeg. A century later, Neal O'Donnell was the landlord, collecting rent from the inhabitants of the area, and his son Sir Richard O'Donnell inherited Achillbeg amongst the rest of this property in 1827. In 1852, he sold it to the Achill Mission Society, who bought it with the assistance of donations from others - one William Pike being one of these. Pike became the landlord for Achillbeg and southern Achill. Pike lived on Achill, just outside Achill Sound.

County Mayo as a whole was one of the poorer counties in Ireland for many years. In the mid-19th century, *An Gorta Mór* (the Great Famine) decimated the population of the area, and the effects of this were worsened by the political circumstances of the day. Achill, and Achillbeg, suffered along with much of the rest of Ireland, though somewhat later. While the worst effects of the famine and the attendant deprivation, disease and depopulation were felt in the 1840s and 1850s elsewhere, the potato crop was worst affected in this area some 10 to 30 years later.

This, in fact, illustrates the nature of the famine - it was not a single event, brought on by one specific circumstance; there were successive failures and part-failures of crops, over a period of several decades. In some years a small area of Ireland would be affected, with minimal hardship due to the fact that food could easily be brought in from other areas, but in other years, perhaps for several successive years (as in 1847-1850), much of the country was severely affected and starvation followed.

During and following the famine, mass emigration took place from the area, again as in other parts of Ireland. Emigrant ships left Westport, Sligo and Galway taking local people to far shores in search of work, hope and a new life. Mayo people arrived on the shores of Britain, New Zealand, Australia, Canada and the United States and their families became established there. Relatives at home would join them, and many families in Ireland became very dependent upon 'money from America' - funds sent home by the former sons and daughters who had left Ireland. With continuing economic depression well into the 20th century, this system was commonplace for a century or more after the famine had first hit hard - an indication of the seriousness of it.

The effect of the Great Famine on rural populations in Ireland, on Irish social history and national consciousness cannot be understated. Between 1841 and 1851, out of a total Irish population of 8.1 million, one million souls died of starvation and related diseases, in their homes, in their fields and even in the streets of towns. Almost two million more emigrated, mostly to Britain and the

United States, and contemporary reports describe those arriving in Boston or New York as being 'more dead than alive'. Many hundreds of thousands more suffered from malnutrition and serious illnesses associated with malnourishment and poverty - many of those dying as a result. With the eastern side of Ireland having better farmland, and being closer to the cities of Belfast and Dublin where some relief was to be had, it was the west and south-west that suffered most.

Despite this, Achillbeg does not appear to have been directly affected by the potato blight, therefore a full description of it lies outside the scope of this book. There are a number of reasons for this - apart from the fact that disease cannot cross water as efficiently as it crosses land, the islanders (of necessity) tended to be less reliant on the potato crop alone in comparison to the mainland population. The blight may not have taken hold, but the attendant economic deprivation did. In the 60 years after 1841, the island's population declined by 42 per cent, from 178 to 104. While the islanders had carefully cultivated what little arable land they had, and to a very high standard, they also fished and kept cattle. At the height of its populated era, every available strip of land in the central valley was used for potato crops, and traces of lazy bed ridges are still apparent today above and around the beach and on the sheltered eastern and northern sides of the island, facing the Blind Sound. Grains and cereals were also grown for both human and animal consumption. In common with the people of Achill and Corraun, another aspect to the situation was that due to severe poverty in the region as a whole, there was widespread seasonal emigration (mostly to Britain). Young boys and girls would accompany older siblings, relatives or parents to work in the potato fields of Scotland or fruit farms elsewhere. Generally, young people made their first trip aged 13 or 14, but on occasion children as young as 9 travelled as well. The wages and the working conditions were poor, the hours long, but the money earned was a lifeline to the families of those who went.

Other islands off the west coast suffered from the Famine to a greater extent though. Inishark and Inishbofin, to the south, are mentioned in a British Government report in 1886 in connection with plans being made to send a supply of seed potatoes there, as the harvests were still failing sporadically. In southern districts of Achill, the same report described a Government Inspector's visit to Dooega, where he found a population of some 600 people who were almost all existing on bags of meal supplied as wages for public works. They were unable to sell their cattle as they could not feed them to a standard that would be acceptable to a buyer. The one shopkeeper in the village had no supplies to give the villagers, as having handed out everything he had on credit he had no money to buy further supplies. Despite this, not one person asked for money or handouts - all they wanted was a pier built for them so they could fish, and employment schemes set up. Elsewhere along the coast, the Royal Irish Constabulary raised funds which were used in providing a seed potato supply to Clare Island, Inishturk, and the Aran Islands.

Throughout Ireland, emigrants often left with little money, little more than the clothes they stood up in, and a total lack of knowledge of the outside world. A contemporary report describes a teenage youth who was found sitting by a roadside in Connemara, physically weak, and with two pennies, a little food, and nothing else. He was spotted by a well-to-do traveller, who asked him where he was going. He answered in Irish, having no English whatsoever. He said he had been walking for days to catch a boat to America. He was completely lost, cold and frightened. The anonymous traveller picked him up and took him to Westport, paid for a passage for him, and fed him in his hotel. The youth had never encountered roast meat or hot water before, and according to his rescuer's diary, 'ate enough to fill a horse'.

A new influence on island affairs appeared from the 1830s in the form of The Achill Mission Society. This was a unique experiment in what some would call Christian evangelism, and others would call extremist Protestant proselytising. From the outset, the 'Mission' and its colourful leader, Revd Edward Nangle, was controversial. Nangle came to Achill in 1831 from Co. Meath, and established a colony at Dugort aimed at converting what he saw as a primitive and superstitious people to Protestantism. He acquired land at Dugort and built a church, a school, printing press and other facilities. He did much work in improving agricultural efficiency and circulated a newspaper partly to publicise what he had done, and partly to circulate to suitably affluent supporters elsewhere in order to raise funds. Nangle built St Thomas' Church of Ireland in Dugort, where the Mission was based.

Nangle's conviction that he had been sent to Achill to convert the people to Protestantism was naturally destined to bring him into conflict with the local population. While the full story of this belongs elsewhere, it is worth recording that no instances of any sectarian tension are known to have taken place on Achillbeg. Although the island never had any locally-based Protestant population, the Coastguard staff were recorded as being almost entirely Protestant. Nonetheless, in 1854 the landlord, William Pike, wrote to Achillbeg and South Achill residents warning them that he would have them evicted if they were guilty of 'persecuting or annoying' people who had converted to the Protestant faith on account of Nangle's influence.

To be fair to Nangle, Achill and Achillbeg were indeed in need of help. In 1831, famine had stalked the land thereabouts, and Achillbeg was as poor as its neighbouring areas even though the crop did not fail directly there. During famine times in the 19th century, offshore islands were likely to escape the blight which caused the potato crop to fail, however the accompanying economic hardship affected them just as much. Extreme poverty was the norm as islanders struggled to pay rent to their landlords, often with little idea of where the money was to come from. Despite this, the people retained their dignity and natural hospitality to outsiders. When Nangle first came into the area to distribute grain to people on the verge of starvation, he visited Achillbeg one day. He was offered accommodation for the night by an islander, in whose house a meal of eggs and a cake was prepared for Nangle and his party. After the meal, before retiring to bed, it was customary to say the Rosary. Given Nangle's personal beliefs, he did not participate. This, however, was seen as bad manners by his hosts, who said to him, 'Are you a man or a mouse? We offered you hospitality and you won't join us in a few prayers!' Nangle and his entourage made their excuses and left - they did not stay overnight in Achillbeg, and as far as is known, never returned.

Right: Early 19th century map, showing two houses on the north side of 'Cregalomen', and the others all in the central valley, or 'village'. The southern hill, Oileán an Sciorta, is crudely anglicised as 'Knockillanaskrha'. *Author's Collection*

Below: The first accurate Ordnance Survey map showing Achillbeg. was published in 1838. This shows the houses and land boundaries as they were then. Apart from the 'Coast Guard Station', which was actually two small buildings side by side, there are no other buildings on the east side of the island. The land boundary running round the hill to the north is approximately where the road to the pier was situated some years later. At this stage, it is likely that there was a footpath of some sort. *Author's Collection*

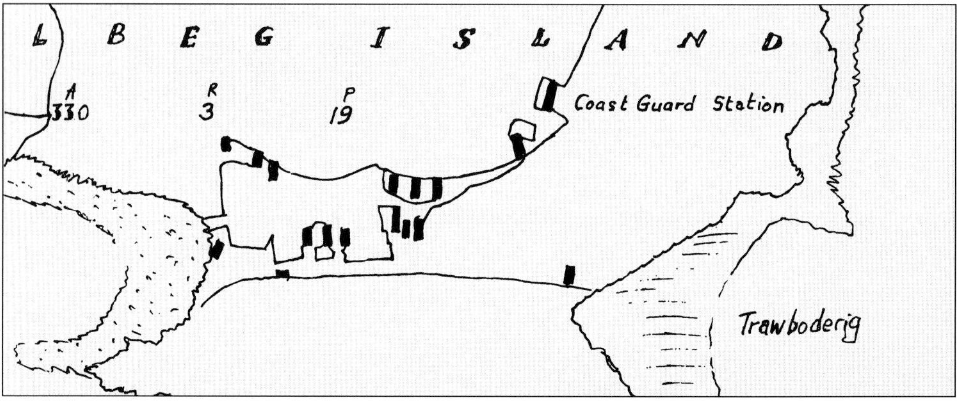

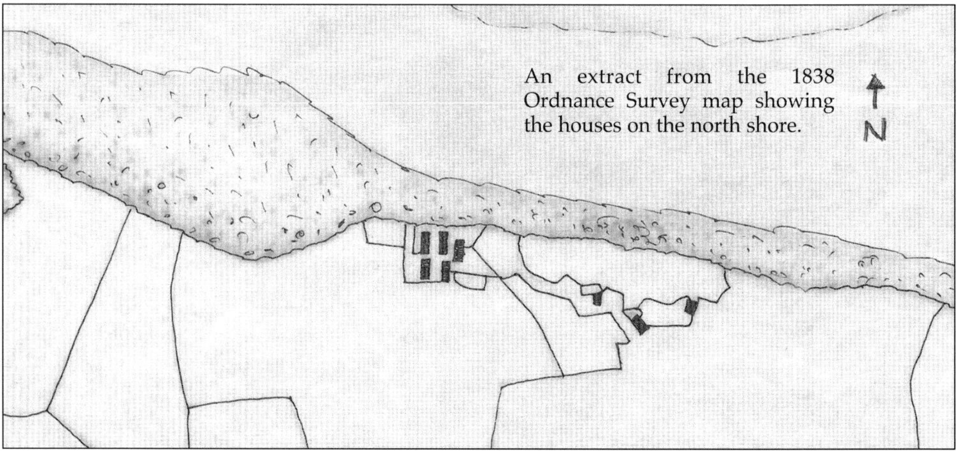

An extract from the 1838 Ordnance Survey map showing the houses on the north shore.

In other areas of Achill, Nangle's influence, fame and infamy manifested itself in a number of ways over the next 50 years. Achillbeg was to remain unaffected directly, and after Nangle died in 1883 the days of the Mission, already in decline, were numbered. Two years later it was gone but ownership of the land remained with William Pike, who lived just outside Achill Sound.

In addition to the seasonal migration already mentioned, permanent emigration had been a feature of life in rural Ireland for many generations since famine times. Having started for relief of starvation, it developed into an ongoing flow for economic reasons. On Achillbeg, the most common destinations for permanent emigrants were England and the United States - Cleveland, Ohio, in particular. To this day, the Cleveland area contains thousands of people of Achill and Achillbeg descent - a glance at a phone book there will reveal Corrigans, Kilbanes and Gallaghers, along with many other names common in the immediate surrounds - Lavelle, Sweeney, Patten, O'Malley and so on. Emigrant ships left from all the major Irish ports, taking those who had managed to save the fare - and who often travelled with little else but hope. Conditions aboard were spartan, with rows of people accommodated in what were essentially large dormitories, on bunks which were little better than cramped wooden shelves. On arrival in the New World, many were in poor health - and some did not survive the crossing, falling victim to sickness and disease *en route*. On arrival, the lucky ones had relatives or friends already there, or had come with their families, but many others were completely on their own in a strange land. Work was plentiful, and pay good compared with home, but hours were long and conditions harsh. Nonetheless, once established, our emigrant would save hard and send money home - a lifeline to his or her family at home.

The wild nature of the southern coastline of the island has already been commented upon, this being a feature of much of the West of Ireland. This fact was not lost on smugglers in past times, and although Achillbeg did not have the notoriety of other places for activities of this sort, a Coastguard presence was established on the island in the 1830s*. It was situated just north of Trá Bó Deirge beach, with a pathway leading up from near there. This path was known to some islanders as the 'Watch House Road'. One early census entry refers to a 'Watch House' apparently as distinct from a Coastguard station. This 'Watch House' possibly took the form of a type of sentry box, and possibly little else - this type of edifice was to be found at other stations elsewhere. Achillbeg islanders with personal memories prior to 1915 insisted there had been a coastguard station of some sort, although it was abandoned before 1900, probably as a result of the new one (1864) being opened across the water at Cloghmore on Achill. Island memory suggests that the Achillbeg building was burnt down about 1920, yielding many finely cut stones which were used up during the construction of new homes for several islanders. There is not the slightest trace of any sort of a building of this type today, and islanders whose childhood was from the 1930s onward have no idea where it might have been, as even they know of no trace of it.

A coastguard presence is mentioned in the Ordnance Survey Field Name Books of 1838, and is shown on the Ordnance Survey map of that same year.

* The coastguards were already well established in the island by 1837, as they are mentioned in '*A Topographical Dictionary of Ireland*', Vol.1, (Samuel Lewis, 1837).

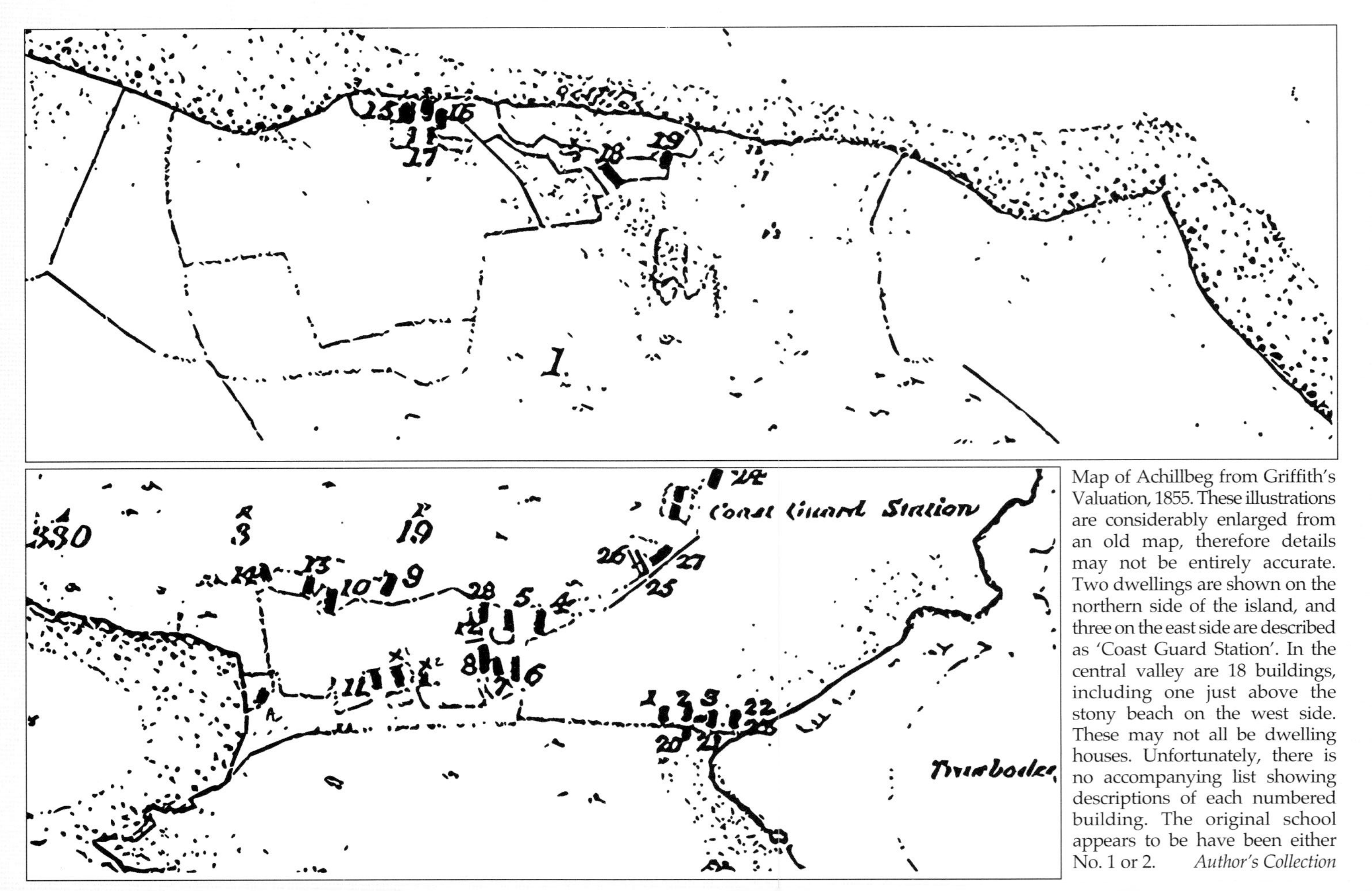

Map of Achillbeg from Griffith's Valuation, 1855. These illustrations are considerably enlarged from an old map, therefore details may not be entirely accurate. Two dwellings are shown on the northern side of the island, and three on the east side are described as 'Coast Guard Station'. In the central valley are 18 buildings, including one just above the stony beach on the west side. These may not all be dwelling houses. Unfortunately, there is no accompanying list showing descriptions of each numbered building. The original school appears to be have been either No. 1 or 2. *Author's Collection*

Some later maps between the 1840s and 1910s show a location at the top of the 'Watch House Road' described clearly as 'Coast Guard Station'. The likelihood is that the coastguards rented an ordinary house on the island at one time - again, this practice was to be found elsewhere. The coastguards would have used the Watch House Road to bring supplies up from the beach, and the house(s) they rented may have been known as the 'station', especially prior to the construction of the purpose built one at Cloghmore.

After the coastguards had moved to Cloghmore, they maintained a connection with Achillbeg, as according to one islander who was taught by the *Paorach*, it was coastguard staff who built the school in 1903. By this stage a woman was living in the former coastguard's house at the top of the Watch House Road.

By 1855, islanders were renting several buildings to the Coastguards, an indication that more space was required. Griffith's Valuation of 1855 records two buildings owned by the Board of Customs as 'Watch Houses' - one of which was under construction that year. In addition, seven other houses were rented to people whose surnames show that they were definitely not originally from either Achillbeg or the general area. (Names such as Aspinell, Adwards, Bowdan and Brech which appear in Griffith's records are attributed to coastguard staff.) This doubtless led to the construction (in 1864) of the full station across the Blind Sound at Cloghmore, which probably replaced the watch house, or whatever had been there previously. This station was one of six in the general area, administered from Westport. It was variously described as 'Achillbeg'or 'Darby's Point' on the plans, indicating the area it covered, rather than the actual location. This station could be said to have been a replacement for the Achillbeg one, but both appear to have been occupied simultaneously for some years. One possible reason for the construction at Darby's Point is that the rented accommodation on Achillbeg was too small for all the personnel and equipment needed. Another possibility was that at this time improvements were being made in telegraphic communication between coastguards, and it may be that the isolated nature of the Achillbeg site was unsuitable for this.

The Cloghmore station was constructed as a long two-storey house with some outbuildings (described on a census form as 'offices'). Its style of construction was very similar to other structures of this nature to be found elsewhere in Ireland, but it was utterly different from anything else to be found locally.

Apart from containing an upper storey, it had a yard around it, and a slated roof - local houses were all thatched at that time. The station was manned by a number of officers, up to eight - thereby bringing new people to the area. Folk history recalls that some were Irish and some English, and the surnames of some of these would appear to bear this out. Census forms listed the religion of most coastguards as Protestant - in some cases Church of Ireland, in others Church of England - indicating Englishmen who had been posted to the station. Just across the water, Achillbeg's population was entirely Roman Catholic. In some areas of Ireland, coastguards were not welcomed by local people for political reasons, though there is no record of any such difficulties at the Cloghmore station, although the officers and islanders tended to lead fairly separate lives. The coastguards had a rigidly militaristic discipline - they had to

Photographs of Achillbeg in its inhabited period are very rare, and few are known to have survived showing any people living or working there. This group photograph is of a rural community further up the coast in Co. Donegal, and was taken about 1885. It is of interest in that it shows very clearly the surroundings of western Irish rural communities of the time. While it may not have been taken in Achillbeg, it could have been: every detail shown corresponds with what a similar scene on the island would have looked like at this time when the population was at its peak. The clothing is all of traditional Irish pattern, and the stone flags used outside the houses may just be seen. All the children are barefoot and while some are obviously clad for the occasion in their 'Sunday best' others wear the plain smock-type clothing in which young children were dressed in summer months at the time. The houses have their thatched roofs tied down with ropes to prevent winter damage. This practice was adopted in most western parts of Ireland, including Achillbeg. Some 50 years before the Land Commission houses were built, the traditional Irish cottage shown here was the only house type in Achillbeg. The ruins of many remain to this day across the island, roofs fallen in, and with nettles growing where children once played. A turf pile may be seen in the top right of the picture outside the house in the distance, which has been newly-thatched. Contrast this with the house behind the group in the foreground which has copious amounts of weeds growing on its roof.

Lawrence Collection CAB4586, Courtesy National Library of Ireland

wear a uniform at all times on duty, and they held drills and paraded for inspection by a senior officer regularly.

They were not encouraged to socialise with local people, lest they become too familiar with them, thereby compromising their ability to carry out their duties. However, anecdotal evidence suggests that one coastguard, possibly named Richards, married a local girl around 1900. The coastguard station at Darby's Point, or Cloghmore, survived in derelict state until the early 1980s, when it was demolished to make way for a fish farm.

The presence of coastguards in the area was doubtless one reason why almost the entire population of the island could speak English as well as Irish, certainly from the late 1800s.

It is interesting to compare the few maps which clearly show land divisions and the positions of houses throughout the 19th century. Several maps are shown which cover the period 1826-1901, during which the population declined from 178 to 104, corresponding with the severe economic deprivation accompanying the Famine. The earliest, dating from the 1820s, shows two houses on the north side of the island, and 13 in the middle, but as the original was on a very small scale this may not be entirely accurate. In the middle of the island, up to 20 buildings appear by 1855, as illustrated on the map taken from Griffith's valuation that year. By the 1960s a map used by the lighthouse authorities shows twelve. On the island's north side, there are seven buildings shown by 1855, two having been there many years earlier, and these remain until the 1960s. However, examination of the locations of the houses shown on the 1960 map indicate that the information is very much out of date, as no map shows the positions of the houses which currently exist, and which were built in the 1930s with 'Land Commission' assistance. While the remains of many of the earlier houses are to be seen, particularly on the north side, these had not been used as dwelling houses for some years.

A British Admiralty survey in 1893 recorded that a gunboat named *Orwell* had been stationed at Achillbeg for a short period in 1882 to assist the coastguards. It was anchored in the bay off 'Traboderig' (Trá Bó Deirge) strand. It was used in 1922 to take new fishing equipment to the island, accompanied by a senior British civil servant who had been entrusted with ensuring that an anonymous donation was used for the benefit of island fishermen (*see Chapter Three*). On another occasion in the 19th century a boat owned or used by coastguards is reported to have capsized just off the island.

Apart from prevention of smuggling, coastguards kept a watchful eye on any attempts by local people to make *poitín*. Folk memory suggests that while Achillbeg did not have a big *poitín* industry, enough for home consumption was made there at one time. Given the small size of the island, the manufacture of the illegal spirit was all but finished by the turn of the 20th century.

At this stage, the community in Achillbeg was well established, though times were hard. Popular folklore recalls the glory days of the 1910s when the *Paorach* taught the islanders, introducing them to a whole new world, and doubtless preparing them for seasonal emigration elsewhere, but one beneficial by-product of the Achill Mission was that the Achill area graduated from one with little or no educational facilities to one with many such opportunities for local

ACHILLBEG, or Little Achill, 349 feet high, forms the north point of the north entrance to Clew bay. When viewed 3 or 4 miles from the eastward or westward it appears as two hills, the middle of the island being very low and nearly overflowed by the wash of the sea. It is separated from the main by a narrow channel called Blind sound, which is navigable for boats excepting when there is a a heavy sea running.*

Eastward of it the south entrance of Achill sound opens; and here, off a small sandy bay, vessels of not more than 9 feet draught may anchor in fine weather, but in south-west gales the sea breaks right across the entrance. The anchorage off the coast guard station, inside Achillbeg island, locally called the Pool, is confined and only sufficient room for a gunboat; the tides are very strong, and in the centre of the Pool there is a whirlpool from half flood to half ebb. Those going in or out should do so at high water as the tide slackens for about a quarter of an hour before and after that time. There are 16 feet over the bar at high water ordinary spring tides; the bar is exceedingly narrow, and be careful to avoid a rock awash at low water, just inside the first point. This rock is marked at high water, but not very distinctly, by the long seaweed which grows on its surface.

In 1882 H.M. Gunboat *Orwell* anchored here, with the coast guard staff bearing N.E. by E., and the south extreme of Achill island bearing N.W. by W.

Tides.—It is high water, full and change, at Achillbeg, at 5h. 14m.; springs rise 10¾ feet, neaps 8 feet.

See Admiralty plan :—Achill head to Roonagh head, No. 2,667; scale, $m = 1{\cdot}7$ inches.

* *See* Admiralty plan :—Achill sound, No. 934.

Extract from *The Irish Coastal Pilot* (from Admiralty Surveys), 1893.

people. In fact, by the 1880s, while the building of Achillbeg's schoolhouse was some 20 years away, island children were already being taught by visiting teachers, and may also have travelled to Corraun or Achill for education. By 1901, the population census listed almost every person living in Achillbeg, even the elderly, as having fluency in both Irish and English. Ten years later the entire population were fully bilingual, though Irish remained as the primary tongue.

In past times, without road systems, island life had thrived on Ireland's west coast in general. The sea, with all its occasional treachery, was safer and easier to travel across than land in many cases - it was only in later years when wheeled vehicles and roads were commonplace that islands appeared to be more isolated places to live. In truth, prior to this many 'mainland' locations were every bit as remote and difficult to get to - much of Ireland consists of boggy or rocky terrain. Well into the 20th century sea transport was used in some coastal areas of the mainland in preference to road transport on occasion. It was important to Achillbeg residents that boats, fishing facilities and equipment were at their best. The importance of sea transport (as opposed to land transport) in the area is well illustrated by statistics for the usage of Cloghmore pier and harbour: which were published in a British Government report in the early 1800s. At this stage it was frequented at its busiest by 50 sailing boats, averaging 8 tons each, and some 100 yawls, averaging 2 tons. Some 500 people were reported to be engaged in fishing in the area by the same report. This figure would have included those from southern Achill and Corraun along with most able-bodied Achillbeg folk.

Towards the end of the 19th century, a number of improvements were made to life in the area. In the 1880s a road bridge was built to link Achill Island with mainland Corraun, and in 1895 the railway from Westport arrived at Achill Sound. Nearer to Achillbeg, the *Parliamentary Gazetteer of Ireland* records a pier being built - this would have been at Cloghmore. It was started in 1822, and by the time the *Gazetteer* recorded it in 1843, it was functioning though incomplete. In 1899 the Congested Districts Board (CDB) provided a nurse on Achill Island - her sphere of operation covered Achillbeg as well. The CDB also carried out various improvements to piers in the locality, most notably at Darby's Point in 1909. A year later, the coastguards called for this pier to be enlarged to cope with tramway wagons laden with marble which were being shipped down from the quarry nearby. Nothing substantial was done, and the horse-worked tramway ceased operations after a few years. The small pier on Achillbeg facing it was first discussed by a Government Famine Relief Committee in the 1880s, but it was not to be built until the early 1920s; islanders had previously hauled their boats up onto the strand. These improvements may have been a reaction to local pressure, as market prices for fish were particularly low in the first few years of the 20th century, and bad weather had made matters worse for Achillbeg fishermen. According to some former islanders, there were fewer mackerel than normal in these waters for a few seasons around this time.

Improvements were also made to Cloghmore Pier at various times throughout the 20th century - ironically, major improvements were made for the benefit of local fishermen just after the last residents had left Achillbeg in the 1960s.

Achill Sound, looking from the island side towards Polranny, on the mainland side, about 1880. The array of shops, hotels and businesses here today have yet to arrive, as have the road bridge and the railway. While in Achillbeg'slast years of habitation this was both the site of a monthly market and a busy place to do business generally, it can be seen that in earlier times this was not so. This explains the Achillbeg islander's habit of sailing across to Corraun, and doing business there, just as frequently as they would have travelled to Achill Sound. A small boat manoeuvres the treacherous currents of the Sound - in a few years time afterwards, Achillbeg's heavily laden turf boats would have to take down their masts as they passed this point on their way (from left to right in the picture) from Saula back to the island.

Lawrence Collection N58551, Courtesy National Library of Ireland

Kildownet Castle, Achill Island, looking towards Corraun, This photograph was incorrectly labelled 'Achill Beg, Co. Mayo' by the photographer, William Lawrence. No historical study of Ireland between 1880 and 1910 is complete without reference to this large archive of photographs which is held in the National Library in Dublin, and may also be viewed on microfilm in several other archives nationwide. Labelling and description of locations, while sparse, is generally very accurate. However, Lawrence took a team of photographers with him on some of his photographic forays, and it may be that this was one taken by one of his assistants who was perhaps not as well-informed about local geography. It is known that Lawrence, or at least some of his staff, made at least three visits to West Mayo and Achill. This picture dates from the first visit. In the context of this book, there are several points of interest. Firstly, the boats shown may well be locally-owned, or they could be from Achillbeg which is not far behind the photographer. The small pier this side of the castle is where Achillbeg people would have landed if they were visiting this area. The cart may well be the mail car, taking mail to Cloghmore Post Office, a short distance down the road - the individual standing beside it appears to have a cap which would be part of his uniform. There are suitcases on the cart as well - do these belong to William Lawrence?

Lawrence Collection CAB6795, Courtesy National Library of Ireland

Kildownet Pier, Achill, about 1885. Belfarsad townland on mainland Corraun is opposite; this picture is taken from near Kildownet Castle (*on the left*). The group landing at the pier are in the traditional dress of the time and include two women - are they from Achillbeg? The boat is a traditional Achill yawl, of the type used by Achillbeg's residents.

Lawrence Collection NS 8448, Courtesy National Library of Ireland

Islanders never had the benefit of any kind of ferry service - in common with the vast majority of Irish islands, transport to and from the island was left to the residents and their privately-owned boats.

Accidents at sea were always an unfortunate feature of life on islands off the west of Ireland. The earliest casualty of Achillbeg's waters to have been reliably recorded was a Spanish Armada ship which was wrecked not far from Achillbeg. This was the *San Nicolas Prodanelli,* a large ship of 834 tons, carrying 26 guns and 355 men. She foundered off the island and was wrecked at Toorglass on the Corraun Peninsula in September 1588. Only 16 men survived and were rescued; but their relief was to be short lived as they were later executed by Crown forces. *

On 13th January, 1894, a barque named the *Jenny* sank off the southern tip of Achillbeg in just four hours. She was travelling from Jamaica to Hamburg, carrying softwood logs. The *Jenny* was registered by her owner, A.F. Kolderup, in Christiania, Norway, and carried the Norwegian flag. She was a wooden sailing ship of 41 metres in length, built in 1865 by J. Jorgensen, of Drammen in Norway, and weighing 510 tons. Her master was Captain L. Andersen. In stormy weather she was smashed to pieces against the rocks on the island's southern side, though fortunately the crew of 10 were saved by the islanders and taken up into their homes for rest and shelter. Some 20 years later, an islander told of seeing cups and saucers from the ship on the seabed while diving off rocks at a very low tide. The tragic drowning of an Achillbeg resident in the early 1960s was one of the deciding factors in the final evacuation of the remaining population, testament to the fact that among boatmen everywhere there is the knowledge that the sea must be treated with great respect. Over the years, Achillbeg folk had many a hair-raising crossing, rescued many a person in difficulties in the water, and, sadly, occasionally lost relatives to the Atlantic. While crossings to and from the island could be treacherous due to the strong currents in the 'Blind Sound' separating Achillbeg from Achill, it was very occasionally possible to cross on foot at an exceptionally low tide. One islander recalled her uncle crossing the few hundred metres between the two in the 1920s. By contrast, the western side of the island was described by *Lewis's Topographical Directory of Ireland* in 1837 as 'very wild, and in consequence of the swells running to a great height, is unapproachable even in the calmest weather'.

Much debris from ships was washed ashore over the years and put to good use by the islanders. Many salvaged parts of the *Jenny* were used to build and repair roofs on island houses. Other cargo would be washed over the side of boats, ending up on the beach.

The 19th century ended on Achillbeg much as it had started, though with a smaller population. The coastguard station had come and gone, but modern housing and the school building had yet to appear. The 20th century would bring all this, along with a world class teacher; but also abandonment some 60 years later.

* *Shipwrecks off the Irish Coast 1105-1993,* by Edward J. Bourke, published 1994 by the author at 24 Coolmine Woods, Dublin 15.

In this picture, described by the photographer as 'Achill Beg Bay', we see a pleasant view of the western tip of Achillbeg ('the Tail'), on the left of the picture, which is taken from the townland of Carrowgarve, on Achill. In between is the rocky outcrop of the islet known as Dunnaglas; this is the site of the remains of part of the Iron Age fort complex which appears to have spanned the area across to Achillbeg in earlier times. It is at this point that Achillbeg appears to have been connected at one time to Achill via Dunnaglas. Over on Achillbeg, and just out of view, are the remains of Dún Chill Mór. In the distance the looming bulk of Knockmore mountain on Clare Island dominates the horizon. The road surface here is narrower than today, and gravel-surfaced: this is how Achillbeg's roads were finished throughout the inhabited life of the island. Though overgrown, they remain today.

Lawrence Collection CAB6801, Courtesy National Library of Ireland

Chapter Three

The Twentieth Century

Comparison of census returns for the first 10 years of the 20th century show a fairly stable population of some 100 people, though over the next 50 years it would halve. It is convenient to treat this period separately from the earlier history of the island, because it is within this period that the earliest first-hand memories of islanders can be quoted extensively, giving a picture of life on Achillbeg through the eyes of its inhabitants.

In 1922, the former Vice President of the Local Government Board for Ireland, Sir Henry Robinson, wrote an account of his experiences during his long working life in Ireland, which covered the end of the 19th century and start of the 20th. Amongst his duties had been the administration of British-sponsored famine relief measures in the area. He recalled how Lady Cavendish, the wife of the former Chief Secretary for Ireland, Lord Frederick Cavendish, had approached him with a small donation which she wanted to be used for the benefit of the people of Achillbeg. After consultation with island fishermen, Robinson decided to buy them some more fishing equipment, as their own was inadequate. He recalled that the islanders were 'good boatmen, but who had no proper appliances for fishing, and were in very great distress at the time'. He purchased a quantity of spillets and nets in Musselburgh, Scotland, and had them transported to Glasgow, then on to Westport. Robinson personally accompanied the equipment on board the HMS *Orwell* to hand them over. A Civil Servant to the last, he methodically recorded the names of the recipients and sent the list to Lady Cavendish, who in her reply mentioned that she wanted her donation to remain anonymous. However, Robinson had already told the local Curate who spoke of it at Mass the following Sunday, having asked Robinson to attend to hear him speak. As Robinson wrote, '. . . he (the curate) referred to Lord Frederick's sympathy (for the islanders) in such moving terms that the whole congregation fell down on their knees . . .' The day was stormy, with dark skies - but the packed congregation included as many from Achillbeg as could go. Robinson referred to 'a little dark chapel' - this would have been the old church at Cloghmore which was replaced by the present structure in the 1960s, and which the islanders used to attend, weather for boats permitting.

There was an interesting sequel. Years later, Lady Cavendish wrote to Robinson asking him how the recipients of the equipment had fared. Robinson asked the then Parish Priest for the Parish Register, and mindful of Lady Cavendish's request for anonymity he simply said that he wanted to ask about the welfare of some families. One by one, the priest told him - one family was doing well, another had emigrated, one had bought two boats, another was sending money home from America, and the daughter of another had become a doctor. With two exceptions who could not be traced, all had progressed well. Robinson was taken by surprise when the priest asked, rather indignantly, why he was only enquiring about the well off! He told Robinson that Achillbeg was

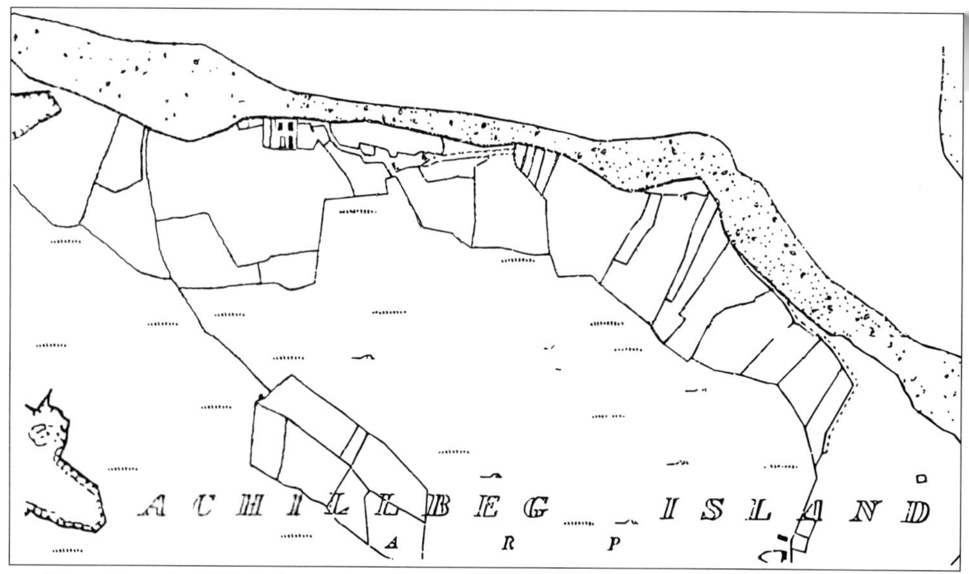

ACHILLBEG ISLAND
ARP

Extract from the 1901 Ordnance Survey map, showing the housing and land boundaries on the island's north side.
Author's Collection

Extract from the 1901 Ordnance Survey map, showing the housing and land boundaries in the centre of the island. The old school is still shown: a few years later, the new one would be built just south of the dotted line, which indicates the extent of possible winter flooding.
Author's Collection

BEG ISLAN
ARP
26 1 29
Achillbeg School

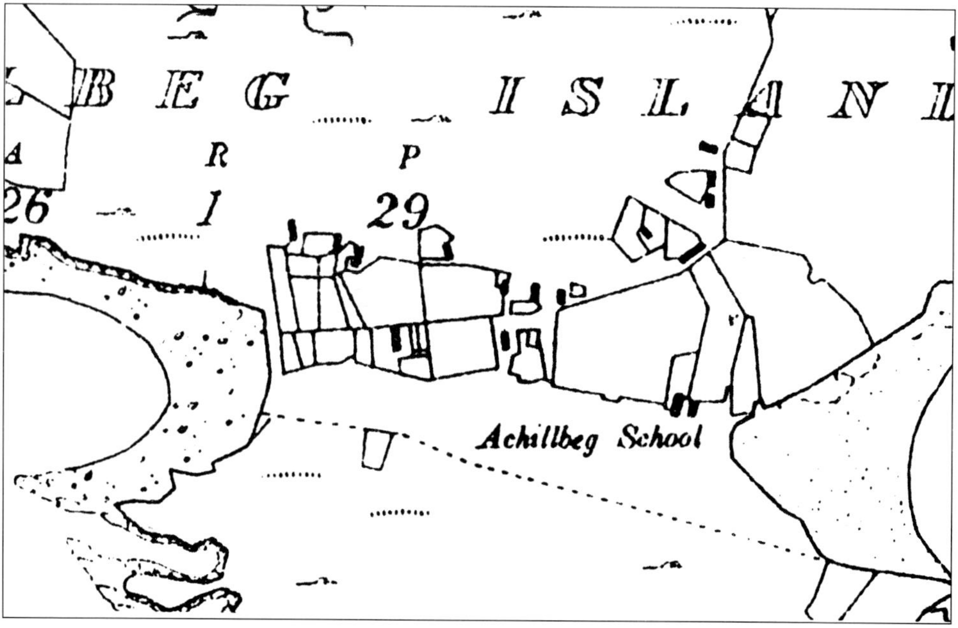

a very poor place, and suggested 'if you are going to do anything at all for the people, it's not those people that's wanting help. Someone has given you teetotally [*sic*] wrong information!' In consideration of Lady Cavendish's wishes, Robinson did not tell him the rest of the story.

Life in Achillbeg was at times hard, but any surviving accounts of outsider's visits portray the islanders as hard working, decent and dignified people - those words being used by a visitor in the early years of the 20th century. The archaeologist T.J. Westropp wrote in 1911, 'The natives, during our two visits, treated us with the utmost kindness and courtesy . . .' and commented that those who guided him around the island were more than willing to answer his every question, and tell him all they knew of the various landmarks that Westropp wanted to research.

From the turn of the century until the island's evacuation some 65 years later, seasonal migration continued to be a feature of life for almost every able-bodied person. During that period most went to Scotland or Lancashire to work in the potato fields. Others went to work on building sites in England or America. For a potato harvest worker the journey would begin with a trip in a local boat to Westport, where an emigrant ship would await. In recalling his youth in the 1910s and 1920s, an Achillbeg resident spoke of being unaware of a single island family who did not have sons or daughters who had gone 'out' to find work of this nature. (In common with other Irish islands, Achillbeg people refer to a traveller coming to the island as coming 'in', while somebody leaving the island is going 'out'.) Another, speaking of the 1930s period, remembered only two young people from the island who did not go 'out'. His summer days were spent with those too young or old to go - and soon, at 13, he joined his older brothers too. When they came back in the late autumn, they would have saved some money and would sometimes arrive home wearing a suit of new clothes that they had bought.

Another islander described his own experiences in the mid-1920s:

> 'I was 13 years and 3 months. We went to Ayrshire, from the 10th June - I first went in 1925. There were bad conditions. A Donegal teacher called Peadar O Donnell - he got the tattie hokers* to join a union and improve their conditions. The pay was sixpence an hour. We worked nine hours a day, five and a half days a week. We got £1 and five shillings a week . . .'

In 1925 the boat fare from Achill Sound was 19 shillings - just six shillings short of a week's pay. One islander, in his 90s in 2003, recalled that the first time he went to Scotland, he travelled by boat the whole way, the boat picking up harvest workers from several locations on the west coast of Ireland. It appears that there were two ways this was accomplished - in earlier days, a ship left Westport for Glasgow, and islanders would sail into Westport from Darby's Point to connect with it. It was on one such journey, in 1894, that such a boat capsized as it entered Westport Harbour, resulting in loss of life. The unfortunate victims were mostly in their teens and early twenties, and their remains were brought back to Achill on the railway, which was then almost complete but not yet open to the public. None of the victims were from

* Tattie hokers = potato diggers.

Achill Sound in the early years of the 20th century. A local yawl is in the foreground. This is the type of boat used for carrying turf from Saula (to the left of this picture) to Achillbeg (to the right, under the bridge). The picture is taken looking from Sweeney's yard, on Achill's shore, towards the mainland Corraun district which is across the bridge connecting the two. The stone building opposite is a fish store built by the Midland Great Western Railway Company for Alexander Hector, a Scottish fish merchant who shipped his produce by rail. The railway station (1894-1937) is just to the right of it. On the right-hand side of the bridge is the hotel premises of Alice Sweeney. The modern hotel on the same site is owned by a descendant of hers.

National Library of Ireland VR3974

While this picture is not of Achillbeg folk, it shows a typical gang of Mayo people in the potato fields of Scotland in the early years of the 20th century. Long hours and poor conditions for low pay, but even the youngest boy will have a valuable financial contribution to make to his family's income back home in the autumn.

Joe Kilbane

Achillbeg, but many were from neighbouring districts on Achill and would have been known to, and related to, Achillbeg people. In later days, a boat left the Bulls Mouth (on Achill Island) and headed up the west coast, picking up more passengers in Donegal, and eventually sailing to Glasgow. From the 1920s the journey consisted of a long walk to Achill Sound railway station, which was in operation from 1894 to 1937, and a train to Dublin, where a boat would take the migrating passengers onwards to Glasgow. From there, another train journey was made to the place of work. There was a train service of two to three trains per day from Achill, but on occasion many hundreds from all over Achill and Achillbeg would travel on the same day, and the railway company would lay on a special train to take passengers and their luggage from Achill to Westport, to connect with the Dublin train. These special harvest workers' trains would leave Achill station as early as 6 am, and those travelling had to have a work permit (or 'passport') which was issued at Achill Sound by the local policeman at the 'Barracks'. A shopkeeper in Sweeney's stores would take a photograph of the applicant for this purpose.

During World War I, while Britain ruled all of Ireland, the Government had introduced conscription in Britain, but due to the unstable political situation did not do so in Ireland. However, many Irishmen voluntarily joined up, including one or two from Achillbeg. One Achillbeg man died in the Battle of the Somme. After the war, those who had fought for Britain had no trouble gaining a work permit, or 'passport'. One man recalled that others were sometimes refused them, if they were known to have refused to join the army. In at least one case, a local man returned temporarily to Achillbeg after spending some time working in England, but when he wanted to return there, his application for a permit was turned down.

After a day's travelling from Achillbeg the exhausted passengers would arrive in their dormitories in Scotland late that evening. Their host would sometimes provide each person with a large sack, which was placed on a bed of straw. Having brought their own pillows, sheets, mugs, cutlery and heavy tablecloths, they would settle in, ready to have good night's sleep on the straw bed. Their work permits had to be examined, and they were given yellow identity cards.

In the morning, the harvest workers were roused early, and set to work in the fields. Working in pairs, one would dig the potatoes up, and the other would collect them in a type of sack worn around the waist, called a 'brath'. Once muddy, these 'braths' were heavy and unwieldy to manoeuvre, especially for a 13- or 14-year-old girl, who was expected to do as heavy a day's work as anyone older. As referred to elsewhere, working conditions were somewhat improved about 1930 due to the participation of the workers in a union, but were still very demanding. Following the disastrous fire in Kirkintulloch in 1937, in which many young people from Achill and Corraun lost their lives, conditions were further improved. One Achillbeg farm worker who had been there recalled going back to the same farm in 1938 and finding conditions and accommodation there to be much better - 'the whole place had been done up', he said. Evenings were free, and workers would meet up with other squads, play cards, and socialise. Savings were carefully accumulated and sent home by 'TMO'. A TMO was a Telegraphic Money Order - the money was paid into a local post office and could be withdrawn from the post office in Achill. Some post offices in Achill opened specially on Sundays to allow local people to receive payments made the previous evening when the workers had been given their pay. There was no exchange rate problem: Ireland continued to use a sterling value pound after independence in 1921 until 1979.

One contemporary report dating from the mid-1910s describes a group of Achill and Achillbeg people meeting a group of German prisoners of war who had been put to work on the same farm. The Germans were adept at making spare sackcloth into pairs of slippers, so their Irish companions did their best to supply them with suitable material . . .

Another islander who was in her teens around 1910-15 described her own experiences thus, '. . . We left Ireland in June and returned in October. I worked there for a few years. If we were picked to wait on winter work we would.* We rose at 3 am in the morning to get the horse and carts ready and filled the carts with potatoes. We worked nine hours. Sleeping quarters were straw beds and one fire in the middle of the floor'.

One lady recalled being paid five old pennies per hour for picking potatoes in Scotland in the mid-1920s. In her group, a dozen or more islanders travelled together, some as young as 12 or 13, and none older than 40. 'The journey on the boat was the worst', she said, 'it took 10 hours to get from Glasgow to Dublin'.

Thirty years later things were much the same. One young worker described saving £5 a week along with two companions. They bought new clothes, which they wore when travelling home. Their pay was £2 and 14 shillings per week, and they were given free coal for the fire in their bothy. Potatoes were also free, but they had to buy milk at the local dairy, and other food. They were able to 'pinch a few eggs' from the farmer's hens, and when the gamekeeper was not about, they used to catch rabbits to eat. They did not kill weasels, as this was considered bad luck in Ireland, but they noticed that Scottish farmers did, and would hang dead ones out to warn off others.

The Scottish farmers who employed harvest workers would sometimes pay their passage over if they did not have the money, and would deduct it from their wages at the rate of 3 shillings per week. Some farmers treated their workers better than others, and often a farmer would take on the role of 'looking after' the younger teenagers - ensuring they sent their money home and did not fall into 'bad habits'!

Other islanders went in search of work on building sites and road-building gangs in England. One told of paying sixpence to travel from Dublin to Liverpool on board a coal boat, and having little to eat on arrival, but work was usually available. In the 1920s, one Achillbeg man spoke of living in rough digs in London, having found nowhere else to stay. In those days, equality laws had yet to be enacted - many boarding houses would exhibit signs saying 'No blacks - No Irish'. The digs he found had a broken window; it was winter, and the only bedding provided was a single rough blanket. He slept fully clothed, watching snowflakes drift through a broken pane in the window, and rose early to find work. 'They'd only give you one egg in that place' he said, 'and I had to offer to pay them more for two'. A meagre start to the day for a construction worker!

* Some workers remained well into the winter months, others came and went in summer and autumn months.

Contracts on a construction job could last for several years, rather than a few months, so workers thus engaged would travel home to Achillbeg at holiday times to visit their families. Christmas would be a time of great reunions: 'I always looked forward to a big Christmas dinner at home' said one man . . . Another islander remembered a homecoming party for a relative being held in a shed, but she was told she was too young to attend it - it was for 'grown ups' only!

An islander who left to work in both the USA and Britain in the early 1920s described similar conditions to those above in Britain, but said that in his experience American work conditions were even worse for a teenage emigrant. Within Britain, England was seen as a better option than Scotland for farm work.

The political turmoil in Ireland at the time has already been referred to. With a cat and mouse game in progress between the Irish Republican Army (IRA) and British forces in western Mayo, it was perhaps inevitable that sooner or later a remote location such as Achillbeg should be seen as a suitable hiding place by one side or the other. Islanders recalled several incidents which spanned the period just before and after independence - the War of Independence itself, and the Civil War in the early 1920s. On one occasion, a group of 20 IRA men came into Achillbeg to hide from the 'Black and Tans'*. They took over a house, and paid several young boys to keep watch for boats coming over, presumably containing the 'Tans' in hot pursuit. One of the youthful occupants of the house, interviewed many years later, said 'They were a nuisance - they ate all our food and sat up playing cards all night'!

After several days of this, the boys became bored one evening and ran up to the house saying they had seen lights of boats coming across. The IRA men departed rapidly, only to come back to hide out at other times. A deputation of 'Tans' and regular British soldiers did call into Achillbeg once, but departed empty handed. The 'Tans' occasionally burned houses and property as they retreated, presumably to prevent, as they saw it, their enemies hiding in them. It was at this time that the former Coastguard's house was looted and burnt down. It is unclear whether the 'Tans' or the IRA started the fire. This house seems to have been used to house several families after the Coastguards had left some years earlier, but it is believed that it was empty from shortly before the 'Tans' came.

After independence, the Civil War followed in the early 1920s. The conflict now switched to that between the pro- and anti- treaty forces. On one occasion, the IRA came to Achillbeg, hid a cache of rifles under a rock near the road, and left. This time the Free State forces came into the island, and found the rifles.

* Ireland was at this stage in the throes of the struggle for independence. By the late 1910s the Royal Irish Constabulary (RIC) were no longer able to maintain British rule on their own, and extras were recruited, some from Ireland and some from England. These men were frequently drawn from the ranks of ex-soldiers who had taken part in World War I. In the hurry to have them placed on duty, their police uniforms were not ready, and they wore a mixture of whatever RIC black uniforms were available, and ex-army khaki 'tan' uniforms. Many received little or no training. They were first deployed in Co. Tipperary where they were nicknamed 'Black and Tans' after a local team of hounds, and the colour(s) of their makeshift uniforms. They quickly developed a reputation for ruthlessness and brutality, immortalised in political history.

This postcard, dating from the 1920s or 1930s, shows two yawls laden with turf. Both have a two man crew. *John Sweeney*

Cave above Garraí an Tuair Mhóir. Were IRA guns hidden here at one time? *Author*

They departed, pleased with their find. One former islander who remembered the incident many years later observed that the rifles were not well hidden and might have been a decoy. Another islander claimed that the Free State Forces made several visits. A recollection of a young girl in the 1940s was of an older cousin taking her to a small cave above the fields on the south side of the island. He told her that this cave might contain buried guns. 'Why?' she asked. 'Because that's where I saw them (the IRA) hide them', he replied. The cave is still there, of course, though it is hardly big enough for anybody other than a small child to squeeze into. Another islander recalled playing hide and seek in it in the 1930s.

Following these incidents, little need arose for officialdom to visit the island for the remaining 40 years of its inhabited period. The Garda Síochana (police) appeared from time to time to check for radio or dog licences, and County Council officials took an occasional look at the road.

Severe hardship continued to afflict the district in the early years of the 20th century. In 1918 a very severe epidemic of flu hit the island, and two teenage boys died as a result. A local newspaper described 'stunted, ill-nourished children . . . people starving and near naked' on neighbouring Inishbiggle Island as late as 1929. It was not as bad as this on Achillbeg, but life elsewhere often looked easier. As late as the early 1960s, a newspaper report on living conditions in Achillbeg pointed out the fact that islanders did not have access to a nurse or health care unless they made a long journey away from the island.

Achillbeg was unable to benefit from tourism to the extent that neighbouring Achill did, as there was no overnight accommodation for visitors, unless they had been invited to stay in a house by a friend or relative living in the island. In the 1910s the *Paorach* took in guests who had come to study, and tourists were known to camp on the island occasionally in the 1920s. In contrast to this, it was long after the last permanent residents had left that several of the houses were sold to people from outside the area, who use them now as holiday homes. Leaving the island after a day visit one autumn evening in 2003, the author noted some 14 people in three groups staying overnight in two houses and a tent.

Any Government interest in Achillbeg, its residents and their welfare appears to have been sporadic at best. In the early 1920s access to the island was improved by the provision of the pier - this was built by John McHugh, of Dooagh, Achill Island. It was enlarged in later years. An offer to build a bridge to Achillbeg from Cloghmore was turned down by the islanders in the 1930s as the plans did not suit everybody. Had a road been taken by bridge across from Cloghmore, the added convenience to islanders would have been offset by a loss of privacy, and a loss of some of the small amount of good arable land on the north side of the island. On several other occasions over the next 20 years, the County Council again mentioned a bridge as a possibility, but nothing came of it.

Achillbeg's population lived for many years in traditional stone-built cottages with thatched roofs. Examination of the 1901 Census shows that almost all were of the same type - two-roomed, with two windows on the sheltered (east) side, and all with stone walls and thatched roofs. However, some had only one room, but still housed a whole family. These were the last survivors of an older type, prevalent in the 19th century. A description of those to be found in the general area has survived from that era: '. . . Habitations still in too many instances poor indeed; most of them now begin to be built with lime and stone; . . . however, the cow, calf, etc. inhabit the same cabins with some of the poor; but in this, too, improvement commences, and detached huts are made to separate the brute from the human species . . .' By the time of the 1911 census, all inhabited houses were two-roomed. A few early Ordnance Survey maps show houses, often as barely distinguishable black dots, and it is interesting to compare these over the years. At one stage there were more houses in or around the central valley, and it seems that building along the east side of the island came later, as did the road. This, and the fact that the building of the pier came later, suggest that earlier settlements were based around the valley only, perhaps before land on the east side was properly prepared for cultivation. The strand was used for access by boat. Later, the road was built from the centre of the island to the pier on the north side and houses began to appear there. However, the earliest maps available show a very small number of houses on the north side, facing Cloghmore on Achill. At this time, most houses would have been one-roomed. As time progressed and two-roomed houses became the norm, some with one room would have been converted, others built new to the same style. Conversions appear to have been the norm, as comparison of maps surveyed at different times show houses in more or less the same positions.

An elderly resident recalled islanders storing any sizeable timbers that were washed ashore from wrecks, so that when a young couple married and set about building a house, there was an adequate supply of roofing timbers.

Originally, house interiors would have been similar to elsewhere in Ireland - inside the main room was a dresser, which contained most of the household crockery, cutlery and utensils, and a small table and chairs. The dresser was an essential part of any Irish kitchen, and by custom always stood either against the side wall in the main room or kitchen, or else against a partition used to separate the room into two parts. Traditionally, the left hand side of the hearth was where the woman of the house sat, while the right was the man's place, often with his clay pipe kept on a shelf (or *dugín*) there. Cooking was done on an open fire, with a cooking pot held on an iron support over it. A bed was made up next to the fire, sometimes recessed slightly into the house walls. Examples of this may be seen all over Ireland, and on Achill at the 'deserted village' on the slopes of Slievemore mountain. Over the years, Achillbeg houses were modernised - returning emigrants brought with them the latest accessories to be found elsewhere.

The house formerly occupied by, and built by the famous teacher, the *Paorach*, was the only two-storey house on the island, though some other houses had small attic-type rooms. In later years this house was the nearest thing Achillbeg had to a shop. The most basic consumables such as tea, sugar, butter and tobacco could be bought here, and on occasion sweets, tinned food and drums of paraffin oil. One former resident recalled a relative of the householder (Ned Kilbane) having come from America, and who lived there for a while - this lady was popular with island children, as she would give them sweets.

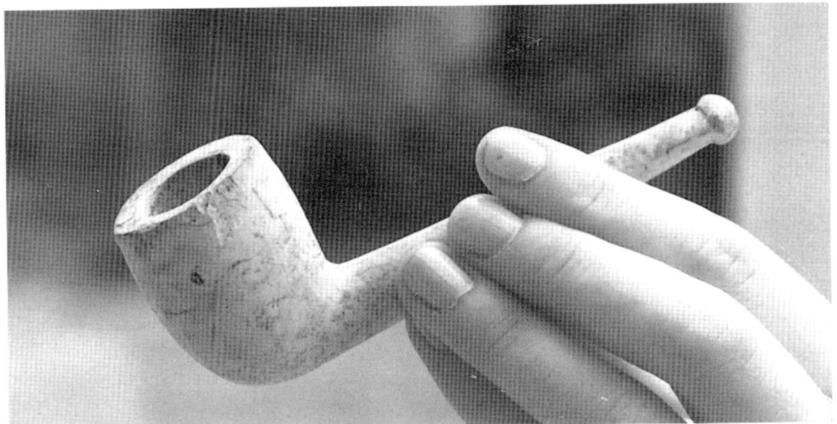

A traditional clay pipe, used widely in the past. When finished with, pipes were often buried near a gatepost outside a house, to give the occupant something to smoke in the afterlife. This example, while not from Achillbeg, is the same as those used there. It was dug up near Achill Sound in recent years. *Author*

The Government was keen to encourage the preservation and stability of Irish speaking areas, and consequently Achillbeg was officially designated as a Gaeltacht (Irish speaking) district in the late 1920s, in common with adjacent districts on Achill and the mainland. This meant that certain grants or loans could be made available to the inhabitants. These were administered through the Land Commission, a government body which had succeeded the Congested Districts Board. As a result of these loans, radical changes took place to the island's housing accommodation in the 1930s. A number of islanders received loans of around £200 (charged at 4 per cent per year) plus a once-off grant to enable them to build new houses to a more or less standard design, which were locally known as 'Gaeltacht houses'. The new houses were warmer than the old cottages, and were very solidly built. It is believed that the elegant cut stones from the abandoned and burnt coastguard buildings were used in the construction of some of them. The 'Gaeltacht' houses had a central living room with fireplace, on the right of which was one large bedroom, and on the left of which were two smaller ones (*see drawing*). Like the old houses, they were immaculately kept. They were whitewashed inside and out, with door and window frames painted in bright colours - green, red or blue. However, one inhabitant described how the walls would 'weep' when there was a south wind, and salt would seep through them. It was not a major problem, as it would dry quickly. At the time these were built, another Government initiative to assist the preservation of the Irish language elsewhere involved an offer to rehouse the islanders on Achill. This was of no interest to the people of Achillbeg, nor indeed were other similar offers made some 15 years later.

For some time, the traditional thatched cottage had been in decline throughout the country, as occupants emigrated, moved to towns, or modernised their properties. The Government made grants and loans available through the Land Commission for new houses to be built, and many of these are be seen in rural areas nationwide. Achillbeg received its share, and for the last 30 years of the island's occupation the islanders gradually moved into these. The old houses

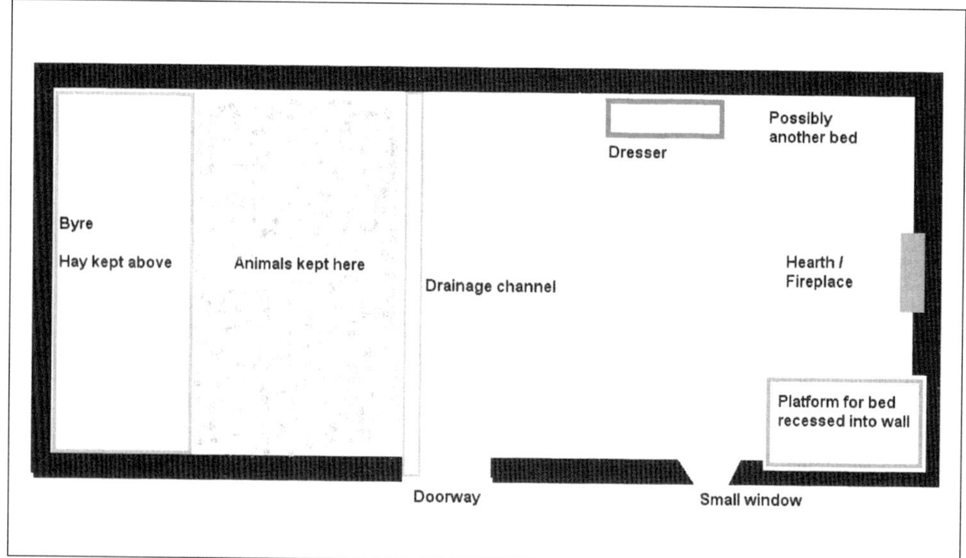

One-roomed stone house of traditional design. Some examples were still inhabited in the first few years of the 20th century.

Detail from 1960 map showing land boundaries and housing as they were, probably, in the 1930s, just before the more modern houses were built. No published map shows the modern houses.

Commissioners of Irish Lights

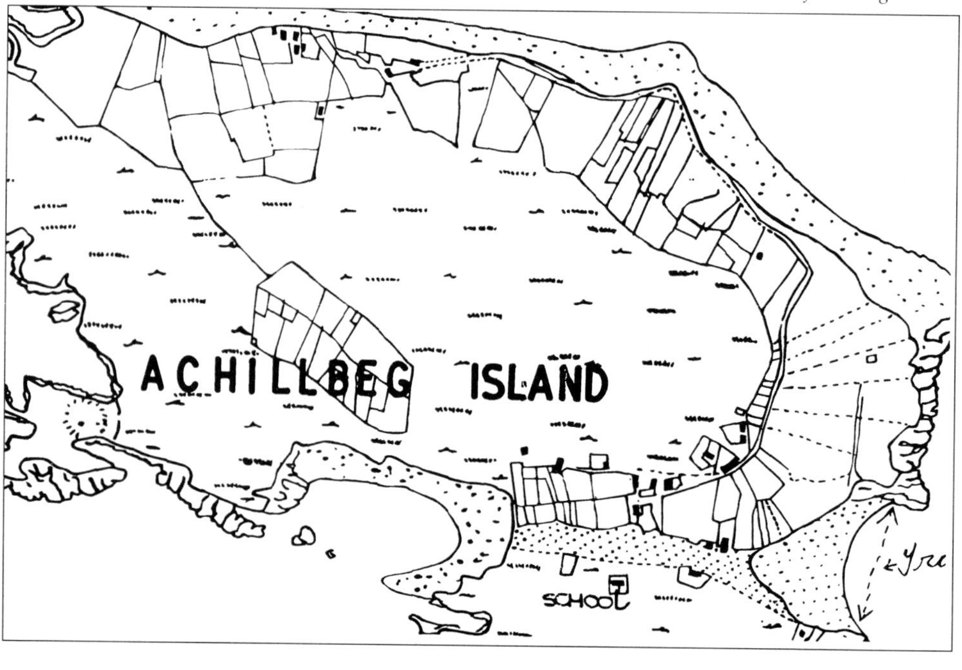

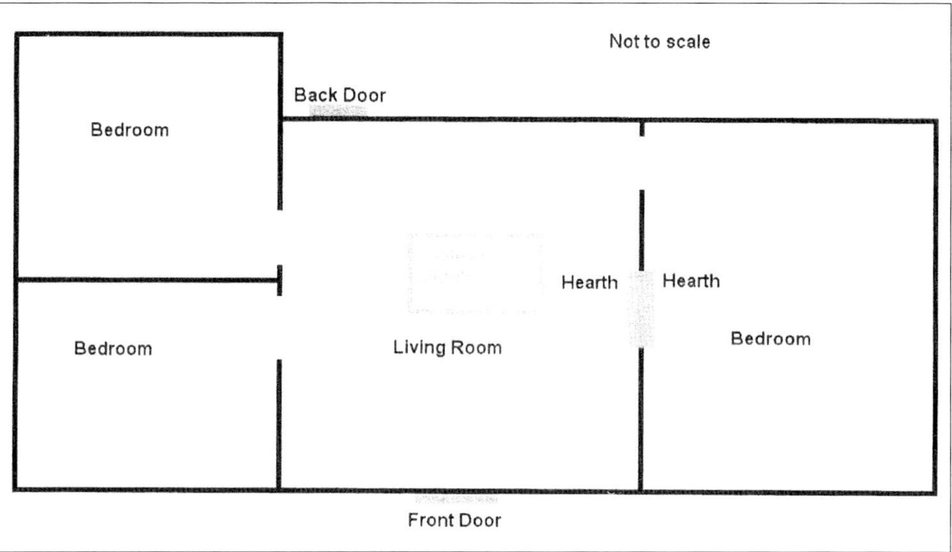

Plan of typical Land Commission (or 'Gaeltacht') house built in the 1930s. The central room had table, chairs, dresser, cupboards, and (in later years) a gas cooker. Cooking was originally done over the open fire.

Land Commission house below Learagán, at the end of the island road. Across the water is the southern end of Achill Island. Some of the houses in this area are home to former Achillbeg residents, who may now look across at their former home. *Author*

A typical Land Commission house at Baileamuigh. Many of these houses still exist, and while this one has been restored, others have not. Despite this, in almost every case the roofs and windows are intact. *Author*

The ruins of an old stone building of traditional design stands in front of two Land Commission houses dating from the 1930s. The protruding extension at the back was a feature of all of these houses, and was to allow two bedrooms to be built at this end of each house. The island road runs from the bottom left-hand corner of the picture, along behind these houses, and towards the one in the distance. It is now covered in nettles. One islander told of riding her bike down this road in the 1950s, and losing her balance, resulting in a nasty fall down into the field on the right. She ended up bruised, and wiser! Trá Bó Deirge beach is on the right, and yes, there are a couple of people on the beach. *Author*

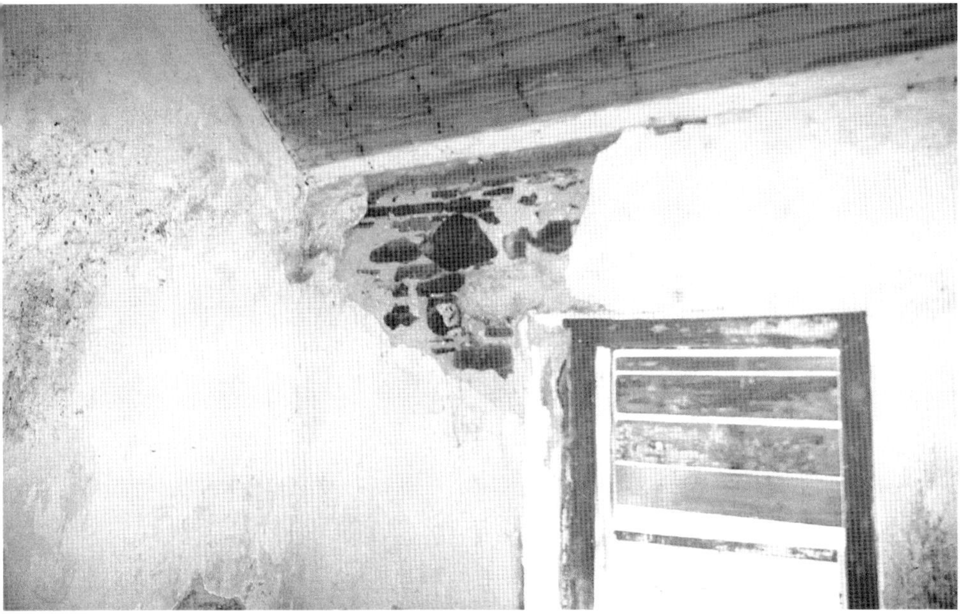

Above: Interior of a Land Commission house. After 40 years of emptiness, the current floor level is perhaps half a metre higher than it was when the house was occupied. This, it has to be said, is due to the ongoing deposits made by sheep, walking unhindered in and out of this house! The solid construction of the house is clear - where plaster has now fallen off the wall above the fireplace, the solid stonework may be seen. The ceiling is of matchboard planking, and the sash windows keep the weather out still. *Author*

Left: Interior of a Land Commission house - detail of interior of an empty example in 2003. The solid stone walls were plastered over. *Author*

were left in some cases to fall into ruins, and in other cases to be used as farm outbuildings. Prior to 1920 all of the houses on Achillbeg were thatched, except the *Paorach's*, which had a roof covered with tarred felt. During the 1930s, slates began to replace the thatch, though the recollection of one resident is that only a few had been thus treated by the end of the decade. During the 1940s almost all thatched roofs on houses still inhabited were remade with slates.

By the 1950s, islanders lived with basic but adequate comfort, gas or solid fuel cookers having replaced open fires in the kitchen, but there was still no electricity or telephone - these facilities did not arrive until within a year of the last residents leaving the island. One of the older houses retained its thatched roof until the 1960s, though by this stage it was not lived in - its owners had moved into one of the new houses nearby, and it was used as an outbuilding.

The multitude of small caves had been used from time to time by smugglers in which to store their pickings. Occasional visits by the Royal Irish Constabulary, or after 1921, the Gardaí, were not unknown. That said, there were other places in the West of Ireland, and other islands, with greater notoriety for piracy and smuggling - whereas there is little record of anything other than what might be termed 'salvage' brought ashore in Achillbeg. One resident remembers a case washed ashore, thought to be off a small fishing boat which had foundered, which was found to contain tins of Ovaltine. This was carefully stashed by the children who found it, in case any of their peers wanted a share of it. On another occasion during World War I, what was thought to have been another gift from the sea turned into a disaster - a young woman found what she thought was a drum of paraffin oil, and she took it into her house. She poured some into a lamp and set it alight. It was petrol, not paraffin, and the unfortunate woman and her baby were burned to death.

While World War II was in progress elsewhere, a British ship was wrecked off Achillbeg. Live mines and bodies of the unfortunate sailors were washed ashore. Gardaí and an official from the Western Health Board attended, and coffins were lined up to take the victims' remains, which were buried at Kildownet Cemetery on Achill. Later, they were taken to Britain for reinterment. As the mines washed up with them were dangerous, island children were taken to a house deemed to be a safe distance away while the mines were dealt with.

Another shipwreck lies just over 2 km offshore, to the north-west. This was a Greek freighter which was torpedoed during World War II. The remains of a winch used in its salvage lies on the shore of Achill Island. One islander remembers scouring the shore around Uaich na Sionnach with her father some years later. Some wooden planks from the wreck had become jammed in rocks. As soon as the tide was at a suitable level to recover them, they did so, and they were able to make wooden pins for the oars of their yawl with the high quality hardwood they rescued.

In the 1950s the Government offered to rehouse the islanders in Co. Meath. The reason that such a location was chosen was that an attempt was being made to establish a thriving Irish speaking community in an area where daily use of Irish was rapidly declining. While this experiment did eventually succeed in creating a small Gaeltacht in Meath, it was done by offering to move people from other places instead. It is hard to imagine how an island people could have settled in an inland environment so different to their own - indeed, a memorandum between Government departments* at the time mentioned this, almost as an afterthought. Hardly surprisingly, the islanders declined the offer.

As the 1960s dawned, the people of Achillbeg were very conscious of the rapidly modernising world outside. This decade brought about major changes nationwide with improvements in education, health and transport. Neighbouring Achill had been connected to the electricity grid in 1952, but this facility would only reach Achillbeg a year or so before the last people left, over a decade later. Twelve Irish offshore islands, including Clare Island, had radio telephone facilities installed in 1953, but again Achillbeg was left out, for over 10 years more. Growing car ownership and the advent of radio and television helped to emphasize the isolation of many rural communities. While visitors to Achillbeg might have found such a life quaint, the realities of living in these conditions eventually became too much - in such circumstances, it was only too understandable for the islanders to want to improve their way of life elsewhere. For some time, the island's age profile had been increasing.

But new activity was afoot. For many years, the lighthouse on neighbouring Clare Island had been considered to be unsatisfactory. While its location high up on the side of Knockmore mountain was ideal in clear weather, it had been found that mist or fog could obscure the light completely. In addition, comparison with other lighthouses showed that it was expensive to operate, and it had no fog light or radio beacon. Therefore, the Commissioners of Irish Lights decided to move the light to Achillbeg, and a suitable site was identified above Oigh na Gabhair, near the southernmost point of the island, in 1960. Notwithstanding the financial case already referred to, further savings would be made by designing the new lighthouse to be unmanned from the outset. As long ago as a century earlier, a proposal had been considered to place an oil lantern on Achillbeg, but this had come to nothing.

A test platform was erected, and the Commissioners set about acquiring the necessary land, both for the lighthouse itself and for a right of way up from the beach. However, this part of the island was held as commonage by 22 islanders, one of whom was by now living elsewhere. In May 1961, the Commissioners instructed their Solicitors to investigate what was involved in acquiring the necessary land. The Solicitor advised them 'This is not at all a simple matter . . .' and nor was it. For some time the Commissioners discussed whether to try to negotiate with 22 landlords, one of them an absentee, or attempt to have a Compulsory Purchase Order served on all of them - with the attendant risk of causing upset to those who would be neighbours of the lighthouse. As it happened, the relevant islanders expressed no objection as the amount of land required was very small and was of little or no use or value. Indeed, the Commissioners' notes mentioned in 1962 that 'the route which the right of way will follow is very rough and only suitable for pack animals . . .'

By this stage the former *Paorach's* house was empty, the last inhabitants having recently moved to the mainland. The Commissioners arranged to rent it from the owner for storage of construction materials and tools. Estimates were drawn up for the lighthouse, the total cost of building it being projected as £12,800. It was estimated that against Clare Island's lighthouse costs of £4,167 annually, those for

* Dept of the Taoiseach Archives, National Archives, Bishop St, Dublin.

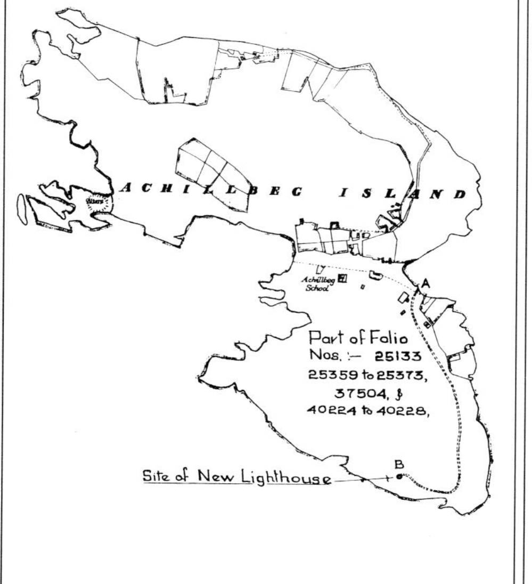

Left: Land Commission map showing the propsed right of way to the lighthouse agreed with Commissioners of Irish Lights in December 1963. *Commissioner of Irish Lights*

Below left: Final estimate prepared in connection with the construction of Achillbeg lighthouse. *Commissioner of Irish Lights*

Below right: Letter from the Commissioners of Irish Lights to a local man appointed as an agent for them during the construction of the lighthouse. The language of the time '. . . you are therefore to have a short ladder available . . .' sounds somewhat authoritarian nowadays. *Commissioner of Irish Lights*

COMMISSIONERS OF IRISH LIGHTS

ACHILLBEG

FINAL ESTIMATE

JOB 2 - MATERIALS & EQUIPMENT			
Concrete materials, concrete blocks, joinery, etc., for concrete hut		£200.	
Stone-Chance quotation - Equipment	£6,972.		
Spares	126.	7,098.	
Lister quotation - Mains Failure Diesel Alternator Set		348.	
E.S.B. - Capital Contribution	£2,500.		
Installation of Pilot Wire Cable	265.	2,765.	
Curved shutters, made up in L.D.		60.	
Indicator Panel and Failure Panel, L.D.		250.	
Miscellaneous Materials		125.	
Earth wire and lightning conductor		100.	
Scaffolding and Lifting Tackle		54.	£11,000. 0. 0
JOB 3 - LABOUR			
Building Hut.			
1 Tradesman. 6 weeks @ £24.16. 6d. p.w.		£149.	
3 Labourers. 6 " @ £11. each		198.	
Erect lantern and install engine.			
2 L.T.M's. 3 weeks @ £23.15. 0d. each		142.	
3 Labourers. 3 " @ £11. each		99.	
Erect optical apparatus.			
1 L.T.M. 2 weeks @ £23.15. 0d. p.w.		48.	
1 L.T.E. 2 " @ £23.15. 0d. "		48.	
2 Labourers. 2 " @ £11. each		44.	
Electric wiring, including warning lights and earth system and testing.			
1 L.T.E. 4 weeks @ £23.15. 0d. p.w.		95.	
1 Labourer. 4 " @ £11. p.w.		44.	
		£867.	
Insurance and holiday pay	11%	£95.	£962. 0. 0
JOB 4 - TRAVELLING & TRANSPORT			
Tradesmen travelling		£100.	
Stevedores and crew unloading, etc.		150.	
Local Boating		50.	
Transport of materials across Island		400.	£700. 0. 0
			£12,662. 0. 0
Contingencies			138. 0. 0
			£12,800. 0. 0

Irish Lights Office,
DUBLIN.
13-4-64.

ENG/WFS/MP/~~[illegible]~~104/58.

7th July 1965.

Mr. J. Kilbane (Martin),
Cloghmore,
Achill Island,
Co. Mayo.

Dear Sir,

The Commissioners of Irish Lights left this morning on their Annual Tour of inspection and expect to arrive at Achillbeg on July 15th. Please arrange to meet them when they land on the Island.

Please also select the best landing place for the lighthouse, which is probably one of the two sandy coves south of the beach and stand-by to direct the boat to it.

I understand there may be some difficulty in reaching the grass bank from the landing beach as it has a fairly steep face about 5 or 6 feet high. Some of the Commissioners are not young men and you are therefore to have a short ladder available so that they can get up this steep face without too much trouble.

Yours faithfully,

W.F.S.

for Engineer

Achillbeg would be £3,851, including the Attendant's wages. The savings were due to a number of factors, not least the fact that Achillbeg lighthouse would be a much smaller structure, and would have no lighthouse keepers living in it, thus allowing further savings. New tools were bought, delivered to Cloghmore, and taken across to Achillbeg for storage. An Achillbeg man was hired as a foreman to act as a local contact for the Commissioners and their agents, and to select and hire two or three men to assist in the construction work.

But two obstacles remained. Transport of heavy materials across Oileán an Sciorta from the beach would be impossible by the island's usual means of transport, the donkey. In addition, electricity would be needed, not only during construction, but afterwards when the lighthouse was fully functional.

The first problem was overcome by the purchase of a 'reconditioned' 1959 Fordson Dexta tractor, with a transport box fitted to the back, for the sum of £450. It carried a Mayo registration number, EIZ 278.

A man named Michael Keane, employed by the lighthouse authorities, was directed to build a suitable raft to float it across, and the tractor arrived at Cloghmore in May 1964 for storage until the raft was ready. The question arose as to who would drive it following its maiden voyage to Achillbeg. Since the island had no road vehicles, the only islanders who could drive were those who had experience of doing so elsewhere. With very few able-bodied men left permanently living on the island, only one man was found who could drive it, and even he expressed some reluctance to take on the job. Accordingly, an outside driver was brought in. The raft was ready for action by October 1964, and the initial mode of transport by donkey and pannier was discontinued. Achillbeg had received its first road vehicle.

The other problem, that of electricity supply, was being addressed at the same time. In the 1950s the Electricity Supply Board (ESB) had offered to introduce electricity to the island, but with the settled population down to some 50 people, housed in no more than eight houses, they said that it would only be cost effective if everybody on the island wanted to be connected. This was not the case, as a small number of elderly people were happy with what they had, so nothing came of it for several years. Towards the very end of the island's populated days, in the early 1960s, plans were again made to bring in electricity - the case was more urgent now, despite the population being now under 40 in number - it was needed for the planned lighthouse at the southern tip of the island. This would be all-electric and unmanned, so electricity was essential. To the ESB, a lighthouse was a different matter to half a dozen houses, and negotiations were opened with the Electricity Supply Board to lay an undersea power cable across to the island. This was ready during 1964, and poles were erected to take overhead wires from the north shore around the side of the hill towards Trá Bó Deirge, and onwards towards the lighthouse. A second line left the main one near the beach and continued towards a few houses in the Baileamuigh area. Under the Government's Rural Electrification Scheme, the opportunity was taken to kill two birds with one stone, and four island homes were connected at the same time. Despite the number of houses to be connected barely half that of five years earlier, Christmas Eve 1964 saw an electricity supply in place.

During installation of the electricity poles, it was necessary to carry out a small amount of blasting, and during one such attempt to enlarge a hole for one

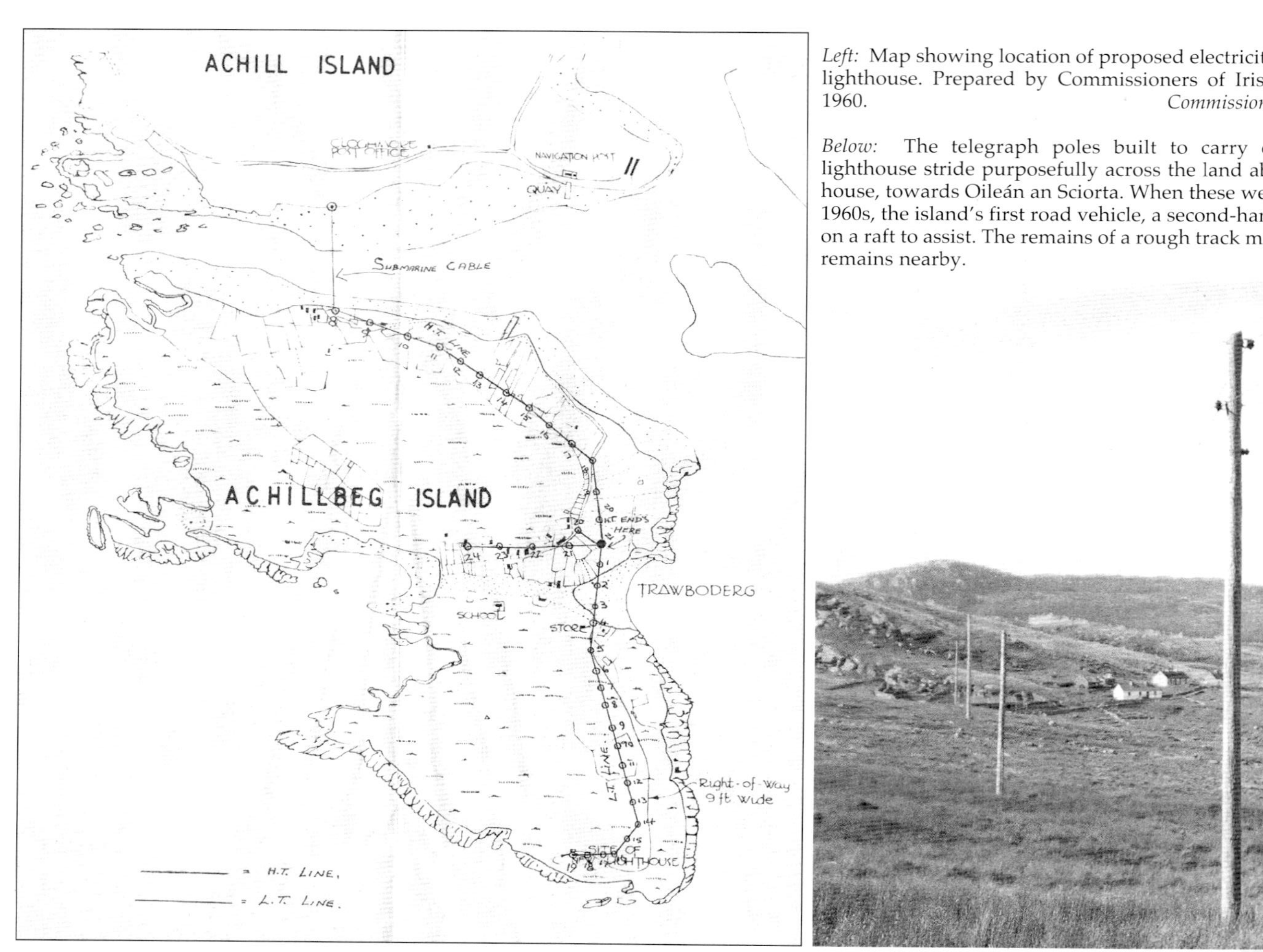

Left: Map showing location of proposed electricity line to serve the lighthouse. Prepared by Commissioners of Irish Lights, August 1960. *Commissioners of Irish Lights*

Below: The telegraph poles built to carry electricity to the lighthouse stride purposefully across the land above the *Paorach's* house, towards Oileán an Sciorta. When these were installed in the 1960s, the island's first road vehicle, a second-hand tractor, arrived on a raft to assist. The remains of a rough track made for the tractor remains nearby. *Author*

The southern end of the island, with the lighthouse visible above the rocks. The cove below the lighthouse is Uaich na Gabliair, the 'cove of the goats'. To the left is Uaich Reille. Depending on translation, this may either mean 'Reilly's Cove' or the 'cove of the roll of wool' - possibly, testament to an incident in which a sheep showed that it was not as adept as a goat at negotiating this sea-battered and rocky terrain! The rocks just under the lighthouse were named Sceilp an Eala by one former resident, though others did not recall the name. The meaning is uncertain. *John Eagle Photography*

The lighthouse in May 2003. Commissioned in 1965, the light was unmanned from the outset and has a range of 18 nautical miles. *John Eagle Photography*

Right: Few pictures survive showing the centre of the island when inhabited. This view was taken in 1960 by the surveyors for the lighthouse, hence the reference number '10' in the foreground. Most of the remaining inhabited houses can be seen across the central valley. Behind them, Achill Island's southernmost highlands can be seen.

Commissioners of Irish Lights

Below: This is the view from the east side of Trá Bó Deirge beach, as it was in 1960. The house on the right is where the *Paorach* lived, and is still inhabited in this view. It is whitewashed, and has a tarred roof. The population is in decline though: while sheep graze in front of the left-hand house, its occupants have recently emigrated.

Commissioners of Irish Lights

of the posts one of the new window panes for the lighthouse was smashed by the blast. The undersea cable proved to be unsatisfactory and was replaced with an overhead line a few years after its introduction.

The several men employed full time on the construction work required accommodation in Achillbeg, and the Commissioners asked their 'man on the ground' to seek suitable accommodation, as they realised that it was unrealistic to expect their workmen to travel in and out of the island every day. Conveniently, one island family had just moved across to Achill Island, and they were in a position to rent their former house to the Commissioners for £3 per month. The Commissioners observed that all that would be needed for the house were a few gas cylinders and a cooker.

By October 1964, work had ceased for the winter months, and the tractor was taken away to the mainland for a badly needed servicing. The raft was taken up onto the beach in Achillbeg to avoid damage. The Commissioners arranged to continue to rent the house while unoccupied for £1 per month.

With electricity now in place, a newspaper report described how islanders would be able to have fairy lights on Christmas trees for the first time in December 1964. Little did the islanders know it, but only a year later the newly lit houses would all be empty: electric fairy lights were to have but one Christmas to light up Achillbeg homes.

As 1965 dawned, and work was due to resume, a preliminary report by the foreman stated that 'The cables that go under water from Cloghmore to Achillbeg taken [*sic*] the electricity to the lighthouse are all smashed by the storms. A pole on the Strand where we unloaded the material for the lighthouse . . . has a list . . . of 45 degrees . . . We had terrible storms here since 1st January 1965.' Remedial action was necessary, and quickly; the work could not be held up as the lighthouse needed to be in a serviceable state as soon as possible. The under water cables were repaired, but this system was clearly unsatisfactory. It was not until 1967, two years after the last residents had left, that a pole was placed in the middle of the short stretch of sea separating the island from Achill, enabling current to be carried overhead. This was more reliable for a while, but ultimately no match for the winter forces of sea and wind. The lighthouse authorities were forced to use the lighthouse's standby diesel generator for a time, and a recently-evacuated former island resident was employed to take drums of fuel into Achillbeg to be stored in the former *Paorach's* house.

During 1965, work proceeded on target with three Achillbeg men being employed. They started each day by rowing across to Cloghmore to unload the supply lorry, and bring in supplies and materials. Even at this stage, consideration was given to improving the transport situation by hiring a helicopter to lift major components of the lighthouse across. However, no firm could be found in Ireland who were willing or able to undertake this, so a London helicopter hire firm was approached. While their price per lift was deemed to be reasonable, the cost of flying the helicopter from London was prohibitive. It would have had to come via Belfast, and with several other stops *en route*, to Achillbeg. Thus, Achillbeg failed to add air transport to the list of innovations that the 1960s brought!

By autumn, work was nearing completion, and in August a party of officials from the Commissioners of Irish Lights visited to inspect the work, staying overnight at

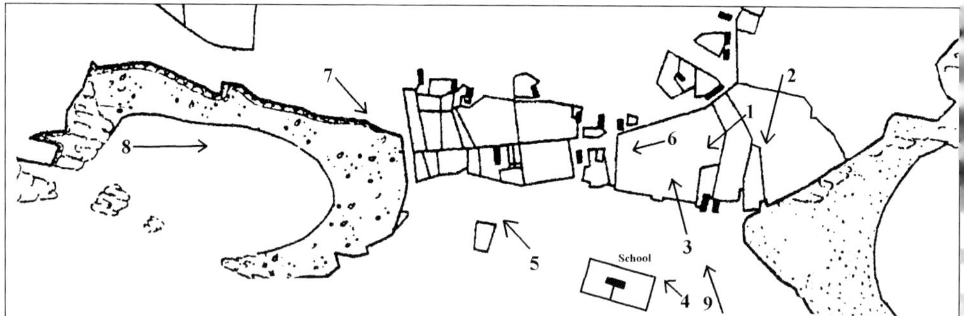

To give an idea of the layout and geography of the central valley, the following series of pictures show the area from the angles shown in the accompanying map.

No. 1. Looking from the houses (Baileamuigh) towards the school. The school can be seen on the far side of the valley on the right, and the top of the beach (Trá Bó Deirge) is just visible on the left, under the rocks. The small field just above the far side of the beach is Garraí Éamiann (Eamonn's garden), and the flat area above the rocks is Macalla ('echo'). The field in the foreground on the right is Idir Dhá Chlaí ('between two ditches'). *Author*

Above: No. 3. Looking from the bottom of the valley up towards the houses. These are 1930s Land Commission houses, and it will be seen from the accompanying map that they do not relate at all to the buildings shown on it. In fact, most of the island's housing stock was replaced with houses such as those in the photograph during the 1930s and 1940s. The white-painted house on the left was in the process of renovation as a holiday home when this picture was taken (2003). To an islander brought up in the 1920s this, the island's principal housing area, acquired a completely new appearance in these years. The rocky outcrop above the houses is Sceilp an Chapall (the 'scalp' or rocky outcrop of the horses). Did an early resident see a shape or image of a horse in this formation, or did somebody once keep horses here? During research for this book, several former islanders were interviewed who had clear memories of events in the 1910s and 1920s. Despite having a detailed knowledge of what their parents and grandparents told them about all aspects of life on the island, all insisted that there was no tradition of horses on the island. Another name for this area was Cam Leac, and the area above the rocks was referred to on an early 19th century Ordnance Survey map as 'Cregalomen', which is probably a loose translation of Creig an Lomáin, a name which refers to an outcrop of rock. The white house on the horizon on the right is another Land Commission house, but it is situated approximately where the coastguards had rented houses of an older type in the 19th century. The field in the foreground is Idir Dhá Chlaí. *Author*

Left: No. 2. View looking south towards the central valley; the beach is on the left. The small roofless building just above the beach is of interest, in that it occupies the site identified as the school on a 1901 Ordnance Survey map. It has all the appearance of an ordinary traditional two-roomed house, but this is what the island's original school did consist of. The house has a tragic story in its past - it was here that a young mother and her child were burned to death following an accidental fire in the early part of the 20th century. Her family moved to a house near the pier after that. The purpose-built school (1903) is on the extreme right. *Author*

No. 4. The view from the *Paorach's* house looking towards Baileamuigh. The school may be seen on the left. The flat area in the foreground is Macalla. *Author*

No. 5. A mixture of housing, Baileamuigh, with abandoned fields in the foreground. The three roofed buildings, which are of 1930s origin, stand with their gable ends facing east to west, while the older houses, such as the roofless ruin on the left, are at right angles to them. The older houses had to be this way round for maximum shelter, despite the slope of the hill favouring the later orientation. The flat area in the foreground was known to some islanders as An Fraoch ('the heather'). Above the houses was Scailp (an Eala?), the meaning of which is obscure. Just above this was simply known as 'the rocks'. *Author*

No. 6. This flat area in front of the school divided the two parts of the island. Frequently wet and soft underfoot, and windy always, it was here that lumps of foam off the sea's waves would blow across the island in winter. *Author*

No. 7. Legacy of Achillbeg's educational system - the school, now roofless and empty, still defies the elements. In the distance, just above the beach on the right, may be seen the gable end of the *Paorach's* house. The field boundaries in the foreground date from the mid-1800s, as Ordnance Survey maps from the 1830s do not show them, but later editions do. *Author*

No. 8. Looking from near Cill Aill Taghnaigh across towards Aill Taghnach. The exposed nature of the small central valley is evident here. The sea can be seen no more than a few hundred metres beyond the stony beach. The Holy Well is on top of the cliff on the left. *Author*

No. 9. The central valley in 1960. The black tarred roof of thePaorach's house may be seen in the centre of the picture, with the other houses across the valley. The fields have neatly maintained boundaries, but few are now freshly tilled, as most of the remaining population are elderly. The line of the island's gravel road may be seen passing behind the houses on the left. Above the houses on the far side, and just under the rocky outcrop may be seen the island's last thatched building, now used as an outhouse. On the edge of Europe, an island community hangs onto its existence - for just a few more years. *Commissioners of Irish Lights*

the Great Southern Hotel in Mulrany. The Commissioners' ship, the TSS *Isolda*, was sent to test visibility of the light from the sea, and as a result of this several final adjustments were made, including the removal of a protruding rock near the lighthouse. At sunset on 28th September, 1965 the Achillbeg light was lit for the first time, that on Clare Island being decommissioned simultaneously. An Achillbeg man, Patrick Kilbane, was appointed as Attendant, and wore full uniform at the opening ceremony at the lighthouse - to which a Commissioner, Ernest Benson, was taken in the 'VIP seat' - the transport box on the back of the tractor! Everybody else walked through the mud and rocks, as the local newspaper put it! Poignantly, the opening ceremony took place on an island finally deserted by most of the few remaining residents only a few weeks before. By November 1965, the tractor had been taken away and sold for £225. The Commissioners cancelled the rental agreement for the house used to accommodate workmen, but retained the *Paorach's* house as a store for oil drums. Instructions were issued to pack away all cups, saucers and utensils which they had brought in for use elsewhere.

The lighthouse had cost £15,908, 15*s*. and 9*d*.; just £308 15*s*. 9*d*. over the final estimate of £15,600 (the original estimate had been £12,800).

The Lighthouse Attendant was not a lighthouse keeper as such - he simply had warning lights attached to an electricity pole 'which he could see from his kitchen window'. If a fault occurred, the lights would alert him to attend to it. However, very soon after the lighthouse opened, he moved to Cloghmore, and the warning lights were transferred to a place near his new house where he could see them. A UHF radio link was maintained between the lighthouse and the Attendant's house until 1991, when remote control commenced from the Commissioner's central monitoring office in Dun Laoghaire.

The lighthouse was not as high as the old one, but had a more powerful light with an intensified red sector to mark the dangerous Bills Rocks. This was an innovation - normally, a red light had a reduced range. It was unmanned from the outset, and is located on 53°51.5'N and 9°56.8'W. The tower is 9 metres high.

As the lighthouse was being planned and built, the remaining population were planning and building too. Achillbeg had become home to a declining and ageing population, with few children in the community as young people continued to emigrate. Some families moved out at this time, leaving fewer still behind. By this stage many houses were already closed up, and only half a dozen or so were inhabited, often by a single elderly person. Many of the carefully tended fields of earlier years were becoming overgrown, with nobody to look after them. An elderly population needed proper care in their twilight years, and with few young people left it was clear that the island community's days were numbered.

A number of local people formed a Committee to seek out the views of each islander, and make plans accordingly. These were Fr Ryan, the Parish Priest, and four islanders. They came to the conclusion that evacuation was the best way forward. Dáil Éireann records in 1961 and 1962 show references in debates to plans being made to evacuate the remaining population, though in the March 1962 Dáil records it was minuted that '. . . the matter has been under consideration . . . and a decision may be reached fairly soon . . .' Reading between the lines, it was known in official circles at this stage that the remaining population were by now willing, if not eager, to leave; but were awaiting governmental assistance. The Government did little to assist them. In other parts of Ireland, examples existed of local authorities providing new houses for island populations who had collectively decided to evacuate their island. The people of Achillbeg were largely left to their own devices.

In recalling the formation of the island's Committee, a former resident recalls a lighter side of the meetings which were held in her parent's house. As a child, she remembers that the children were told not to disturb the adults while they were talking. But the children wanted to stay, so they hid in the attic when meetings were in progress, and threw small items down on the assembled company to amuse themselves . . .

Correspondence between islanders and Government bodies continued with a view to obtaining help in rehousing all concerned elsewhere. Other than assuring the islanders that their case had been 'referred to a Committee', little was done by the County Council. Gradually, the islanders began to leave, one family now, another some months later. In some cases, Council houses were made available nearby on Achill or on the mainland Achill Sound area. The writing was on the wall; the community had now fallen below a sustainable level.

Some islanders already owned land on Achill, Corraun or elsewhere; others made arrangements to rent houses on Achill or Corraun while they bought or built new homes of their own. Many islanders resettled in the southern end of Achill in many cases overlooking Achillbeg, and their land. Achillbeg names such as Kilbane and Gallagher are nowadays common in Cloghmore, Derreens and Sraheens. Some islanders took the opportunity to emigrate, while others had already established a lifestyle in which they worked elsewhere and only returned to Achillbeg at holiday times to stay with relatives.

Even at this late stage, a final act of modernisation was to take place. Despite having been recommended by a Government Committee in October 1960, and approved by a Cabinet minute in July 1961, it was not until April 1964 that a radio telephone was installed on the island. It was situated in one house (owned by Peter Gallagher), but could be used by other island neighbours by arrangement with the householder. The phone number was 'Achillbeg 50'. It was to last little more than two years - after the island was abandoned it was removed again, in July 1966.

Recent closure of the school meant that the few children left would have been faced with a daily boat journey to school in Derreens if their families remained. The Government's Secretary in charge of Gaeltacht affairs visited Achill in June 1965 to discuss improvement of the piers at Cloghmore and on Achillbeg's north shore. But this was the very month that the school closed its doors. It was too late to give much consideration to daily commuting to and from Achill, as the last residents were making preparations to leave. They spoke with mixed feelings about their departure. Happy childhood memories contrasted with the stark reality of living in a place of this sort, where it was necessary for almost everybody to leave to find work, and where life was still hard.

The autumn of 1965 became the autumn for Achillbeg's population - by the end of October, they had all left the island, though one house at least was occasionally occupied for another year or so. A few former residents made occasional visits to their old homes after that, but gradually nature reclaimed the island.

Chapter Four

After the People Left

I came to rest upon your shores
O island now deserted
The silver sea laps at water's edge
where houses tower overhead.
The cry of the gull pierces the stillness
of an island now deserted

Children play by the old school yard
now empty and in ruins
Farmers tilled their lands
now graced by lazy beds.
Laughter rang, throughout the homes
on an island now deserted

(*The Deserted Land*, Noírín Gannon, July 2001)

By the autumn of 1965, the remaining houses were closed up, inhabitants gone. The stillness of the island was punctuated now by the sounds of sea birds and the sheep still grazing there. Several residents continued to make the daily journey in to Achillbeg to tend sheep and land which they still owned, but the little fields and gardens gradually became overgrown, and reclaimed by nature. The neatly gravelled road became a grassy track, and many of the walls around the fields fell into disrepair.

Meanwhile, the old school building lay empty but intact. It was used for a while as a store by the lighthouse authorities, but over the years became derelict as the ravages of time and the weather took their toll. By the time the school reached its centenary, 35 years had elapsed since it closed and the roof and floor had given way. The children's coat-hooks, now exposed to the sky, had dust replaced with rust, as the neatly matchboarded wall they were attached to lost its green paintwork, and became bleached with sun, wind and salt.

But not all of the island's buildings have met with this fate. The *Paorach* had been well known in his day for taking in guests, as did other islanders from time to time: the tranquil beauty of the island was not lost on early visitors. It was not long before one or two of the old houses had been sold to 'outsiders' as holiday homes, and several are used as such today, with others showing signs of being under restoration. On one visit in 2003, the author left the island one summer evening having counted at least 14 people in three groups staying overnight. Two of the houses were occupied, one by quite a large party, and one young family was pitching a tent near the strand. One wonders if a modern green and purple vinyl tent keeps the midges at bay any better than the old peaked-topped canvas type which one elderly islander remembered visitors erecting on the same spot in the 1920s.

It is hard to imagine a more peaceful and beautiful setting for a holiday to 'get away from it all'. Naturally, the holidaymaker will have to bring all his food and

Hard winter weather was best kept out by blocking up doors and windows - like many island houses of traditional design, all open windows and doors were on the east side of the building. On the west side, either none were ever provided, or if they had been, they were later sealed up, as in this example. *Author*

Interior of traditional design stone cottage, Baileamuigh. The furthest gable contained an open fireplace, and the room nearest the camera may have been used for livestock in latter times as a doorway on the left-hand side of the middle wall has been closed up at some stage. The school may be seen in the distance. *Author*

A pair of lonely ruins. Few of these homes were occupied after the Land Commission ('Gaeltacht') houses were built in the 1930s. *Author*

The view from the window of an old cottage. Did the occupants look out of it and ponder for a moment on their new life, as they closed up the house for the last time? *Author*

The 1965 evacuation of the island did not mean the end of all life there - nearly 40 years later, a sheep dip is seen here, built on to one of the old houses, and clearly still in use. Several former residents still keep sheep on the island. *Author*

The view from Gort Breac towards An Baile Amuigh (Bailemuigh) and the school. The stony beach in the foreground, and the sandy one (Trá Bó Deirge) in the background, show how narrow the island is in the middle. Islanders spoke of this area being a 'natural wind tunnel' in winter. Many a storm must have battered the gable window of the school while those inside, barely warmed by a turf fire, struggled with maths and English verbs by the light of oil lamps. The flat area behind the school was known as Macalla ('echo'), on account of the acoustic conditions in that place. *Author*

Trá Bó Deirge beach, late summer 2003. The much smaller sandy cove on the far side of the beach is Maolán na mBan, the 'bare rock of the women'. Traditionally, girls and women bathed here, the boys occupying the larger beach, where boats were also brought in before the pier was constructed. Above the beach is the cultivated area known as the 'páirc', through the middle of which a small path leads from above the beach up to the left. This was the 'Watch House Road', a path believed to have been built by the coastguards in order to carry supplies from their boats up to the houses they rented, which were situated just out of the photograph on the left. On this warm evening, two small boats are present - we are not alone! Just across the narrow stretch of sea is mainland Corraun. *Author*

supplies, and be content with the company of his own party, or none. Not everybody wants a fortnight in the Costa del Sunshine, Shops, and Nightclubs! While houses have been sold in this way by a few former residents, the land has largely remained in their ownership. In the 21st century, sheep are still tended by members of the families who left and their descendants. No cattle are kept in Achillbeg now, and no crops are grown, but the remains still exist of tilled fields and their boundaries, firing the imagination and adding to the rich but compact landscape of the island.

The electricity line had been installed just before the last people left in order to service the lighthouse. Following several unsuccessful attempts to use an undersea cable the Electricity Supply Board advised the Commissioners of Irish Lights that since there was no longer a resident population they could not justify repairing it after its most recent savaging by stormy weather in March 1967. Attempted repairs had failed, and the ESB suggested that a permanent generator be installed. The lighthouse authorities again rented the house that they had housed their staff in during construction and held discussions with the owner about placing oil storage tanks at this property. The householder raised some objections, but before any serious negotiations needed to begin, the ESB relented and provided a new supply consisting of lines carried over the water on poles. This new supply was commissioned in October 1967, despite the engineer in charge observing that the poles would be 'subjected to very wild weather' His words came true - in 1971 they were badly damaged by severe winds and were reported to be drooping dangerously. However, the Commissioners had removed their temporary generator in 1968, and ended their rental agreement for the house used for workmen's accommodation. As an added precaution, given the difficulties in maintaining an electrical supply, 1971 saw the introduction of radio monitoring of the lighthouse, replacing the original arrangement made with a local attendant. This had suffered from poor reception.

The Commissioners had retained the former *Paorach's* house as a store until 1974, when they asked the owner if he would be willing to sell it to them. However, as both parties agreed, the roof was in very poor condition and it was uncertain what the house was worth, so nothing came of it. Rental continued until March 1979, after which another winter battering had reduced the house to a state of 'rapid deterioration'. The roof has since fallen in completely and some walls are no longer sound. By this stage the lighthouse had adequate storage space itself, and it received a new storage area in 1986. This time a helicopter was used to ferry in the necessary materials. In 1998 the Commissioners for Irish Lights established a helicopter landing pad adjacent to the lighthouse. The rough track made from the beach to the lighthouse for access during construction was by now barely discernible, and certainly impassable by any means of transport other than on foot.

Some of the former islander's houses fared better. Not long after the last residents had left, several houses were sold to holidaymakers. Several are now used as holiday homes and avail of the electricity supply as does the lighthouse. Drinking water is still available in several wells, for those who know where to look.

Some of Achillbeg's only permanent residents, 2003. This view as at Creigh Mhór, above Garraí an Dúna. *Author*

Gort Breac, the 'speckled field'. Above it was Gort Breac Ard, the 'high speckled field', and Bearna Ghort Breach Ard, the 'gap/way out of the high speckled field'. The numerous rocks are the probable reason for the area to be described as speckled. The island road, having come round the hill from the pier, and past the houses, ended up here. *Author*

On a beautiful sunny evening this is the view from Garraí na Loinge, the 'garden of the ships'. This is the more sheltered side of the island and nature has attempted to allow a few bushes to grow in the shelter of the walls, but even these are not native. After the permanent population had left, some of the former homes were sold off as holiday houses. The new owner of one of these planted a few fir trees here as an experiment, and they have survived - though without the shelter of the wall this would have been unlikely. Inside the wall is Garraí Uachtair, which may mean the 'upper garden', or alternately a garden for dairying. If the latter is the case, it might give a clue as to one former use of the ruined building in the foreground. However, one islander identified this as 'Ned Jim's Cró (hen house)'. This former owner, at least, used it to shear sheep in. *Author*

The last house on the island, still in good order some 50 years after the occupants left for a new life in England in the 1950s. The road runs past it, but ends shortly afterwards. A rough track was constructed in the 1960s for some distance further to allow access for a tractor when the electricity poles were being erected from here towards the lighthouse. *Author*

Between the pier and the houses, the road and its boundary walls have withstood nearly 40 years without maintenance in this 2003 picture. *Author*

Down the road towards the pier. The fields on the left, in the area called the 'Páirc', are still well maintained, fenced and gated. *Author*

The island road, still in excellent condition, winds round the hill from Leargán towards the pier. Cloghmore pier is to the left, in the distance, on Achill's southern tip. *Author*

The road just east of the pier on the island's north side. The stone retaining wall on the right remains, but coastal erosion is eating into the road surface on the left. The stone surface of the road may be seen, though this part looks as though it may fall into the sea at any time. It is believed that this stretch of the road required repair following storm damage about 1930. *Author*

A small dumper truck rots away silently today near Leargán. This was brought to the island by a former resident after the permanent population had left, in order to carry out some work on his property there. However, it broke down and had to be abandoned. To the author's knowledge, this is one of only three motor vehicles ever to run on the island's roads. The other two were a tractor used in connection with the lighthouse construction in the 1960s, and an old motor bike with sidecar which was taken over some years later by a holiday home owner. With only one small road from the north side of the island to the centre, such vehicles would always have a limited range. In 1999 a mechanical digger and cement mixer were used on the pier during repairs. *Author*

An old sheep shears lies rusting inside the ruins of one of Achillbeg's old houses. *Author*

By July 1999, the old pier had deteriorated badly. This small digger and a cement mixer were brought to Achillbeg to effect the necessary repairs. *Joe Kilbane*

The old and the new: repairs underway at Achillbeg's pier, July 1999. *Joe Kilbane*

Family picnic party leaving the island from Trá Bó Deirge strand, 1993, almost 30 years after permanent habitation ceased. Behind may be seen the overgrown remains of land formerly cultivated right down to the shore. Near the rocks below there were several fresh water wells. The hill above the house is Oileán ne Sciorta. The house, though long unoccupied, was still structurally sound, roofed, and intact. *Author*

The pier on the island's north side. Though overgrown with seawood, the pier has had some repair work carried out in recent years. Cloghmore pier on Achill Island is across the water. *Author*

Cloghmore pier, taken from the boat coming out from Achillbeg. *Author*

Cloghmore pier in 2003; Achillbeg lies beyond. The pier has been considerably enlarged since the last days of the island's occupation. *Author*

What does the future hold for Achillbeg? Conventional wisdom tells us that no matter what world economic circumstances throw at us, no matter what types of investment come and go, land will always be valuable sooner or later. If this is the case, the descendants and families of those who own the land in Achillbeg do indeed hold a very unique asset. Some Irish islands which are in much more remote locations have thriving communities, and on some of these the Irish language is very much the primary one. Examples of this would be Tóraigh in Donegal, Óilean Chleire (Cape Clear) off Co. Cork, and the three Aran Islands in Co. Galway to name a few. Through history, there are examples of Irish islands which have had a viable population and community for some time, and many years after this has died out, or moved on elsewhere, another community appears and establishes itself. This, indeed, happened to Achillbeg: there seem to be few signs of habitation between the early settlements on the north and west coast and the more recent population of the 19th and 20th centuries. Several Irish offshore islands which lost their populations in the 20th century have been in more recent times re-colonised, albeit by a small number of people. In theory, this could also apply to Achillbeg - maybe in 50 years, maybe in two hundred.

For the present, Achillbeg's use to mankind is as a grazing ground for the sheep of former residents, and as a holiday location, albeit a very quiet one indeed, for those who own holiday homes there or camp occasionally above the strand.

In the very long term, there is another factor at work: the sea continues to relentlessly batter this western outpost of Europe - as on neighbouring Achill and on the mainland. The south-western coast of Achillbeg and nearby areas on Achill are literally falling into the sea - the writer has witnessed a huge chunk of many tons of rock falling into the sea off Achill in bad weather. In the 1990s, an entire sandy beach was swept away in the tide one night at Dooagh, some miles away along the coast of Achill - only to reappear in part after another storm at a later date. Achillbeg's southern hill, Oileán an Sciorta, acts as a shelter for Baileamuigh, the central valley, and the northern hill adjacent to Cloghmore. But down at the southernmost point of the island, a winter storm is a spectacular pageant of nature as the thundering energy of the Atlantic and the wind fling waves against the rocks while the spray stings the observer's face . . .

Now empty, fields of present
embrace the memories of yesterday
now, decked by dock and thistle

(from *Memories of a childhood summer*, Noírín Gannon, 2001)

Chapter Five

Island Life and Culture

Achillbeg had a close knit community, as befitted its size and population. Many of the families were inter-related, though there were equally many examples of outside people marrying into the island. The fact that almost everybody in Achillbeg emigrated at some time, even if only temporarily, contributed to one of the island's characteristics - its bilingualism. In other districts in Ireland, English was still very much a secondary language well into the 20th century, and there were of course other parts where even by then locally spoken Irish was a detail of history. The Irish spoken in Achillbeg was the same as that spoken on Achill - there was a distinct dialect, which gave a clue to the island population's origins in the fact that it contained many features found in the Ulster dialect. Despite that, a native speaker from, say, Donegal or Tyrone was considered by Achillbeg (or Achill) people as having too quick a style of speech. Certain sayings, phrases, or words were found elsewhere only in Antrim, Donegal, or other Ulster counties in between. In the early 1960s G. Stockman recorded a very comprehensive list of similarities between the Achill dialect and that of Ulster, which was published by Queen's University in Belfast in 1974*. In this study, words are recorded as being in use in Ulster and Achill only; other examples exist of a form of a word used throughout Ireland being used alongside a 'local' word, and so on. The dialect thus associated with Achillbeg was also associated with Upper Achill, i.e. the central and southern part of Achill, adjacent to Achillbeg; but Lower Achill (the western end of the island) had its own dialect, and at one time even the people there were seen as being different from those of Upper Achill.

Between 1911 and 1925 there was a gradual national decline in the percentage of Irish people speaking the native tongue, and a corresponding increase in the day to day use of English. This was due to two things; firstly, in 1911 the educational system was still the British one, which was conducted entirely in English. The use of Irish in general had been actively discouraged by the authorities for so many years that an almost irretrievable conversion to the English tongue was under way. Secondly, increasing emigration of Irish people to English speaking countries resulted in greater interaction with these countries. In Achillbeg this trend was reversed, mainly through the efforts of the *Paorach* who, as mentioned, was a strong supporter of teaching in the native tongue - and did so meticulously, whatever officialdom thought. In the general area of Corraun and Achill, the equivalent figures were:

Proportion of population speaking Irish as their first language

	1911	*1925*
Corraun	87.5%	87.5%
Achill Island	56.0%	53.1%
Achillbeg	83.3%	97.2%

* A copy of this work is also held in Castlebar Library.

A drawing of a soot house from a 19th century publication *Irish Folk Ways.*

At Garraí an Dúna, near the north-western tip of the island, this smoke house, or 'hen-cró' remains. The building is not much over a metre in height, and was used for slowly burning sea shells and seaweed through the winter to make fertiliser for the fields. In summer, these small buildings were used as hen houses. This one was used by the Gallagher and Corrigan families. One resident recalls it being used for her own hens, which were taken away from this exposed site in winter, to spend the darker months of the year scratching around her house a short walk away. In the background may be seen Achill Island's southern end, just across the water. The adjacent coastal erosion encroaches - how long will it be before this ruin is despatched into the Atlantic? *Author*

To the end bilingualism was maintained on Achillbeg, and one of the pleasures of talking with a former islander today is the rich variety of Irish words that are in their vocabulary, used in everyday conversation.

In 1838, just before the famine, the Ordnance Survey recorded some details about land use and agriculture on the island thus: '. . . It is the property of Sir Richd. O'Donnel, Newport, and is let to tenants by a lease of lives at £64 yearly . . . The cattle all graze in common on the uncultivated ground, their owners paying a sum proportionate to the number they respectively have grazing. The arable land is held in divisions respectively. The island is in general very rocky, only 80 acres being capable of cultivation; the remainder is rocky mountain . . .'

Islanders worked hard to maintain the fertility of their land, and were very skilful in getting the best out of it, but farming implements were simple. At the start of the 19th century, a survey of the island indicated that there were '. . . five or six common ploughs, harrows with wooden pins, very few with iron, and very frequently a hand rake which is used for harrowing in the grain . . .' Even in later days no mechanised equipment was used at all since there was neither electricity nor any road vehicles. However, many parts of the island had been painstakingly cleared of stones, fertilised, and cultivated. Most cultivation was on the north slope of the central valley, along the east side of the island, and on the northern coast, overlooking Achill. Fields were surrounded by well-built stone walls, many of which are still standing.

Fertiliser was made from crushed sea shells and seaweed. The seaweed was gathered in large bundles and taken into the island by boat, while barnacles were scraped off rocks and crushed, before being placed on the drills of potatoes. This added lime and minerals to the soil.

The method of fertiliser manufacture had interesting origins. In the very early 19th century and earlier, the poorer houses in the general district were made of clay or turf sods, with a roof of similar materials. They had neither chimneys nor windows - in fact, the only source of light and ventilation was the open doorway. While no remains of any such houses are known to exist specifically in Achillbeg, it was common practice where these houses did exist that when roofs became unstable, and they were due to be replaced, the sods from which they had been made were used for fertiliser. The reason for this was that owing to the lack of ventilation, soot would gather on the inside of the roof after a period of time. It is believed that in northern Scotland, and probably also in Ireland, houses were in some cases deliberately constructed in this ventilation-free fashion for this reason.

In any event, when in later years house construction became more sophisticated, small 'soot houses' were built. A description of one in 1880* is of interest:

> The smoke oozes out over the whole roof, giving the house, when seen from a distance, the general appearance of a dung-heap in warm wet weather. The object of the roof is to . . . accumulate soot [The description went on to say] The soot-huts are rectangularly gabled structures measuring some ten by five feet externally and about eight feet high. They are built either out in the fields, where peat and sods are at hand, or near the farms, in which case they often serve in summer as hen-houses. The low side-walls are of dry

* *The Past in the Present*, A. Mitchell, 1880.

stone construction though when built in the fields they are more usually of sods: the entrance, in the gable, is only some two and a half to three feet high. The roof structure is of the simplest, consisting of a ridge pole against which bits of driftwood serving as rafters rest without ties of any kind, the whole being kept in place by a great thickness of sods laid horizontally, the lowest layer resting on the thick wall-tops.

At the end of the harvest season the hens would be removed to spend the winter closer to the farmer's house, which would be in a more sheltered location, and the roof would be built up as described. The fertiliser ingredients would be burned as described, smouldering away all winter. No wonder the smoke houses were located well away from the houses! The roof would become soot-encrusted and charred, and would eventually fall into the ashes. The mixture provided a very good fertiliser. In summer, the building would be lightly roofed, and used as a 'hen-cró' or hen-house.

Many different crops were grown in Achillbeg's fields. Turnips, wheat, oats, rye, beetroot and potatoes were all used to feed animals and humans alike. Cabbage, onions and carrots were also grown.

An early 19th century description of the diet in the general area was thus: '. . . potatoes, a little oaten bread, milk, butter, herrings and on two or three grand festival days in the year, some bits of flesh-meat.'

An 1892 description of an island diet for those less well off was:

Breakfast - Tea and flour bread; very poor people had potatoes instead of flour bread
Dinner - Potatoes and milk or eggs
Supper - Potatoes and milk or eggs

It was noted that 'the custom of taking four meals a day . . . is now creeping in'.

An interesting insight into the overall economy of a family unit has survived - this dates from 1892, and refers to two typical families in the Achill/Achillbeg area. These statistics came from a British Government survey, and show a comparison between the annual income and expenditure of a well-off family with four teenagers, and a poorer one with five children under 14:

Family in Ordinary Circumstances

RECEIPTS	*£*	*s.*	*d.*	*EXPENDITURE*	*£*	*s.*	*d.*
Father's migratory earnings (with clothes)	9	0	0	Rent of holding	1	0	0
				Grazing for Cattle/Sheep	1	0	0
Above for sons	9	0	0	County Cess		2	6
Above for daughters	6	0	0	Clerical charges		10	0
Sale of 1,800 eggs	4	1	0	4 bags of meal	3	0	0
Profit on sale of pig	1	10	0	6 bags of flour	3	12	6
Sale of one bullock	3	0	0	Groceries: half a pound of tea and 1 stone of sugar per week	7	10	0
				8 ounces tobacco per week	5	14	0
				Clothing	3	0	0
				Sundry household expenses	2	10	0
Total:	*32*	*11*	*0*	*Total:*	*27*	*19*	*0*

Family in Poor Circumstances

RECEIPTS	*£ s. d.*	*EXPENDITURE*	*£ s. d.*
Father's migratory earnings,		Rent of holdings	1 0 0
with clothes	10 0 0	Grazing of cattle	10 0
Sale of eggs	4 0 0	County Cess	2 6
Sale of pig	1 10 0	Clerical charges	5 0
Sale of bullock		Meal and flour	4 4 0
(one every 2 years)	1 10 0	Groceries	3 15 0
		Tobacco	2 12 0
		Clothes	3 10 0
		Household	1 10 0
Total:	*17 0 0*	*Total:*	*17 8 6*

It was further estimated that the food that was grown by the family and consumed by them was worth about £18 10*s.* 0*d.* In one year, this equated to four tons of potatoes, 30 hundredweight of corn, and two tons of straw (for bedding and animal feed).

Due to the good quality of what clay soil there was, it was possible for islanders to grow an early potato crop. If there were many spare potatoes they would be sold at Achill Sound market where a good price could be gained for them. Winter feed for cattle was hay which was cut in the autumn and saved in hayricks. This was augmented with wheat stalks, straw and grass. In late summer while the hay was being cut, it was customary to make weatherproof covers for the hayricks out of rushes. Since no rushes grew in Achillbeg, some islanders would travel across to Corraun to cut them (at Belfarsad). These had another more important purpose - they were used for thatching the roofs of the houses until slated roofs began to take over in the 1930s.

One resident recalls summer days spent with her parents in the fields, cutting the grass with scythes, and laying it in rows to dry. Once dried, it was gathered into haystacks and saved. Oats were harvested in similar fashion, with two full stacks being a day's work for one person. They were weighted down with stones to prevent the wind blowing them away. Oats were then threshed by hand, and when the sheafs were moved, mice could sometimes be heard squeaking before running away when disturbed. After threshing, the oats were sieved out as food for the hens.

Much of the harvesting work was done by women and young teenagers, as this was the time of year when their older brothers or fathers could be away working in Scotland or England.

Most households owned a few cattle, pigs and hens along with perhaps 30-40 sheep which grazed the hilltops. A sheepdog, of course, was an essential occupant of most houses. While each household had its own fields or gardens, the hilltop pastures were commonage, used by everybody. Donkeys were also bred, being required for transport. Cows were raised for beef and milk. An islander described the butter making process: '. . . we set the milk in a dish, it was set in the morning. We'd cream it off in the evening and put it in a crock, then into a churn. You had to churn it up and down, then you salted it. If someone called at the house, they had to take a hand at the churn, or there'd be bad luck . . .'

Cattle raised on the island were seen as good quality by buyers elsewhere - several Achillbeg residents recalled fair days at Achill Sound, when they routinely gained the best prices for their cattle. On a fair day, cows were brought to Cloghmore in a yawl at high tide, but could be persuaded to swim at low tide if necessary. Cows are not known for their agility in the sea, and were often afraid to go into the water. When this happened, the cow's head was held under the water until she became used to it, and a rope was placed around her neck and secured to the boat. One man would row, while another man could hold one or two cows on ropes. The cow would be able to float, but would swim when the water got into her nostrils. From Cloghmore pier the cattle were walked the few miles to Achill Sound. The journey in the sea washed them, and the salt in the sea water made their coats shine. This helped their appearance, and islanders would readily sell them at Achill Sound market. One resident recalled bringing a cow across to Derreens this way in September 1937, to visit a bull owned by a farmer there. On his way, he met a lengthy funeral procession on its way to Kildownet Cemetery, and he had to move his cow off the road. The sun shone on the windscreen of the hearse as it made its slow journey along the road. The procession was of the victims of the tragic Kirkintulloch fire in Scotland, where 10 young people from the Achill area had perished in a dormitory which caught fire. The victims were some of the many from Achill, and Achillbeg, who travelled to work there each season. Their remains had been brought by train to Achill, just two weeks before the railway line closed - thus fulfilling the grisly prophecy made by Brian Rua O Cearrbhain, of Erris, many years earlier. The first train to Achill (in 1894) had carried coffins, and now one of the last ones did too. Local legend claims that O Cearrbhain had predicted that 'the day will come when fire carriages on iron wheels would bring death'.

If a cow made several journeys back and forth, perhaps being taken to a bull on one occasion, and back to market on another, she would actually become used to swimming, and some cows were able to swim by themselves behind the boat with little guidance from their escorts. In contrast, pigs took more readily to the water, and could swim, but were inclined to cut themselves with their hooves while doing so. Therefore they were taken inside the boat where possible. Sheep were always taken in the boat. Achillbeg boat men knew their stuff - despite this being a treacherous crossing, expert knowledge of the tides and currents meant that islanders were rarely cut off from travelling.

Achill Sound market took place on the last Friday of each month and was a major business and social event, especially between the late 1890s and the early 1940s. As well as trading in all types of livestock, clothes and household supplies were sold at stalls, and other equipment ranging from building supplies to equipment for boats was available in Sweeney's yard. The day's business done, some refreshment could be partaken of in one of several bars at the Sound, before returning to Achillbeg. This could be quite lively - the owner of one of the bars at the Sound in the 1920s used to close early on fair days as he disliked excessive drinking! The closure of the railway from Achill Sound in 1937 and increasing mobility through road transport gradually reduced the fair to a shadow of its former self. More routine shopping was done by Achillbeg's population at Corraun where flour, tea, jam, clothes and other staple supplies were available. Typically, one trip every second week ensured sufficient supplies of the basics.

One hazard of raising cattle on an island was that of preventing them from falling into the sea. A wall and fence was built along a particularly dangerous stretch of the coastline above the cliffs near Uaich na bPréachán at one time, but occasionally livestock would break through. One islander recalled a dramatic rescue of a cow which had become trapped at the edge of the cliff. The animal was indeed rescued - but at considerable danger to its rescuers. Other cows were not so fortunate - one lady recalled several falling to their deaths off the cliffs near Athoire. *Feanógs* (hooded crows), other birds, and foxes would attack lambs and chickens, and children or teenagers were often asked to keep watch over the flocks in season. On one occasion, a child was asked by her mother to watch their chickens. The girl had been ill, and fell asleep instead. The *feanógs* came and took all the chickens - earning the unfortunate child a telling-off! One way of limiting the loss of lambs and chickens to birds was to dislodge their nests near the rocky coves on the island's western side. This was very dangerous, as that part of the island receives a severe battering from the sea all year round. One time, several children set out to climb up the rocks on a moonlit night, using a long stick to reach out towards the nests and smash them. One child stumbled and only avoided a severe and possibly fatal fall by the quick thinking of a companion, who caught her in the nick of time. Recalling the story some years later, she said that had her parents known where she was, and what she was doing, there would have been trouble! Not surprisingly, parents would not have allowed children to play on these rocks. A sad sequel to the tale was that the young man who stopped her falling was the victim of an accident some years later, when he was drowned crossing to Achillbeg.

Each family salted their own beef, fish and pork as required. The process was laborious, but necessary in the days before refrigerators were available. Members of one of the Gallagher households recalled that in the 1930s they did not eat lamb or sheep - they did not like to see them slaughtered, though they raised them for market elsewhere. The same family did, however, ensure they had a good sized pig killed in advance of Easter and Christmas each year. One family of Kilbanes were often called upon to slaughter animals, earning them the nickname of the 'Butcher' Kilbanes.

Pigs were fed on potatoes, meal and sour milk to fatten them. When the time came to slaughter them, as one resident put it 'We'd get him out of his pig sty by rattling a bucket (of food) against the wall outside. When he put his head out, you had to strike him on the forehead with a mallet to stun him'. The pig was then slaughtered, and salted to preserve it. A wooden casing was made with a hole in the bottom, and the pig was placed in the casing packed in salt. In the case of a very large pig the draining process could take up to 10 days. Once the carcass was drained, boiling salted water was poured over it, and the joints cut. These were put in pots hung over the fireplace. The salted water was prepared by adding salt gradually to boiling water, and when it was judged to be approaching the right consistency a potato was placed into the water. If it floated, the water was salty enough, but if it sank, more salt was added. One islander described the process, when he was a child in the 1940s:

Local boatmen at work: this group was photographed near Achill Sound about 1880. All have hats or caps, and at least one has a tie. These are not fishermen; they could be tourists, or part of Lawrence's party. While Lawrence did not visit Achillbeg Island itself, he did take a boat trip around parts of Achill's coastline. The yawl and boatmen are typical of the period and of Achill, Corraun and Achillbeg. *Lawrence Collection CAB6787, National Library of Ireland*

A traditional yawl near Achill Sound, about 1900. This boat is of the type used to carry turf from Saula (on Achill) to Achillbeg. Once in danger of disappearing, the Achill yawl has reappeared in recent years, and every summer a Yawl Festival is held with up to 20 yawls racing in the area. Some are owned by former Achillbeg residents. This picture was taken behind what is now the Ostán Oileán Ácla - the Achill Island Hotel. *Lawrence Collection 4083, National Library of Ireland*

> The pigs were usually about 8 stone in weight, maybe 10. I remember the odd one could be up to 20 stone. We used to get 8 lbs of salt, and brown sugar. You had to mix them, and put salt petre on the bones. Then we drained the pig and preserved it. Sometimes, if it was a big one, you had to take it out, renew the salt, and put it back.

In telling the story of how this was done, another islander who recalled this process in his youth in the 1920s said 'And ye talk about cholesterol nowadays!'

Island transport was by donkey and cart. Many families had donkeys, and they were used to carry supplies up to the houses from the pier or the strand. Shopping was sometimes done at McCann's shop at Derreens, a couple of miles up the road on Achill. Paraffin, which was used for lamps in the houses, was taken to Achillbeg from a shop at Darby's Point in 10 gallon drums. These were brought over by boat and harnessed two at a time to a donkey, one either side. The island's roads were more than adequate for this type of transport, and of course made travel on foot convenient. The roads were few, but well built and maintained. At the time of writing, this is still evident even after almost 40 years of disuse - the surfaces may now be overgrown, but are solid, level, well drained and secure. From the pier, one road headed west, towards the end of the island known as the 'Tail', as far as the coastal area just below Leargán. To the east of the pier, another road headed along the shore line along the bottom of some fields, and then turned sharply south, going uphill past where most of the newer houses were, towards Baileamuigh and the middle of the island. The road continued past the houses to the central valley, turning westwards up the hill towards Gort Breac. The surfaces were of stones and gravel, and sound stone walls bordered them where appropriate. The County Council had a contract with members of the Kilbane family to maintain the roads for a fee of £6 per annum. A Council inspector would call up to twice a year in order to check their condition. Today, the roads remain in good condition structurally, though overgrown, except for a stretch immediately east of the pier where the road to the island's centre heads along the edge of the coastline. At this place it is beginning to be eaten away by coastal erosion, and has narrowed to about half its original width at one point. One islander believed that this stretch of road gave cause for concern in the past, and it was his understanding that major repairs had to be undertaken at this point about 1930. A Council employee came to the island to rebuild it, boarding with John 'Tommy' Gallagher for the duration of his stay.

Transport in and out of the island originally depended on a small natural shelter near Cloghmore (on Achill), and various points along the coast of Corraun, with Achillbeg's beach being used by islanders as a landing place. In 1822 the building of Cloghmore pier and slipway improved facilities on the Achill side, though Achillbeg was to wait nearly another century for its own pier.

The boats used locally were known as yawls and punts. The yawl was favoured for heavier transport, while a punt was a smaller boat some 15 feet long, for lighter use, for example a quick trip across to Corraun or Achill.

Yawls were a feature of coastal life along the west coast of Ireland, with a distinctive double-ended type used in Achillbeg and surrounding areas of Achill and Corraun. These were carvel built, whereas in most of the rest of Ireland clinker-built boats were the norm. They therefore resembled ships

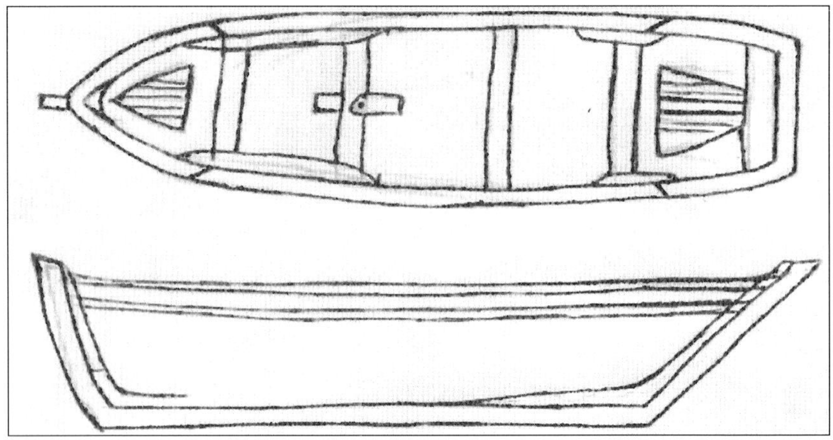

Achill transom stern boat. *Folklore Commission*

Double-ended Achill yawl. *Folklore Commission*

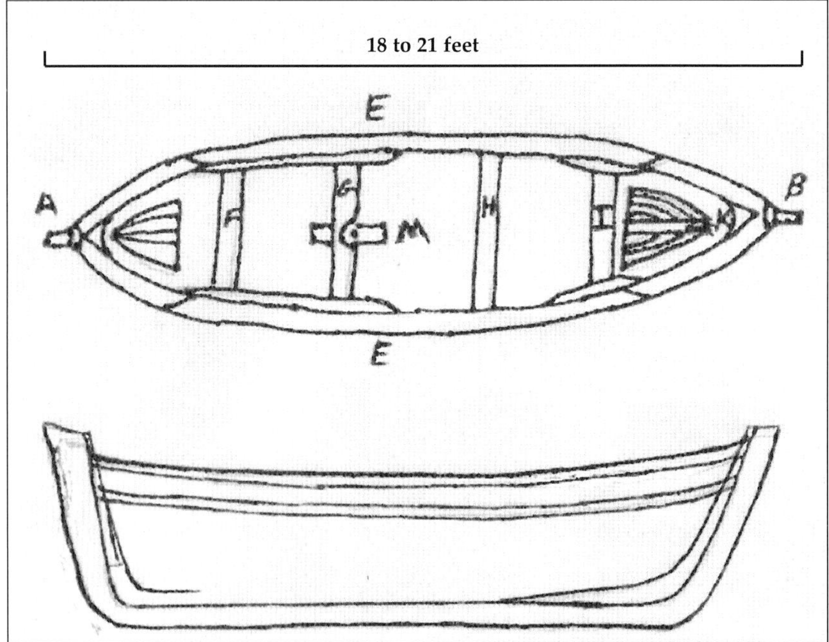

In 1941 the Folklore Commission recorded some details of the traditional Achill yawl. Rough drawings were included as shown. A detailed study of these boats was undertaken by James Kilbane (Achill Sound) in 2001. The difference between the double-ended yawl and the transom stern boat is evident.

A Bow stem or fore stem
B Stern stem, aft stem or sternpost
E Gunwale (in 3 sections)
F Bow thwart, bow seat
G Mast thwart or mast seat
H Removable thwart - a seat that may be removed when carrying a cargo
I Aft thwart
J Bow floor (*An tseile tosaigh*)
K Stem floor with movable centre board (*An tseile deridh*)
M Mast step. Note the hole for the mast foot.

boats, and were easy to land on the island's strand.* They were ideal for local conditions for a number of reasons. Being double-ended, the stern cut approaching waves when they were landing, whereas a transom stern would receive the full force of the wave, making it harder to land in a bay, such as that at Ashleam on Achill, where strong waves washed onto the beach. They were very manoeveurable, an ideal weight and size to easily pull out of the water, but sturdy enough to be used in the open sea in all weathers. They were affordable and easy to build and maintain - a thoroughly practical design, ideal for the strong currents and dangerous waters surrounding the island. This was not lost on the officials of the Congested Districts Board, who encouraged their use from their inception in 1892 onwards†. The CDB had specifications on file for the yawls, and would give grants or loans for their construction. The specifications had to be strictly adhered to in order for the builder to claim the grant. The grant aid was £9 for a boat 18 feet long, or £12 for one 21 feet long. This was, by the standards of the day, a considerable sum of money and would have made a major contribution to the personal circumstances of the recipient.

A Government report on the local fishing industry reported in 1836 that those in use by Achillbeg folk were 14 feet long, 5 feet wide, and 2 feet 6 inches deep. Yawls around the coast of Ulster tended to be about 26 feet long, while the Achill version was between 18 and 21 feet long, and 5-6 feet wide. The mast was about 18 feet high. A boat builder interviewed in 1941§ said that each boat he built had 22 'intimbers' or ribs, and conformed to these dimensions. His oars were 18 feet long. One former islander believed that at least one of Achillbeg's yawls had been of a longer length. In reality, the length of any boat from time to time was governed by the availability of wooden planks the right length. A boat which approximated to the dimensions described above was big enough to be suitable for all traffic, but light enough to pull easily onto the shore.

The yawls were extremely well built to a traditional pattern, some in Achillbeg, others elsewhere. Combined with the skill, strength and experience of island boatmen they provided a most efficient form of transport. In the early part of the 20th century they were built by Michael Corrigan of Achillbeg, or could be purchased for £20 from two men named Burke, at Derreens and Achill Sound, or a member of the Kilbane family at Cloghmore. There was also a boatwright on Corraun. In later years, they were built by a local family named O'Malley. Many experienced boat builders carried their plans in their head - despite no drawings being made, and no measurements taken, their boats always turned out the right length. To some extent this was dictated by the maximum lengths of timber available, but to a greater extent it was the manifestation of a skill now rarely found.

The yawl had a seat at each end, and another between the mast and one end. Between the mast and the other end was a removable seat, which was taken out when the boat was to be loaded with fish, livestock or turf.

* Carvel-built and clinker-built boats differed visually - carvel-built boats had outwardly smooth sides, whereas clinker-built boats had overlapping planks. While carvel-built boats were to be found elsewhere, clinker-built examples were more numerous around Ireland's coastline.

† References in various annual reports of the Board.

§ Interview with Sean O'Malley, part of the collection of the Folklore Commission, details of which may be viewed in UCD, Dublin and Castlebar Library.

ROINN IASCAIGH

AIREACHT UM IASGACH

Department

(~~Ministry~~ of Fisheries).

P G

J McG

J. K.

No. Appn. 299/24 Mayo

Loan 288 S.L.R

Promissory Note.

witness. D. O'C.

We, and each of us hereby jointly and severally or any two or more of us promise to pay to the ~~Ministry of Fisheries~~ DEPARTMENT OF FISHERIES, at 3 Kildare Place, Dublin, the sum of *Five Pounds Sterling* with interest thereon at the rate of £5 : 0 : 0 per cent. per annum for value received, by *Four half-yearly* instalments, payable as follows, viz. :—the sum of £1 :7 :1 on the first day of *November* 1925, and the sum of £1 :6 :7 on every succeeding first day of *May* and first day of *November* in each year, until the first day of *May* 1927.

And should default be made in payment of any of said Instalments the whole amount then remaining unpaid shall immediately then become due and payable.

Dated this 16th day of March 1925.

£5 :0 :0.

SIGNATURE.	ADDRESS, POST TOWN.
Peter Gallagher John	Achill Beg. Island. Achill Sound. Co. Mayo.
John McGinty	Cloughmore, Achill Sound
John his x mark Kilbane Pat	do. do.

Witness to Signatures *and marks* of *... Peter Gallagher John McGinty and John Kilbane ... with whom I am personally acquainted, *and I truly, audibly, and distinctly, read and explained the nature hereof to marksman, who seemed perfectly to understand the same and put* his *mark thereto in my presence.*

*The Names of the Persons whose signatures or marks are witnessed, to be inserted here by Witness.

N.B.—If there are no marksmen, the part in Italics may be struck out.

D. O'Colcuy Sergt ... Witness.

Achill Sound Co. Mayo ... Address.

This document records a loan made by An Roinn Iascaigh (the Department of Fisheries) to three local men, one from Achillbeg, for fishing equipment in 1925. The loan amount was £5, and repayments of £1 6*s*. 7*d*. were to be made at six-monthly intervals. Many islanders availed of these loans.

John Sweeney

In the 19th century virtually all island households had a yawl or punt, but they were not necessarily in good condition. An 1836 survey found Achillbeg's stock of boats to be generally in a poor state with some lying on the beach rotting, beyond repair. Of those in use, many were positively dangerous, and it is testimony to the island boatmen's skills that fishing expeditions arrived home safely. The survey reported rotten timbers in many operational boats and frayed rotting ropes. Some boats had no sails. This is indicative of the extreme poverty prevailing at the time. After the Famine, conditions improved somewhat, but islanders still struggled to keep an adequate fleet of good boats afloat. Government Fishery Board loans were introduced, but the terms, conditions and methods of application were not communicated efficiently, and many local people were unaware of their entitlements to them. Later, the Congested Districts Board gave grants for the purchase of boats, but during times of extreme poverty, when islanders 'couldn't procure one shilling', as the 1836 report put it, the uptake was again less than it should have been for the same reasons.

Following a boom in fishing in the first two decades of the 19th century there were some 30 yawls based at Cloghmore pier by 1850. These were owned by the islanders of Achill and Achillbeg. Over the years, emigration caused the numbers to reduce - a former Achillbeg resident remembered 'up to 20' pulled up on the beach there in the 1910s. By the late 1920s there were five on the north side of the island and 11 on the beach. An islander with childhood memories in the 1930s remembered that 'the pier held the "punts" or curraghs, and every house had a yawl on the beach. About nine or ten fitted at the pier.' After 1921 the Congested Districts Board was wound up, and as a result the grants were discontinued. The last of the grant-aided boats was in use until the 1950s, by which time there were about seven yawls remaining. By the mid-1960s there was but one. At night the yawls were hauled up onto the beach, or in stormy weather even up to a nearby field.

Despite the surrounding sea currents often being treacherous, it was rare for Achillbeg to be cut off for any length of time. Having said that, the possibility that this might happen was an ever-present worry - for example, on one occasion in the mid-1930s no boats could go either way for a full week. In the 1950s and 1960s, the number of elderly people on the island highlighted the issue of a doctor or priest being unable to cross when needed, especially in view of the attendant shortage of able-bodied boatmen, but island folk history suggests that nobody ever died on Achillbeg without a priest nearby, despite occasional instances of the island being cut off for several days at a time by bad weather.

One Achillbeg resident remembered that in his youth, which in his case would have been the 1910s and early 1920s, many of the island's yawls had no names. However, in later years most if not all had. In some cases these names commemorated world events - another indication of the fact that, on account of almost all the population having travelled abroad to work at some stage in their lives, they had a good knowledge of outside current events.

None of Achillbeg's yawls have survived, but this class of boat has now been saved from almost total extinction by the efforts of a number of Achill Island

An Achill yawl arrives at Achill Sound after one of the annual yawl races, 2003. Some crew members have Achillbeg roots . . . 'Saoirse' is Irish for 'Freedom'. *Author*

residents. Once down to two or three operable boats there are now around 20, new examples having been built to traditional design in more recent times. In times past, regular races were held between local teams, some from Achillbeg, but these had died out in the 1950s, largely due to the permanent and semi-permanent emigration of most of the able-bodied islanders who would formerly have taken part. In 1964 the races were revived by an Achill businessman and local boatmen, and they flourish to this day. Newer models have tended to be slightly larger though - some have masts some 25 feet high made of modern materials costing several thousand euros, though in days past masts were about 18 feet high. An appropriate connection with Achillbeg is that descendants of islanders are involved in the operation of some of these. Every summer the Yawl Festival takes place in the area and beautifully kept yawls are raced. In August 2003, one yawl race was dedicated to the twinning festival which took place between Achill Island and the American city of Cleveland, Ohio - a city where, as already mentioned, many Achillbeg emigrants made their new home. Appropriately, the festival had among its guests that year the Mayor of Cleveland, who was of Irish descent, and a prominent Cleveland Judge (Sean Gallagher) whose father left Achillbeg as a child with his parents and siblings in 1930. Another race takes place annually at Derreens, closer to Achillbeg. Again, former islanders are very much involved.

Like agriculture, fishing was carried out with a minimum of technological help - hard physical labour was the main tool. For this reason, Achillbeg and Corraun men were considered to be the best rowers in the area, according to a local man who regularly witnessed boat races in the 1930s. Indeed, Achillbeg men who took part in a race in 1933 were considered throughout the area to be 'unbeatable on rowing'. Women were not inferior in this regard; many anecdotes were told of what one eye witness once described as 'very strong girls and women' undertaking feats of rowing heavy cargoes in rough weather.

In the late summer or early autumn, herrings were caught. The boat was rowed to a suitable location, often many miles out to sea. Using a shade of some sort, or a box with a glass panel in the bottom, boatmen would look at the sea below them to see where the shoals were. The herrings would be ringed with nets, and the nets lifted. Islanders with memories of the 1920s recall that it was possible to land 5,000 herrings per year at Cloghmore Pier with a yawl and a crew of six or seven. What was needed for home use was salted and stored. On occasion, the process of preparing the fish for storage would go on long into the night, with fish being gutted and packed into tubs or barrels of salt. Fish which were surplus to home use were taken to the pier for sale. £1 to £2 could be obtained for 1,000 fish, and a seasonal profit of £40-£50 was achievable. This would have gone a long way towards supporting an island family in those times, though in a bad year the return would have been much less. There was a curing station at Achill Sound, and between 1895 and 1937 fish could be sent to Dublin on the train from there. Herrings fetched five shillings per hundred in Dublin in 1930. One islander recalls looking forward to eating a herring when he came home from school each day. His mother would soak the fish earlier in the afternoon in order to take the salt out of it, and it would be ready to eat later.

By November, haddock was the main catch, the season lasting until springtime. In summer, mackerel, rock salmon and herrings were to be found in bays locally. In general, trammel nets four metres long were planted outside the bay at night, and collected in the morning. A variety of fish would be caught, some eaten straight away, and some salted. Fish was a valuable and tasty addition to the islander's diet, and any surplus caught was sold.

The catch was sold on Cloghmore Pier to local people and fish buyers alike. Some buyers had a fixed price which they would not vary from, and others were prepared to bargain, depending on the quality of the catch. A curious system of mathematics governed the sale of fish. A 'handful' of fish was three, and boxes were filled three at a time. Cod were sold by the dozen - but a dozen consisted of 13 fish, not 12. Herrings and mackerel used an even less conventional form of measure, being sold by the 'hundred'. A quantity of a 'hundred' fish was in fact 129. The idea was that perhaps 100 would be live, 20 dead, and eight 'for luck'. That left one. The final fish was put in a separate box called a *cliabh*, so that when a quantity of fish was to be counted, the number of fish in the *cliabh* was multiplied by 129, whereupon they were then included with the rest, and a deal struck.

Fishing off Achillbeg could be hazardous, though the island was not short of highly skilled boatmen. There were several 'near misses' over the years when one fisherman rescued another in difficulties. Two brothers set out on a fishing trip in the early 1930s, and a sudden storm forced them to seek refuge on the Bills Rock, some 10 miles from Achillbeg. They managed to pull their boat up onto the rocks, and were stranded there for two days. Fortunately, they had matches with which they were able to start a small fire, over which they cooked some of the fish they had caught.

Another man recalled setting out early one morning for a day's fishing with his brother. They saw a skate, the largest they had ever seen, and tried to catch it. After a struggle, they did so, and once they landed it into their boat, they saw that the fish had a large number of hooks stuck in its underside - obviously, many other attempts had been made to catch it, but unsuccessfully. The fish was quite old, hence the number of hooks and its size, but they took it home anyway, and ate it. With neither electricity or refrigeration facilities, fish had to be salted when caught, and could then be preserved for consumption when required. Once cured, the fish were hung up and dried in the air until needed, or stored in layers in a barrel of salt.

One day a conger eel almost two metres long was seen close to the pier. Two Kilbane brothers, then aged about 11, took a lump of bacon and tied it to a line and a hook. They managed to entice the eel out of a crack in the pier, and they caught it. It provided a substantial meal for the boy's family.

While fishing was a major occupation in Achillbeg, as in other areas nearby, few if any islanders made their living entirely by this means. As long ago as 1829, a Government report noted this fact. Most, if not all, houses had a small boat, a 'punt' which was used to go back and forth to Corraun and Achill.

Each summer, the island's yawls played a major part in securing the islander's supply of fuel. Many Achillbeg residents owned stretches of turf bog on Achill's east coast, at Saula. There, the islanders would cut turf when they needed it, and leave it to dry before coming to collect it. The transport of turf from there to Achillbeg was a day's job, and an arduous one, in itself. A typical household could expect to make this journey between two and five times a year, starting in March. Ideally, the work would be done by May, enabling the islanders to travel to Britain for seasonal work once the year's turf supply was secured.

The boat crew would start at 4.30 or 5.00 in the morning, and sail from Achillbeg up through Achill Sound and on to Saula, a coastal district in north-east Achill. It was necessary to make the journey with a high tide, as low tide would have resulted in boats becoming marooned on sandbanks. Because the tide was high at the time of the journey, the boat's mast had to be taken down as it passed under the road bridge at the Sound. An islander takes up the story: 'In the 1920s there were up to 20 yawls. Only one or two people didn't have one, and they shared. Occasionally, a boat did two runs a day - very early morning until late evening. We stacked the turf near the strand'.

As a comparison, another report (from the 1920s) describes 'up to 20' boats setting off together for a day's work - this would have meant that most, if not all, of those available were pressed into service. Each boat would need three or four people to load it.

On arrival at Saula at the beginning of the season, turf which had been cut the previous season and stored there would be loaded. This was done by women and children, while the men cut more. One islander recalled being brought in the boat aged nine or ten - her job was to hold the boat while older members of her family loaded it. The cut turf would be loaded carefully - a job which took many hours. It was important to load the boat evenly on both sides and the turf sods were built up like bricks, right over the gunwale of the boat, and surrounding the mast in the middle. A fully loaded boat would have a load stacked four or five sods over the gunwale. Any more than that, and the boat would be too heavy to sail, though one man recalled rowing with 10 sods above the gunwale. Rowing took longer, and was a very strenuous task, and was therefore not favoured. However, physical feats which would nowadays be considered superhuman were often necessary - one witness remembered watching a man and his wife rowing a huge load against the wind.

The loading had to be done evenly and symmetrically, and in such a way that on the return journey the mast could be lifted out of the middle while the boat passed again under the bridge, and replaced without disturbing the large load of turf. This was a skill in itself - and while the fact that there is no record of any serious mishaps during this manoeuvre, there were near misses. One man, in recalling his experiences in the 1930s, told of how he feared for the life of his older brother (who was on the boat with him) as they approached the bridge with a loaded boat. He watched as the youth lifted the mast clear of the load to lower it down to go under the bridge. However, the current was flowing faster than usual that day, and his brother misjudged the boat's speed - and as they approached the bridge he was still standing up with his back to it. He shouted and leaned forward to grab his brother, who only just ducked in time to avoid hitting his head on the underneath of the bridge, which he missed by a split second and a few inches. Had his head hit the bridge at that speed, the impact would have killed him instantly. On another occasion, an unfortunate tragedy did take place when a man fell between two boats being loaded at Saula, Unknown to his colleagues, he was trapped with his head under shallow water, and he drowned. A memorial was subsequently erected nearby.

The return journey had to take place with the evening tide, and once the boats were home the unloading had to take place immediately so that after a few hours sleep, the crew would be able to set out again with the morning tide.

It could be 9 pm by the time the exhausted crew arrived back in Achillbeg with their cargo. One lady recalled her experiences on the 'turf boats' in the late 1920s and early 1930s: 'We'd set out early, maybe half past four. I was about 13 the first time I went. At Saula I sat in the boat and built up the turf while the men brought it. When we got back there would always be a pot of tea above in the house, and then we'd unload the turf'. The unloaded cargo would have to be carried up the beach and stacked in a pile, or brought up to the houses in *cliabhs* (creels) on the back of donkeys. One boatload would fill about 44 *cliabhs*. At one time, there was a large stack of turf just above the beach belonging to the Kilbane family.

Sometimes, if the man of the house was away working in Scotland, women would have to undertake this gruelling journey while pregnant. Boys and girls aged 13 and up also helped - one former resident recalled loading a boat almost unaided when she was that age. Such was life; it was either that or go without fuel to cook, heat water, and warm the house in winter.

Some turf could be sold, though most was needed for domestic use. When the coastguard station at Cloghmore was inhabited, the officers there would pay for a full boatload of turf, provided the exhausted boat crew unloaded it and brought it up to their yard for them, and stacked it there. The price they offered was very low - just a shilling (about 7-9 cents, at 2003 comparisons) per boatload delivered to Darby's Point. So low was the price, that it was hardly worthwhile as a commercial transaction, but times were hard. However, the boat men had one ace card up their sleeve - they used to ensure that a certain amount of wet turf was in each boat, thus making the load heavier and making the boat sit lower in the water. To the purchaser, none too keen at the best of times at parting with money, it appeared he was receiving a larger quantity of turf.

Apart from fishing and turf carrying, yawls were used for the collection of seaweed, which was made into fertiliser. This was harvested at selected locations, often from rocks placed deliberately in places where the weed was likely to grow on them. Cut seaweed is heavy, and the harvester's task a tough one. It was gathered up in large bundles which were generally towed by yawl to where it was required. An 1836 report shows that islanders often had a surplus of seaweed left over after they had gathered enough for their own use, and this was sold locally on Corraun and Achill. By the 1940s, the advent of commercial fertilisers resulted in less use of seaweed for this purpose.

Achillbeg never had a post office. Instead, a contract was given to an island family to collect and deliver mail. In those days, the postal service would have carried documents of value routinely - internet, credit card and electronic payments were decades away in the future! Consequently, postal staff had to be vetted carefully, and even a casual or part time postal worker had to swear an oath of secrecy. The employee's working activities were carefully controlled and regulated. Thus, the island postman had to cross to Cloghmore in the morning and walk up to Cloghmore Post Office where he (or she) would collect a mail bag containing letters for the island at 12 noon. Having brought the mail bag back into Achillbeg, the contents had to be delivered - this took some two hours; and any outgoing mail picked up from residents - there was no letter box on the island. Even if there was no outgoing mail, such was the degree of regulation that the empty mailbag had to be brought back over to the post office that afternoon. The contract for this work was for many years in the hands of the Kilbane family, who were related to the Postmistress at Cloghmore. They left the island about a year before the last inhabitants did, but continued to make the daily journey to deliver mail to their former neighbours.

According to Post Office regulations, if an islander needed to collect a pension payment or allowance of any kind, they were meant to go to Cloghmore Post Office themselves to collect it, but at least one elderly lady in the 1950s was too infirm to cross on the boat. Unofficial arrangements were made for local postal staff to bring her money to Achillbeg for her. Cloghmore Post Office closed in the mid-1970s, by which time it was some nine years since the last post had gone to Achillbeg. Its place was taken by Derreens Post Office, a short distance up the road. This is adjacent to Patten's Bar, itself a familiar place to many an Achillbeg resident on a Saturday night, and both are run by the Patten family.

Special occasions like Christmas brought their own entertainment like the 'Wren Boys'. Wren Boys were a traditional form of entertainment throughout most of Ireland. They consisted of groups of children and young teenagers who would call from house to house, sometimes in fancy dress, and carrying a small box or container in which a wren was supposed to be. Seeking money to 'bury the wren' they would chant

The wren, the wren, the king of the birds
St Stephen's Day she was caught in the furze*
Although she is little her family is great
Rise up the landlady and give her a treat
And if your treat is of the best
I hope in heaven your soul will rest
If your treat is only small
It won't agree with the Wren Boys at all
So up with the kettle and down with the pan
Give us an answer and we will be gone

One former Achillbeg 'Wren Boy' remembered (when in his 90s!): 'We had one big fella amongst us. We used to try to get the price of a football, but the big boys would take the money off the younger ones' . . . In his day (the 1910s), island Wren Boys were aplenty, but by the 1950s there were few, as the population was not only much smaller, but of a much higher age profile as well.

Why the wren was described as the 'king of the birds', and then referred to as 'she', is not known!

* Furze = gorse bushes

The former Cloghmore Post Office. Achillbeg may be seen across the water just to the left of the building. Each day, Achillbeg's postman had to cross to here to collect the mail. The post office was closed in 1974, and is now a private house. *Author*

Patten's Bar and Post Office, Derreens, Achill. For many years, this was a centre of social interaction for those who would make the crossing from Achillbeg on a Saturday night. After Achillbeg was abandoned, many former islanders settled in this locality on Achill, and are thus able to continue the tradition to this day. The post office is the single-storey building on the left - this replaced the post office down the road at Cloghmore, to which mail for Achillbeg was delivered. *Author*

Christmas dinner was a big occasion, with relatives often present from abroad. Preparations were made well in advance. Sons, daughters, uncles and aunts would return to the island with tales of distant city life, and presents. 'They always had new clothes on them, the latest fashions', said one islander of her cousins, who had emigrated to Britain. Butter and cream were made and plentiful supplies of flour and sugar were brought in - as well as tea, of course! Dances were held in the houses and everybody caught up on the year's news; tales were told in front of a roaring fire in the lamp light, while the weather did what it does best in December outside. And the kettle boiled in the fireplace long into the night . . .

After Christmas and the New Year, the next big feast was St Patrick's Day on 17th March. One young witness reported in the 1930s that 'everyone enjoys himself that day, especially the grown up men'!

In the 1910s, the *Paorach* had taught chess and backgammon to children in the island school, and the legacy of this lived on - many islanders were keen and skilful board gamers. Traditional music sessions took place in island houses as well - there were many fine musicians in the small population. In the mid-1950s a cinema opened at Keel on Achill, and a dance hall called 'Mulligans' was another magnet for the young in Dookinella. A visit to 'Mulligans' was a weekend highlight for the young of the island in the heady days of the Showband era of the 1950s. 'We'd set off in the boat', said one eager participant, 'and we'd get across and change into our good clothes. Then we'd cycle the 16 miles to Mulligans - the pair of us on the bicycle, and the dance would go on till about three in the morning. I remember getting back (to Achillbeg) at five or six in the morning - the cock was crowing . . .' The late nocturnal habits of teenagers on weekend nights in the 21st century are clearly nothing new! On one occasion in the 1950s, two brothers set out in the 'punt' (small boat) to collect a 9 gallon barrel of Guinness which they had bought for £5, and which was to be brought into the island to assist in celebration of a forthcoming marriage. They brought the barrel to the island, but they were anxious to go to the dance in Keel, so the barrel was left in the boat overnight. When they returned the next morning, the barrel was in their house, the contents gone (apart from a liberal amount spilled on the floor) and friends and neighbours were sleeping it off in the brother's beds . . .

Dances would also be held in various places on Achill and further afield. Contemporary advertisements for such functions advise that 'Minerals and Light Refreshments will be Available' - a night out at that time was sometimes more sober than many nowadays!

Achillbeg had a good soccer team, and visiting teams came into the island from Achill and Corraun from time to time, games being played in the school yard or on the strand. The *Paorach* had successfully encouraged a revival of Gaelic games, and the island had its fair share of good footballers and hurlers. An elderly man in Achill recalled visits to Achillbeg in summer months to play football in the 1930s - 'they were tough fellas over there, good footballers', he said. One tragic accident took place, however, in 1943, when a young Achillbeg player died of an illness after collapsing on the pitch during a match at Achill Sound.

Aerial view of northern hill, showing the cultivated area known as the Pairc in the foreground. This view was taken within a few years of the island's abandonment, and all the houses are still in good condition. The only tell-tale sign of the lack of habitation is the fact that road is now overgrown with grass. The roofless building on the extreme bottom left, just above the beach, is where the island's original school was situated prior to 1903. *Nick Pollard*

Most households had radios, or 'wireless receivers' by the 1950s. In the absence of electricity, these were powered by large batteries. Once switched on, the 'wireless' had to warm up for a few moments before anything could be heard. The batteries lasted a week or so, and had to be taken over to Michael and Johnny Gallagher's shop on Corraun to be recharged. It was customary to keep two - one for use while another was being charged. While at Corraun, a visit to the *Teach Mór* bar could be included . . . One islander recalled that in order to maximise the life of the batteries, his father only allowed the 'wireless' to be switched on when it was time for the news.

Many islanders have memories of life in Achillbeg in the 1950s. To some, this period meant carefree, happy, childhood days spent playing on the strand, catching lobsters and crabs on their own 'special' rocks, and the occasional excitement of something unusual washed up on the shore. One day, some island children found some messages floating in a corked bottle - they turned out to be from an address in Australia. They had been in the sea for three years; the children's father wrote to the sender to let them know where their bottle had appeared. Of play-filled summer days, 'We were never in the house', one resident recalled some 50 years later.

Inevitably, there was mischief afoot: 'We were full of divilment', said one, recalling an incident in which her father acquired a good pedigree ram, at the not inconsiderable cost of £24. The ram was the family's pride and joy, but the children could not resist telling their neighbours' children that it was bigger and stronger than theirs - which was the only other ram on the island at the time. In order to prove the point, it was arranged that the two animals would be taken by the children to a remote place and set to fight each other. The resident ram took one charge at the £24 newcomer, and tossed him over the cliff! The puzzled owner searched the island for his new purchase, to no avail. He set out in his boat to comb the coastline and found nothing. A pact of secrecy was made between all the children concerned, and it was only some 30 years later that the perpetrators, by now adults, told their father the truth . . .

Another story told by one of the same children concerned an elderly resident of the island who owned a donkey. The children wanted to persuade the donkey to wander into its owner's house, so they helped it along by prodding it with a nail! The owner, as always, took everything in good humour.

But to adult islanders the 1950s meant long periods working abroad, occasional visits back to Achillbeg to visit ageing relatives, and increasing uncertainty about the sustainability of the ever smaller community.

Television's conversation-stifling pleasures did not become a feature of island life: while reception had become available in neighbouring Achill in the early 1960s, Achillbeg did not have an electricity supply until its last year of occupation. Some islanders did occasionally cross to visit friends or relatives in Cloghmore, and one recalled regular visits to a relative there to watch 'The Virginian' - an old black-and-white 'Western' series which was popular at the time. In Achillbeg, social life and entertainment was altogether richer - on dark winter evenings, gatherings would be held in one or other of the island houses, where card games and board games would be played long into the night, helped along with mugs of tea, or a glass of whiskey. Many islanders were good

Photograph taken on the island's road in the late 1950s; Michael Joe Kilbane (with scythe) and John Gallagher. The gravel surface of the road is in excellent condition, a tribute to those members of the Kilbane family who kept it so, even in this late stage of the island's inhabited period. Behind can be seen two substantial stacks of turf, carefully stacked to last through the winter.

Joe Kilbane

The island social life included late night card playing sessions, helped by lots of tea! In 1961, this gathering is in John and Bridget Kilbane's house. *Left to right:* Peggy Kilbane, Maureen Gallagher and her sister Bridget, Hughie Gallagher (*at back*), Patrick Gallagher (*front*), and Jimmy Kilbane.
Joe Kilbane

The same evening, same house - *left to right:* Michael Gallagher (with cigarette), Patrick Gallagher, Peter Gallagher (with cap), Maureen Gallagher, Bernie Gallagher (younger child behind Maureen), Michael Joe Kilbane, Peg Kilbane, Peg's father Johnny Kilbane (with tea cup), Bridget Gallagher, Anthony O'Malley and Patsy Gallagher. *Joe Kilbane*

Former Achillbeg resident, Annie Corrigan, 2002. *Author*

View of the centre of the island painted by former resident Annie Corrigan, many years after she had left. The school is in the centre, with tilled fields above and to the left of it -just as the painter had frozen it in her mind and a contrast to its overgrown state today. Annie's daily journey to school in the late 1920s took her across the western side of the mountain, approaching the little whitewashed building from this direction. The painting is displayed in St Fionnan's Nursing Home, Achill Sound. *Author, courtesy Annie Corrigan*

musicians, and sessions would be held in various houses with singers accompanied by fiddles and accordions. One former resident remembered large amounts of tea being consumed, but then, according to statistics, Ireland frequently (to this day) has the highest per capita consumption of tea in the world! There was no public house on the island, so those who preferred something stronger would cross the water and walk up to 'Kitty's' (or 'Johnny's', as it was known later) - the Patten family's pub at Derreens, which still plays host to former islanders who live in the locality. Pubs kept earlier hours in those days - in the 1930s week day closing time was 10.30 pm, while on Sundays it was 7.00 pm. That said, as in many rural districts, the licensing laws could be interpreted liberally from time to time! One resident recalled the journey back to the island after a night out: 'We went down to the pier and we had to cross over again in the boat. But it was pitch dark by that stage, and also up in the houses when we got there. We had to watch out in case we tripped over a bucket or something when we got in . . .' Care had to be taken not to wake the other occupants of the house in the early hours of the morning . . .

It is interesting to look at the traditional clothing of earlier generations through the eyes of outside observers. The artist, Paul Henry, who lived in Achill Island for some years in the early 20th century, described the colours of the aprons and cloaks worn by local people as having shades of vermilion, while earlier observers had seen various shades of red, and occasionally dark blue in use. One islander described a style common in Achillbeg at one time - a long red garment with three black stripes just above the bottom hem. All this was against a background of black or navy blue cloaks and ankle length dresses. Headscarves were often worn, and were coloured orange or red. Henry described paisley designs and black velvet diamonds sewn in a row along the edge of the homespun flannel dresses. Various roots and natural dyes were used in the production of these garments, and men's suits often had a yellowy brown shade of colour. Fishermen's working clothes would bear salt stains following prolonged exposure to sea water. Henry's observations included Achillbeg folk as he spent some of his time living in the coastguard station at Cloghmore, just above the pier used by the islanders.

As Achillbeg was an island in a remote location, but with a very mobile population, rural Irish culture co-existed very well for many generations with that of the outside world. One resident recalled that during her childhood days in the early 1930s it became customary for young women returning from a period of work in Britain or the USA to bring home the latest fashionable clothes. In her recollection, it was about this time that island women began to abandon the traditional clothing of many generations. After this time, few if any island women made all of their own clothes, and gradually islanders dressed in the same way as anybody in more cosmopolitan parts of Ireland. While traditional clothing may have fallen out of favour, most women kept their 'decent' shawl, even if it was rarely if ever worn. However, every island woman had her own spinning wheel, and one lady, Annie Corrigan, was well known locally for the quality of her work well into the 1990s when in her 80s - and nearly 40 years after Achillbeg was abandoned. The spinning wheels were used to make wool for socks, which was usually dyed black. Wool was washed and teased, before addition of paraffin, margarine or butter to help the spinning process. Thread was made and sent to a weaver on Achill or Corraun. Blankets, bed-coverings and material for suits were also made, in addition to clothes.

Island men returning from work on construction sites in England introduced the ubiquitous donkey jacket to the locality. In the 1950s and early 1960s, when most young people were away working, and doubtless becoming more fashion conscious, one islander arrived home with a friend from England. The visitor was very well dressed, and as he arrived in the house where he was staying, he paused to brush some dust off his sleeve. Unfortunately, his sleeve was draped over a candle and his expensive jacket was badly damaged!

As the 'swinging sixties' dawned, the remaining islanders felt the winds of change blowing as never before. Electricity and telephone communication were still being talked about, and though they would come in the island's last year of habitation, they seemed as far away as ever, as politicians and government bodies prevaricated over what help, if any, was to be given to islanders. Elsewhere, car ownership was becoming more common, especially in rural areas. Achillbeg's road system was unsuitable for road vehicles, and there were no facilities for shipping them to and from the island anyway. The island still had no church, pub, shop or nurse. Unusually bad weather accentuated Achillbeg's isolation in the early months of at least two years around this time, when the island was cut off for days at a time.

But even in these twilight days of the island's population, life continued as normal. The young people may have been 'working away' but would return at holiday times to visit elderly relatives. In these times people were close; families kept in touch, and there was much excitement when an emigrant returned home. The author has been privileged to have been shown personal letters exchanged in 1961 between two islanders - one working off the island, and the other on it, growing older. The resident was keeping his younger correspondent up to date with the 'news', and wrote:

> I am in no position to start moving heavy goods about . . . it's nourishment I want, not punishment . . . Well times are very quiet - nothing to do and all day to do it in. I hear that they are all leaving Achill Beg but it does not look like that to me - they are still running and chasing . . . The Murphys* and the fellow with the side pockets are busy on the road and the smell of the perfume is delightful - it is a grand thing to die a natural death than be poisoned . . . (!)

A two part newspaper article in 1962 highlighted the islander's plight. As the writer put it, 'I have just returned from the lost world of isolated children, a hump-backed island on the edge of the Atlantic . . .' A somewhat dramatic description followed which described the day to day hardships faced by islanders, the difficulties in maintaining a community then consisting of just 30 people. Among the permanent population there was just one young family and only three adult men under 65 years of age - the rest of the population were elderly people. On the 'forgotten island', the lack of manpower resulted in little land being tilled. 'Next year the patches of potatoes will be fewer, the meadows tinier', continued the report. Mention was made of the teacher at the time,

* The 'Murphys and the fellow with the side pockets' referred to a group of workmen who were temporarily working in Achillbeg and a donkey with side panniers - which apparently left nobody with a keen sense of smell in any doubt as to where it was . . .

Patrick O'Boyle, who was just 19. This reflected that fact that, as the Parish Priest had found over recent years, it was practically impossible to persuade a teacher to come and live in Achillbeg as there was no housing accommodation available. A succession of teachers had lodged with island families, but this was hardly satisfactory on an ongoing basis. Mention was made of the fact that the last island wedding had been some 30 years earlier.

'Achillbeg is doomed', announced the journalist; predictably, his words were to come true 3½ years later, but only as far as permanent habitation was concerned. For the island, a cloak of grass and heather reclaimed the fields and paths where bustling human activity had once reigned supreme.

As the summer of 1965 passed, the last people moved out - one family today, one elderly resident next week. The late nights began to draw in, and just one house remained occupied by one elderly man. By October, all of the remaining permanent population had finally left the island - a new life beckoned elsewhere.

Above: Before electricity came to Achillbeg, islanders used old battery-powered 'wireless' radios to keep up to date with what was happening elsewhere. This advertisement shows the very latest mains-powered models available in 1961 - one of the many attractions of a more modern life in the early 1960s

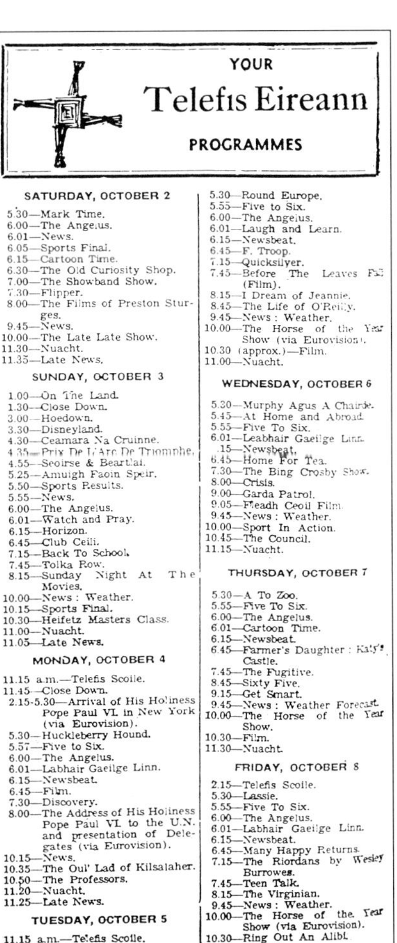

YOUR
Telefıs Eireann
PROGRAMMES

SATURDAY, OCTOBER 2

5.30—Mark Time.
6.00—The Angelus.
6.01—News.
6.05—Sports Final.
6.15—Cartoon Time.
6.30—The Old Curiosity Shop.
7.00—The Showband Show.
7.30—Flipper.
8.00—The Films of Preston Sturges.
9.45—News.
10.00—The Late Late Show.
11.30—Nuacht.
11.35—Late News.

SUNDAY, OCTOBER 3

1.00—On The Land.
1.30—Close Down.
3.00—Hoedown.
3.30—Disneyland.
4.30—Ceamara Na Cruinne.
4.35—Prix De L'Arc De Triomphe.
4.55—Seoirse & Beartlai.
5.25—Amuigh Faoin Speir.
5.50—Sports Results.
5.55—News.
6.00—The Angelus.
6.01—Watch and Pray.
6.15—Horizon.
6.45—Club Ceili.
7.15—Back To School.
7.45—Tolka Row.
8.15—Sunday Night At The Movies.
10.00—News : Weather.
10.15—Sports Final.
10.30—Heifetz Masters Class.
11.00—Nuacht.
11.05—Late News.

MONDAY, OCTOBER 4

11.15 a.m.—Telefis Scoile.
11.45—Close Down.
2.15-5.30—Arrival of His Holiness Pope Paul VI. in New York (via Eurovision).
5.30—Huckleberry Hound.
5.57—Five to Six.
6.00—The Angelus.
6.01—Labhair Gaeilge Linn.
6.15—Newsbeat.
6.45—Film.
7.30—Discovery.
8.00—The Address of His Holiness Pope Paul VI. to the U.N. and presentation of Delegates (via Eurovision).
10.15—News.
10.35—The Oul' Lad of Kilsalaher.
10.50—The Professors.
11.20—Nuacht.
11.25—Late News.

TUESDAY, OCTOBER 5

11.15 a.m.—Telefis Scoile.
2.15—Telefis Scoile.
5.30—Round Europe.
5.55—Five to Six.
6.00—The Angelus.
6.01—Laugh and Learn.
6.15—Newsbeat.
6.45—F. Troop.
7.15—Quicksilver.
7.45—Before The Leaves Fall (Film).
8.15—I Dream of Jeannie.
8.45—The Life of O'Reilly.
9.45—News : Weather.
10.00—The Horse of the Year Show (via Eurovision).
10.30 (approx.)—Film.
11.00—Nuacht.

WEDNESDAY, OCTOBER 6

5.30—Murphy Agus A Chairde.
5.45—At Home and Abroad.
5.55—Five To Six.
6.01—Leabhair Gaeilge Linn.
.15—Newsbeat.
6.45—Home For Tea.
7.30—The Bing Crosby Show.
8.00—Crisis.
9.00—Garda Patrol.
9.05—Fleadh Ceoil Film.
9.45—News : Weather.
10.00—Sport In Action.
10.45—The Council.
11.15—Nuacht.

THURSDAY, OCTOBER 7

5.30—A To Zoo.
5.55—Five To Six.
6.00—The Angelus.
6.01—Cartoon Time.
6.15—Newsbeat.
6.45—Farmer's Daughter : Katy's Castle.
7.45—The Fugitive.
8.45—Sixty Five.
9.15—Get Smart.
9.45—News : Weather Forecast.
10.00—The Horse of the Year Show.
10.30—Film.
11.30—Nuacht.

FRIDAY, OCTOBER 8

2.15—Telefis Scoile.
5.30—Lassie.
5.55—Five To Six.
6.00—The Angelus.
6.01—Labhair Gaeilge Linn.
6.15—Newsbeat.
6.45—Many Happy Returns.
7.15—The Riordans by Wesley Burrowes.
7.45—Teen Talk.
8.15—The Virginian.
9.45—News : Weather.
10.00—The Horse of the Year Show (via Eurovision).
10.30—Ring Out An Alibi.
11.00—Nuacht.

Right: The modern world beckons: as the final residents left the island for a new life elsewhere, these television schedules were available to those lucky enough to own a TV. With one channel only, broadcasting for no more than six hours a day on some days, and finishing before midnight every evening, it was a far cry from today's comprehensive service. However, Saturday night's *Late Late Show* is still on the air over 40 years later! Almost half of Monday's total air time was given over to the Papal visit to New York. The author well remembers Friday night's *The Virginian* . . . memory lane! *Mayo News, October 1965*

Above: Portrait of an islander: James Kilbane (died 1940). *Joe Kilbane*

Left: Achilllbeg man Paddy Kilbane, 1926. *Peg Masterson*

Chapter Six

The People of Achillbeg

The most important aspect of a study of this type is the people who lived in the place. It is they who shaped the land, who built the houses, and who now have left Achillbeg to travel across the world.

The earliest settlers in Achill Island appear to have come some 5000 years BC. As mentioned already, it is probable that Achillbeg and Achill were joined at this time, and indeed a link to the mainland Corraun district may also have been in place. It may therefore be taken that this is the earliest date that people settled on what is now Achillbeg Island. It is thought that some of the early inhabitants of the region had migrated from further north. To this day, the surname Gallagher is associated with the area, and there were many Gallaghers on Achillbeg. This surname is often associated with Counties Derry and Donegal. By the 19th century, the earliest period for which comprehensive records of individual families on Achillbeg are available, three surnames dominated the island population; these were Gallagher, Kilbane and Corrigan. There were Burkes also, though the last family with this name is believed to have emigrated in the early 1930s. A lady whose childhood was on the island in the late 1920s and early 1930s remembered them leaving. As in other rural areas of Ireland, it was likely that several people in a community would have the same name - perhaps a father, son, grandson and cousin. There were a number of John or Johnny Gallaghers, for example, or Anthony Kilbanes - in order to distinguish between one and another, or one family and another, an additional 'nickname' would be added, possibly giving a clue to occupation, father's name, or the like. Thus, one Johnny Kilbane was known as Johnny 'Butcher' Kilbane to distinguish him from other Johnny Kilbanes. This particular nickname had its origins in a family occupation. Under the Kilbane name, there were the 'Nellie' Kilbanes, the 'Roughty' Kilbanes, the 'Mhaggi' Kilbanes and so on. The Gallaghers had, for example, Michael 'Joe' and Michael 'Pat' - references to father's or grandfather's names. Distinctions of this type are still widely used today right across Ireland. These nicknames were used officially on occasion - for example, on census returns.

While seasonal migration was the result of financial hardship, the fact that it was undertaken served to protect the islanders from the starvation and disease that the Famine visited upon so many other areas of Ireland. Thus, we find that having reached a peak population of 178 as recorded in the 1841 census, 10 years later the population of Achillbeg had only dropped by 29 - and this due to permanent emigration rather than direct starvation. However, while the population of many parts of Ireland declined very rapidly after that, by 1880 the decline on Achillbeg had temporarily halted, and with some minor variations the population stayed at around the hundred mark for the next 35 years. This was doubtless a direct result of income from migrational work elsewhere. Mass emigration from all over Ireland was nonetheless becoming an established part of life, and the pattern for the future was set. In the first 50 years of the 20th century,

How the population declined. In the 20 years following the Great Famine, over a third of the island's population left. By the 1870s it had stabilised again, but despite a slow increase until the 1910s, it never fully recovered. By the 1920s, the lure of a more sophisticated life elsewhere became irresistible. Some 40 years later, the last suitcases were packed by the remaining residents.

the population of the whole of County Mayo (including Achillbeg) dropped from 647,000 to 472,000. Against this background, in 1940 the Irish Land Commission sought the views of the islanders on whether they would like to be relocated on Achill, but they declined the offer which was repeated on other subsequent occasions, with the same result. Similarly, an offer to have a bridge built from Cloghmore across to Achillbeg was declined. The bridge would have made access easier for the islanders, but the connecting road would have occupied some of the small amount of arable land on the island, and possibly resulted in some invasion of the islander's privacy. By 1956 there were but 50 people living permanently on the island, though many others whose permanent residence was now elsewhere would come back to Achillbeg regularly to visit relatives. Three years later there were 38, and the island school had only eight pupils - all but one from a single family. The early 1960s saw the population fall to 30 and under before final evacuation took place a few years later.

The years for which population figures are known are:

Year	*Population*	*No. of houses*	*Notes*
1838			No actual population figure, but Ordnance Survey recorded 25 families living in Achillbeg
1841	178	32*	(92 male, 86 female) Immediately prior to the Famine. * 29 houses inhabited, three uninhabited.
1851	149	29*	(75 male, 74 female) Famine at its height. * 29 houses, all inhabited.
1855		32	Information from Griffith's valuation: 21 houses occupied by local people, almost all Kilbanes and Gallaghers, and 7 occupied by coastguard staff. 2 as coastguard offices, 2 unoccupied.
1861	137		
1871	93		Post famine emigration still very high:population almost halved in previous 30 years.
1881	105		
1890	110		Famine hardship less severe, but road transport easier due to opening of bridge onto Achill in 1887.
1891	113	19	
1901	104	20	Railway from Dublin to Achill now operational - emigration and transport easier.
1910	117		School building now open (though education facilities had been available for many years before).
1911	117	22*	(66 male, 51 female) Stable population, era of *An Paorach*. * 21 houses inhabited, 1 uninhabited. In addition, 4 outbuildings.
1921			Unknown: but population halves over 25 year period 1911-36.
1926			Unknown.
1936	67		Economically depressed period, though new Land Commission ('Gaeltacht') houses were being built. Last island wedding about this time.

NOTE: WRONG HEIGHT FOR PATRICK. HE WAS ACTUALLY 6'4" OR 6'5". VERY TALL FOR HIS ERA. NOTE ALSO IMPROPER SPELLING OF ACHILLBEG ISLAND, IRELAND. HERE IT IS ACKERBAT. ALSO NOTE WRONG BIRTH DATE FOR JOHN. ACTUAL DATE 1-28-13. NOTE: FIR AVE IS ALSO MISSPELLED.

No. 88526

UNITED STATES OF AMERICA

DECLARATION OF INTENTION

(Invalid for all purposes seven years after the date hereof)

ss: *In the* COMMON PLEAS *Court* *of* CUYAHOGA COUNTY *at* CLEVELAND, OHIO

PATRICK GALLAGHER (Full true name, without abbreviation, and any other name which has been used, must appear here)

6028 Fur Ave (Number and street) Cleveland (City or town) Cuyahoga (County) Ohio (State), aged 48 years, do declare on oath that my personal description is:

...or White, complexion Fair, color of eyes Blue

..., height 5 feet 7 inches; weight 168 pounds; visible distinctive marks

...; nationality Ireland

...erbat, Ireland (City or town) (Country), on March 15, 1882 (Month) (Day) (Year)

The name of my wife or husband is Mary

... 1905 (Month) (Day) (Year), at Ireland (City or town) (State or country); she or he was

...nd (State or country), on 1885 (Day) (Year), entered the United States

...k N.Y. (State), on July 13, 1913 (Month) (Day) (Year), for permanent residence therein, and now

...with me (State or country) I have 10 children, and the name, date and place of birth,

...ach of said children are as follows Patrick, Jan 17, 1906, Ireland; Peter, July 6, 1910

...14, Michael, Nov 27, 1916, Owen, May 23, 1918, William, Sept, 1919

...9, Hugh, July 27, 1921, Beatrice, Jan 30, 1924, Sarah, Feb 22, 1927

...eland, and now residing in Cleveland, Ohio

...tofore made a declaration of intention: Number ..., on ... (Date)

...idence was Ackerbat (City or town) Ireland (Country)

...United States of America from Queenstown (City or town) Ireland (Country)

...permanent residence in the United States was at New York (City or town) N.Y. (State)

... Patrick Gallagher, on July 13, 1930 (Month) (Day) (Year)

on the vessel SS Carmonia (If other than by vessel, state manner of arrival)

I will, before being admitted to citizenship, renounce forever all allegiance and fidelity to any foreign prince, potentate, state, or sovereignty, and particularly, by name, to the prince, potentate, state, or sovereignty of which I may be at the time of admission a citizen or subject; I am not an anarchist; I am not a polygamist nor a believer in the practice of polygamy; and it is my intention in good faith to become a citizen of the United States of America and to reside permanently therein; and I certify that the photograph affixed to the duplicate and triplicate hereof is a likeness of me: So HELP ME GOD.

Patrick Gallagher (Original signature of declarant without abbreviation, also alias, if used)

Subscribed and sworn to before me in the office of the Clerk of said Court, at Cleveland, Ohio this 21 day of Jan anno Domini 1931. Certification No. 7 9725 from the Commissioner of Naturalization showing the lawful entry of the declarant for permanent residence on the date stated above, has been received by me. The photograph affixed to the duplicate and triplicate hereof is a likeness of the declarant.

...k Gallagher

[SEAL]

THOS. C. COOK Pro Tem
Clerk of the Common Pleas Court.
By ..., Deputy Clerk.

...L-A. ... OF LABOR ... SERVICE

14—2623 U. S. GOVERNMENT PRINTING OFFICE: 1929

Patrick Gallagher's Immigration Papers, admitting him and his family to the USA in 1930. The papers record that he had originally come from 'Ackerbat' in Ireland. Despite variations in handwriting, 'Ackerbat' seems a somewhat liberal translation of 'Achillbeg'! Accompanying him were his wife and 10 children, with dates of birth ranging from 1906 to 1927. Many other former Achillbeg residents would sign their names to papers like these.

Judge Sean C. Gallagher, Cleveland, Ohio

Year	*Population*	*No. of houses*	*Notes*
1946	63		
1951	54		
1956	50		
1959	38		Only one young family left at the school.
1961	38		
1962	30		Arrangements for evacuation being explored.
1964	26 ?		Probably about 26. Few young people resident all year round.
1965	0		By the end of the year - Nil.

As mentioned before, the island had some famous visitors in its day; but it also exported those who would become famous. In July 1930, Pat and Mary Gallagher emigrated with their young family from their house below Garraí Úr just west of the pier. The couple had eight sons and two daughters, aged from 3 to 24. The family settled in Cleveland, Ohio after a long and arduous journey across the Atlantic. Patrick, the father, had been reluctant to leave his homeland; but necessity dictated it. Nonetheless, he made an arrangement with the neighbour who bought his land that should American life not suit the family, he could return and purchase it back for the same price. Life was hard, but they settled in to their new home, never returning to take back their land. As the Gallagher family grew up six of them joined the United States Army. In 1944, they hit the headlines nationally - in the USA, that is. They were the only family in the USA to have six brothers all fighting for their new country in World War II. Later, an eighth member joined up. The local and national media carried the story - on 17th March, 1943 the Cleveland local newspaper quoted the youngest brother, who had not yet joined up, 'Just say that the Gallaghers are proud this St Patrick's Day that they are Irish, and are proud of those six boys, all born on foreign soil, who are fighting for this land of which they are naturalised citizens'. Appropriately, their mother received a medal. Patrick Gallagher lived to be 88, and his youngest daughter survived to 2003. One of her older brothers had said some years previously that his earliest memory of America was tasting Coca Cola for the first time, and Lucky Strike cigarettes! An interesting sequel was to follow some years later: one of the boy's sons, himself an eminent Judge in Cleveland, travelled to Achill in 2003 with an official party who had arrived to celebrate the twinning of Achill Island with Cleveland City.

Cleveland played host to another famous son of Achillbeg. John Kilbane emigrated from the island in the late 19th century, and settled like many others from his homeland in this vibrant American city. His son, Johnny, was born in 1890 in Cleveland. Johnny showed promise as a boxer, and his career flourished. In February 1912, at the age of 22, he took the world Featherweight Boxing title from Abe Attell, who had held it for eight years in succession. Great as Attell was, Kilbane became greater - he held the world title for 11 years. In 1923 he was beaten by Frenchman Eugene Criqui, and he retired from boxing. Like many with Achillbeg ancestry in Cleveland, he later became involved in public life, serving as a Senator from 1941. He died from cancer in May 1957. His name lives on in the Greater Cleveland Sports Hall of Fame.

Cleveland Ohio
Mary Gallagher
6118 Glen ave
May 6th 1939

Dear Bro, Wife & family

Just a few lines to let you know that we are all enjoying good health Thank God. hoping ye are also enjoying good health. times here as just same as usual but expects to be a better summer, than it had being with the past 2 years, the building trade is slack yet but the day you work on it you earn $7.00 + 20c a day I suppose Pat will be feared about going to England this year I hope things will be quieter when it comes to that time, We got the Shamrock all right & so did Michael Get his one day before St Patrick day from Briggie Patrick Michaleen was here last night he say Mary Ned the Tailor from Bolliglan landed last monday, Peter got the Tobbacco from Mike Madden Young Pat was telling us that Tom Vaggy son got severely hurt in a motor car accident or how is he getting along or which of them got hurt how is all the friends + neighbours getting along James will be Graduating from the 12th Grade the End of this month or the beginning of June he will send one or two of his Photo's next week write soon & let us know how everything is going on over there

£ 8 0

Enclosed you will find £ 8.0.0 in
a check, I have sent it same as before
in Anne Redmond's name she knows nothing
it all about it, she was here last until
10 O'clock chewing the rag with old Pat & he gave
her Hell, she don't care. the Eddie's Wife
is not feeling so well with the last 6 weeks
the Eddies Grandson Bernard was buried
on the 18th day of March he was 16 years old
he was sick for long time. the day he was
buried Bridget Vaggy curry came here along
with old Meg from the church the first
time I seen her since I told you before.
I never let on that she wasn't coming
same as always

Breege Johnny was here last week she
is thin & wirey & old looking shawn Biddy
is just landed up now listening to the
Radio & the Ball Game.
John's daughters from Ohio are all
married Winnie has a Baby Girl 6 months old
I have no more to say this time

Write soon again
With love to all
Mary Gallagher

Letter from America. Mary Gallagher, an Achillbeg emigrant, writes to her family back home in May 1939. This letter has been reproduced with the kind permission of Judge Sean C. Gallagher, Cleveland, Ohio. The references to island nicknames like 'Vaggy' and 'Breege Johnny' will be noted.

Pfc Hugh P. Gallagher Pfc James F. Gallagher Sgt John F. Gallagher

Col Michael Gallagher Pfc Owen P. Gallagher Pfc W.T. Gallagher

All the Gallagher brothers would survive the war and return to Cleveland raising families and continuing with their involvement in local Irish affairs. Mary Gallagher died in 1964 followed by her husband Patrick in 1970 at the age of 88. The oldest son Patrick died in 1967, Michael in 1971, Owen in 1973, Sarah in 1975, Peter in 1976, James in 1985, William and John in 1987 and Hugh in 1991. The entire family is buried in close proximity to each other in Holy Cross Cemetery. The last surviving sister, Beatrice, passed away in 2003. There are countless sons and daughters, nieces, nephews and grandchildren of these brothers who now have integrated themselves into all walks of life in America. Their story is representative of the simple contributions of the common men and women of Ireland who helped shape America.

Judge Sean C. Gallagher, Cleveland, Ohio

Approaching Achillbeg: the pier is just underneath the nearest building. The roofless ruin on the right is the ancestral home of the Gallagher family. *Author*

The Gallagher homestead. The road, in the foreground, twists up to the left and around the back of the house towards the 'Tail'. to the left of the house, but just under the road, the family's well nestled under the rocks. It may still be found, if you search carefully . . . The Gallagher family left the house in 1930 for America, where their descendants still live. *Author*

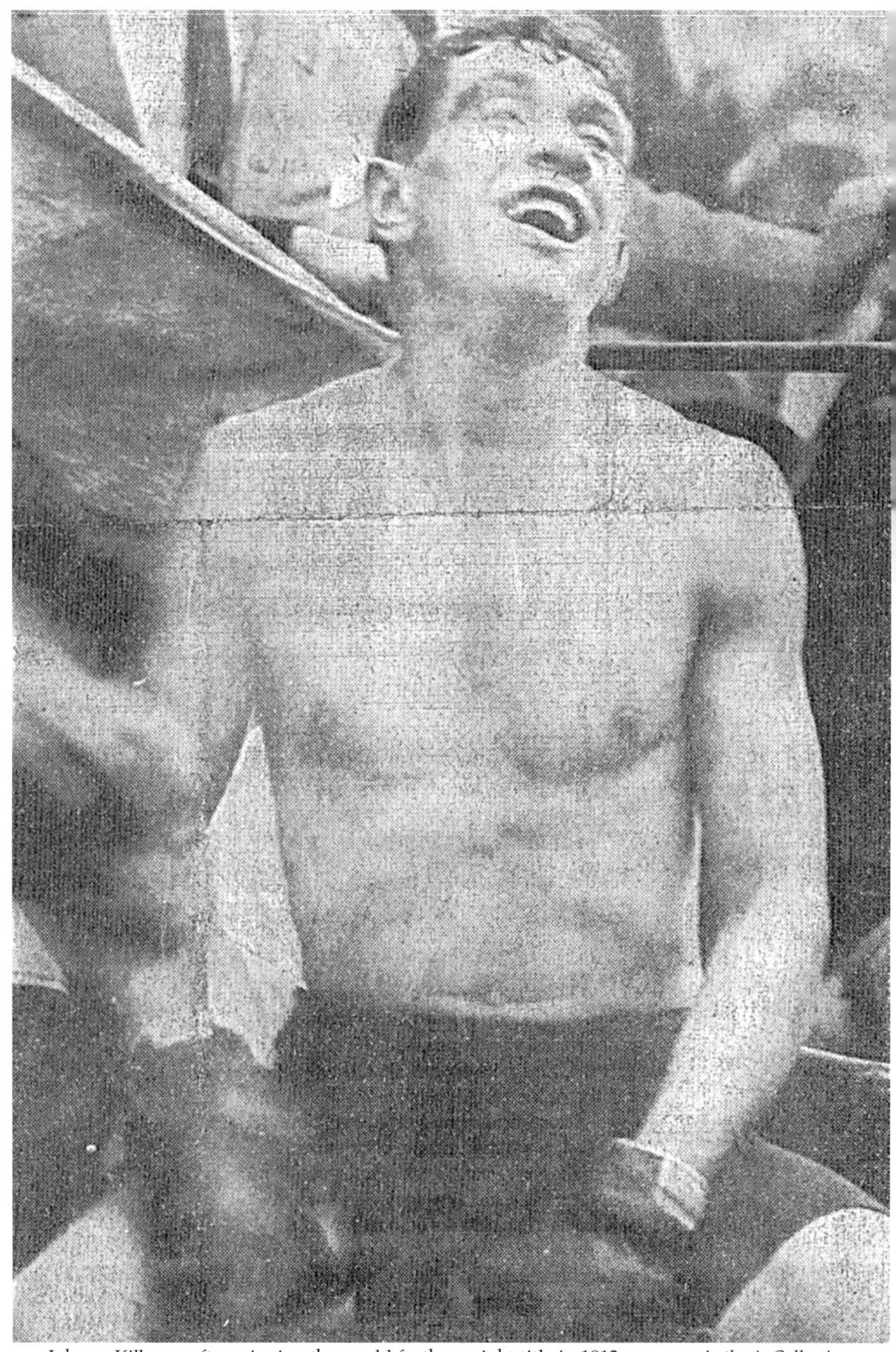

Johnny Kilbane, after winning the world featherweight title in 1912. *Author's Collection*

This book does not set out to provide a detailed chronicle of each family's exact lineage* - to do so would be outside the terms of reference of this study. With just three main family names in most of the island's reliably recorded history, those wishing to study the ancestry of one particular family will gain as much information as is available from normal genealogical channels, such as Parish records and the like. In addition, to bluntly list names, occupations, addresses and the like is to risk invasion of the privacy of former residents, many of whom still live in the immediate mainland locality, or on Achill Island. In any event, even if the above did not apply, census records over the years are either incomplete or lacking in detail for earlier times, and unavailable at time of writing for later periods. Comparison between the 1901 and 1911 census records even show occasional discrepancies over the ages of some islanders: the two sets of records are 10 years apart, but the age of an individual may have been recorded as having changed by less or more than 10 years. To attempt a detailed family tree for each surname would therefore result in a very incomplete picture, and be of limited use in consequence.

However, it is interesting to look at the most detailed census records that are available, as they give a 'snapshot' of life on Achillbeg at various times. In 1855, Richard Griffith, the Commissioner of Valuations, carried out a detailed survey entitled *General Valuation of Rateable Property in Ireland,* known generally as *Griffith's Valuation*. The survey lists each household in Achillbeg, and shows a total valuation of £73 and 17 shillings. It is useful in showing the location of most of the occupied houses, as it is accompanied by a map. The buildings were numbered 1-32 on the 'Valuation of Tenements' listing within Griffith's survey. However, the accompanying map only shows 27 buildings (*see page 34*). It is probable that 29 and 30 are the two buildings just discernible on the location marked 'Coast Guard Station'. That leaves two - 31 and 32, which are not marked. It is possible that they were built after the map had been prepared.

The names allocated on Griffith's Valuation to these houses are:

House No.	*Name of Occupier*	*Immediate Lessor*	*Description*
1	John Gallagher		House & Land
2	Neill Kilbane		House & Land
3	Hugh Gallagher		House, Offices & Land
4	Patk Gallagher (Peter)		House & Land
5	Francis Gallagher		House, Offices & Land
6	Michael Moran		House & Land
7	Sally Gallagher		House & Land
8	Pk. Gallagher (Michael)		House, Offices & Land
9	Ptk. Gallagher (Thomas)		House & Land
10	Patrick Kilbane	Thomas Brassey (Landlord)	House & Land
11	Catherine Kilbane		House & Land
12	Farrell Gallagher		House & Land
13	Sibby Gallagher		House & Land
14	Thos Gallagher (Grace)		House & Land

* For the information of those wishing to follow enquiries of this nature, much useful material is held in Castlebar Library, Co. Mayo, and the National Archives, Bishop Street, Dublin. It is recommended that the Parish records at Achill Sound are also consulted.

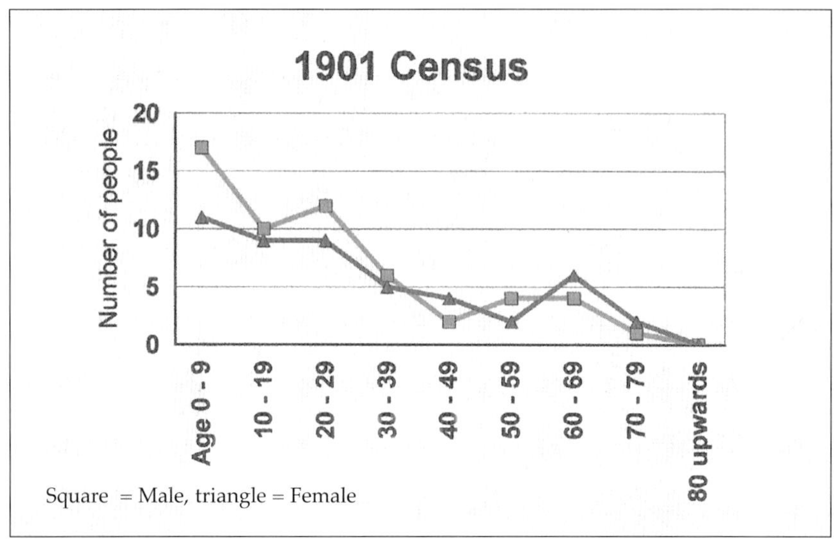

Square = Male, triangle = Female

It will be seen that the population in 1901 was a young one, with 40 per cent under 20 years of age. In addition, there was a distinct male majority among the young, with 27 males under 20, and 20 females.

In 1911, the age profile was even younger. This time, 46.8 per cent of the population was under 20. The slight increase in overall population at this time represented Achillbeg's heyday: after the devastation wreaked by the economic side effects of the Famine, the island had stabilised. It was not to last. As these young people grew up, emigration increased. This led to the gradual decline of the population one generation later: the children in this census were not to live as their parents did, and many fewer children replaced them in the school some years later. A graph based on the above criteria for any year in the 1950s or 1960s would have shown the line of the graph sloping completely the other way, as the majority of those remaining were much older.

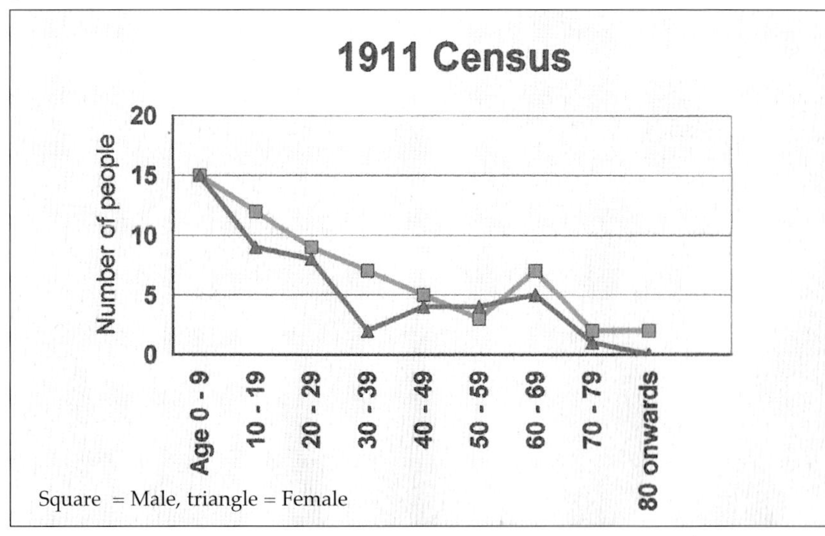

Square = Male, triangle = Female

15	Bridget Lynch		House & Land
16	James Kilbane (Jnr.)		House & Land
17	Mary Kilbane		House & Land
18	James Kilbane (Snr.)		House & Land
19	Hugh Corrigan		House & Land
	Edward Kilbane		Land
20	Richard Lyons	John Gallagher	House
21	John Bomley	Neill Kilbane	House & Office
22	*Unoccupied*	Michael Moran	House & Office
23	William Aspinell	Hugh Gallagher	House
24	Andrew Manning	Patk. Gallagher (Peter)	House
25	William Adwards	Patrick Kilbane	House
26	Patrick Brech	John & Hugh Gallagher	House
27	*Unoccupied*	Patk. Gallagher (Tom)	House
28	Isaac Bowdan		House & Office
29	Board of Customs	Sally Gallagher	Watch House
30	Board of Customs		Watch House (In progress)
31	Anthony Gallagher	Hugh Gallagher	House
32	Thomas Toole	Patk. Gallagher (Michl.)	House

The two most complete and detailed census records available are for 1901 and 1911. The records for these years are reproduced in *Appendix Two*. From these, the following information can be extracted:

1. Age Profile

Age Group		*1901 Census*			*1911 Census*	
	Male	*Female*	*Total*	*Male*	*Female*	*Total*
0-9	17	11	28	15	15	30
10-19	10	9	19	12	9	21
20-29	12	9	21	9	8	17
30 39	6	5	11	7	2	9
40-49	2	4	6	5	4	9
50-59	4	2	6	3	4	7
60-69	4	6	10	7	5	12
70-79	1	2	3	2	1	3
80 and over	0	0	0	0	2	2
Totals:	*56*	*48*	*104*	*62**	*48**	*110**

* The age details of seven of the island's total population of 117 could not be accounted for by surviving records. The actual population of 117 was broken down as 66 males and 51 females.

This aerial view of the east end of the village was taken shortly after the island's abandonment. The field boundaries and houses are intact, but the road has become overgrown. In the distance is Achill Island (*left*) and mainland Corraun (*right*).

Nick Pollard

2. *Housing*

The 1891 census had showed 19 houses on the island. By 1901 the number was 20, one extra having been built. In the 1901 census, there were four one-roomed houses still in use, out of a total of 19 dwelling houses. One of these contained just one person, another held a family of four, and two held a family of six people each. By 1911, all houses were two-roomed. On that year's census there were 22 buildings in all - one was the new school and 21 were inhabited houses. In addition, four 'out offices and farmsteadings' were recorded - these may have been older (one-roomed) houses now in use as farm out-buildings.

The sizes of families in the houses varied. In some cases in-laws or elderly relatives lived with a family, and in one case in both years a single man lived on his own. The following table shows a comparison between 1901 and 1911, but no clear pattern emerges, other than a certain degree of overcrowding in the later year - one house held 12 people, two held 8 people and five held 7 people. It should be remembered that in 1911, a few of the houses extant in 1901 had been replaced with larger ones.

Number of people per house		1	2	3	4	5	6	7	8	9	10	11	12
Number of houses containing that number of people	1901 Census	1	1	1	2	5	4	2	-	3	-	-	-
	1911 Census	1	-	2	5	3	1	5	2	-	-	-	1

One former resident believed that in the late 1920s and early 1930s there were 22 occupied houses, and 30 children in the school. This is 2-3 houses more than in the years quoted above. During the 1930s, Land Commission assistance resulted in new houses being built for most of the remaining residents.

3. *Language and Literacy*

In 1901, out of 104 residents, 101 spoke Irish as their first language, but had a knowledge of English sufficient to classify them as bilingual. One spoke English only - she was a teacher named Norah McHugh who lodged on the island but was not a native. From some years earlier, it is worth adding a comment from the 19th century *Statistical Survey of County Mayo* regarding not just Achillbeg, but the general area: 'Use of the English Language is rather general, and in some state of improvement, but still very defective; many can't speak a word of it'.

Two people, aged 50 and 60, spoke Irish only. The older of the two was listed as being bilingual 10 years later, while the other appears to have left the island as her details do not appear in the 1911 census. It would be unusual for a widow in her 60s to learn a new language, but the explanation in this case may be that Norah McHugh, referred to above, lodged with her. This late education in another tongue was understandable as Norah was the only person on the island who spoke *no Irish*, despite being entrusted with the children's education. This is a very telling reflection of the educational system of the time. With the

Above: Looking west across the middle of the island. The village, Baileamuigh, is on the right, and the school can be seen on the left. This picture was taken about five years after the last people left the island, and illustrates clearly how narrow the middle of the island is, and why the residents knew this area as a natural 'wind tunnel' all too often. *Nick Pollard*

Right: This aerial view taken in the early 1980s clearly shows the roads on the north east side of the island. The road leads from the pier (out of the picture to the right), and divides here. The 'main' route heads over the hill towards the houses in the distance, while the path to the left leads down to the strand. Nature is beginning to reclaim some of the fields. *Nick Pollard*

In the early 1950s, four Gallagher boys and Peg Lavelle leaving the pier for Cloghmore.
Peg Masterson

Peg Kilbane (now Masterson) and Bridie-Anne Gallagher - and Peg's cat - in front of their *hen-cró* (hen house), early 1950s.
Peg Masterson

Island group, December 1959, outside Anthony O'Malley's house. From *left to right*: John Kilbane, Patsy Gallagher, Bridget Kilbane (John's wife), Margaret O'Malley, Mary (Maura) Gallagher (seated), Anthony O'Malley, Johnny Kilbane, Michael Gallagher, Johnny Gallagher (with cap), Peggy Kilbane, Mary 'Jack' Kilbane (Johnny Kilbane's wife, Peggy's mother), Peter Gallagher 'Mollie', Peter Gallagher. The last Peter Gallagher (with dog) was to receive the island's only telephone some four years later. Photograph courtesy of Joe Kilbane, whose father is shown, extreme left; and his mother, third from left.

Family group, 1961. The elderly couple pictured were very popular with the local children and always had time to talk to them. As the children grew up and left the island, they would return to visit periodically and renew old friendships. *Left to right:* Biddy Kilbane, Briege Kilbane (now Armstrong), Johnny 'Redden' Kilbane, and Peg Kilbane (now Masterson). Behind is the year's supply of turf, neatly stacked up. A pile this high would be the result of three boatloads from Saula.

Peg Masterson

householder speaking only Irish, and her tenant only English, it is clear that some form of common communication had to be found. Did Norah's host offer her lodgings in order to learn English?

It is interesting to examine the age profile of those who could read and write, and those who could not. For obvious reasons, those under four years of age are omitted from the following table (though a single three-year-old was recorded as attending the school in 1911!). It will be seen from the following table that literacy increased from some 62 per cent of the population over four years of age to 72 per cent in the 10 year period. No doubt the provision of a proper school building had much to do with this - in 1901 classes were still being held in one of the houses, but in 1911 the National School was open. Only a few years after this census, the island's educational development was to progress much further, due to the efforts of the *Paorach*.

Age group	*1901 Census*		*1911 Census*	
	Cannot read	*Read & Write*	*Cannot read*	*Read & Write*
4-9	*1*	*17*	*3*	*17*
10-14	-	*11*	-	*10*
15-19	*1*	*7*	*1*	*10*
20-24	*3*	*9*	-	*8*
25-29	*3*	*6*	-	*9*
30-34	4	2	*1*	*7*
35-39	2	2	-	*1*
40-44	4	1	3	1
45-49	1	-	3	2
50-54	2	2	5	1
55-59	1	1	-	1
60-64	9	-	2	1
65-69	1	-	5	3
70-74	1	-	2	1
75-79	2	-	-	-
80 onwards	-	-	2	-
	35	58	27	72
Percentage	*38%*	*62%*	*27%*	*72%*

Figures in italics indicate age groups in each year where the majority could read and write.

Examination of the ages of those who could not read or write may give a clue as to when any form of schooling became available to the islanders. In 1901, the majority of those over 30 could not read or write, but 86 per cent of those under 30 could. Of those over 55, just one man (who was actually 55) could read or write. Ten years later, this man would of course have been aged 65, but four people are shown as having this basic standard of education by that stage.

In 1901 and 1911 a similar number of people aged under 29 could read and write. This means that the increase in literacy which brought the island's average up by 10 percentage points was mainly as a result of *adult* literacy improving. The number of adults aged 30-69 doubled in this period. It can be assumed that where figures begin to show a heavy majority of older adults with

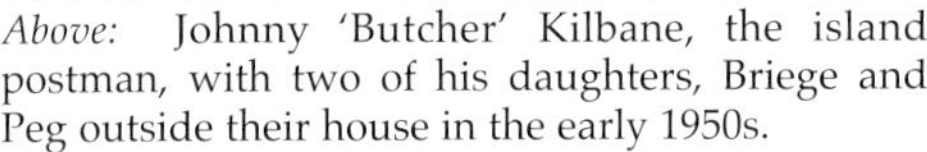

Above: Johnny 'Butcher' Kilbane, the island postman, with two of his daughters, Briege and Peg outside their house in the early 1950s.

Peg Masterson

Above, right: Michael Gallagher, who died in a tragic accident a few years before the island was finally abandoned. This picture of him was taken in the late 1950s.

Joe Kilbane, with permission of Bernie Gallagher

Right: Danny and Mary Kilbane, 2002. Danny was born on Achillbeg and lived there until he reached adult life. *Author*

no ability to read and write, that these adults would not have had the benefit of even a 'hedge school' as children. This is apparent with people over 40 or so in 1901, and 50 or so in 1911. Forty years before 1901 was 1861. A child born in 1861 would have reached school starting age (4) in 1865, and would have reached the normal school leaving age (about 14 in those days) about 1875. It is therefore reasonable to assume that some form of formalised educational facilities came to Achillbeg perhaps around 1870, although travelling teachers had been recorded there as early as the 1820s.

4. *Occupations*

Occupations given in both sets of census results show almost everybody on the island listed as 'farmer'. In 1901, one respondent (James Bourke) described himself as a boat builder. He lived with his widowed mother who, however, was a farmer - and his sisters were classified as 'farmer's daughters' In 1911, a Michael Corrigan described himself as 'Farmer and Seaman' while John Gallagher was a 'Farmer & Butcher'. These last two were more accurate: most islanders did some fishing and some farming. To this day, island people generally need to be much more versatile than their mainland counterparts.

5. *Family units*

Reference has been made elsewhere to the nicknames used to distinguish different families with similar names. While these names are obviously unofficial, the 1911 census in particular relied on these, and as will be seen in the census results, reproduced in Appendix Two, they were freely included. House No. 4 contains John 'Anthony' Gallagher, while House 5 (presumably next door) has John 'Molly' Gallagher, who also has a son named John.

As previously mentioned, most island residents had one of just three surnames. The predominant name was Gallagher. Comparing family units, the following pattern emerges:

	1901 Census				*1911 Census*			
	Gallagher	*Kilbane*	*Corrigan*	*Other*	*Gallagher*	*Kilbane*	*Corrigan*	*Other*
No. of Family units	11	6	2	1*	13	6	2	0
No. of people	57	34	9	4	70	36	11	0

* Bourke.

Some years later, in the 1920s and 1930s, there were O'Malleys living on the island as well.

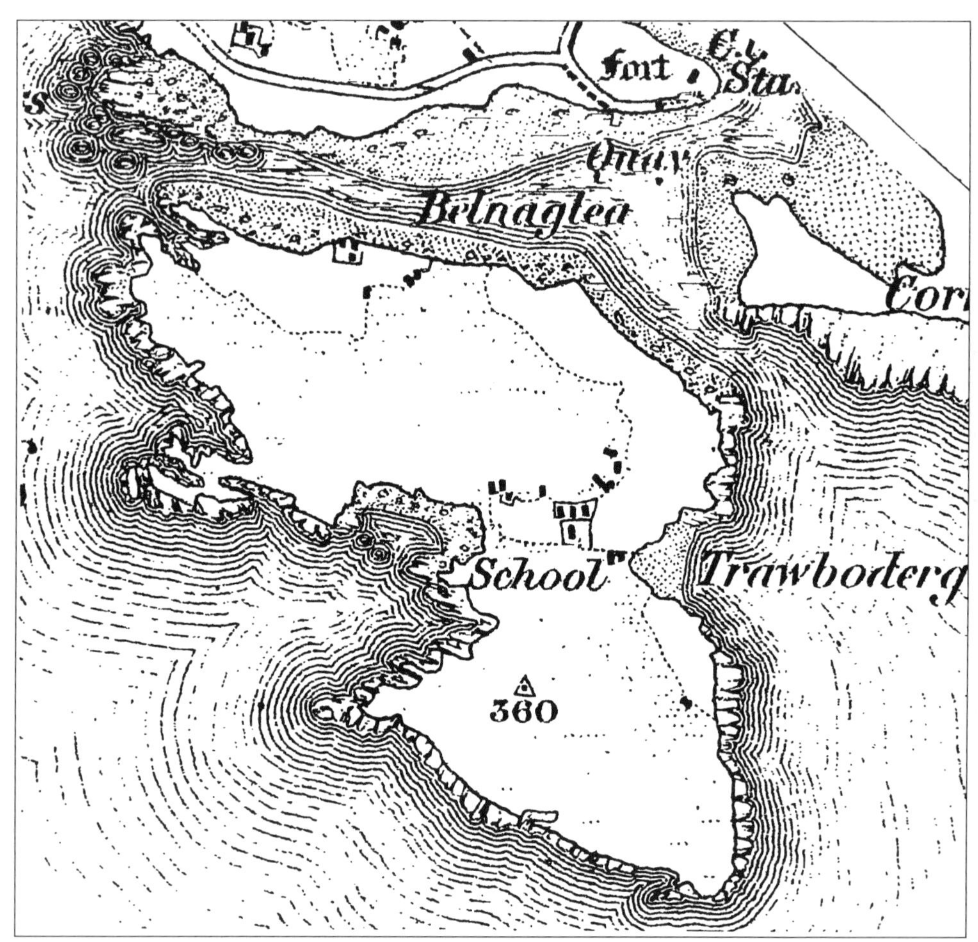

1831 map - the original school building is shown here, though it does not appear on a map a few years later. It is possible that a teacher boarded in the house shown, but had moved elsewhere when the 1838 map was produced.

Chapter Seven

Education and the School

Education in rural Ireland was at one time the preserve of the well to do, though in the 19th century travelling teachers used to teach children in 'hedge schools' - literally, on occasion, at the side of the road - the basics of reading, writing and even classics. There is some evidence of teachers coming to Achillbeg and lodging there while teaching at that time. As far back as 1826 a teacher named Ward was lodging in Achillbeg, and was paid £4 per annum. The school was described thus: 'a dwelling house of the parents of one of the Master's Scholars. The parents of each pupil supply this accommodation in turn'. Pupils, or their parents, had to pay to attend this school. In the census of 1901, a 33-year-old teacher named Norah McHugh is recorded as 'boarding' with John and Bridget Gallagher. She was apparently a qualified teacher, and was the only person on the island on the day of the census who was recorded as speaking English only. Everybody else spoke Irish, though the majority were bilingual. On the face of it, it seems strange that the island's teacher, of all people, could not speak the everyday language of the islanders, but in those days English was imposed upon pupils in almost all schools in Ireland, whether the teachers, parents or children liked it or not. In some areas this was favourably received, elsewhere not. At this stage, Achillbeg islanders were in favour of education being carried out through the medium of English, as most would spend their teenage years working in summer on farms in Britain. However, education in the general area was to undergo a revolution in the later part of the 19th century - and in the case of the Achill/Achillbeg area, with a unique added ingredient - the Revd Edward Nangle.

Nangle, already referred to, had established several schools which provided a good standard of education to local children - although intense pressure was applied to force the families of the attendees to convert to the Protestant faith. In the 1880s his activities came to the attention of the Revd John McHale, the (Catholic) Archbishop of Tuam. McHale saw that in the absence of any other formal schools in the area, Nangle's self-made educational system was winning converts, although it became clear subsequently to both Nangle and McHale that many such conversions were temporary! Consequently, McHale set about establishing a structured system of Catholic education as well, in order to stem the flow of converts to Protestantism, and to regain Nangle's 'converts'. As a result of this activity on neighbouring Achill, the area ended up changing from one with virtually no formalised education at all, to one with facilities far superior to those available in many other rural communities. Doubtless some of today's educational experts would have much to say on the effects of this competition between schools. The national educational system, and the network of purpose-built National Schools came to the area on the back of all this activity, and thus Achillbeg received its own school at some stage in the late 19th century. At first, it appears to have been situated in an existing building just above the beach, and it is marked as being in this location on the 1901 Ordnance Survey map. It is also referred to as such in the 1901 census.

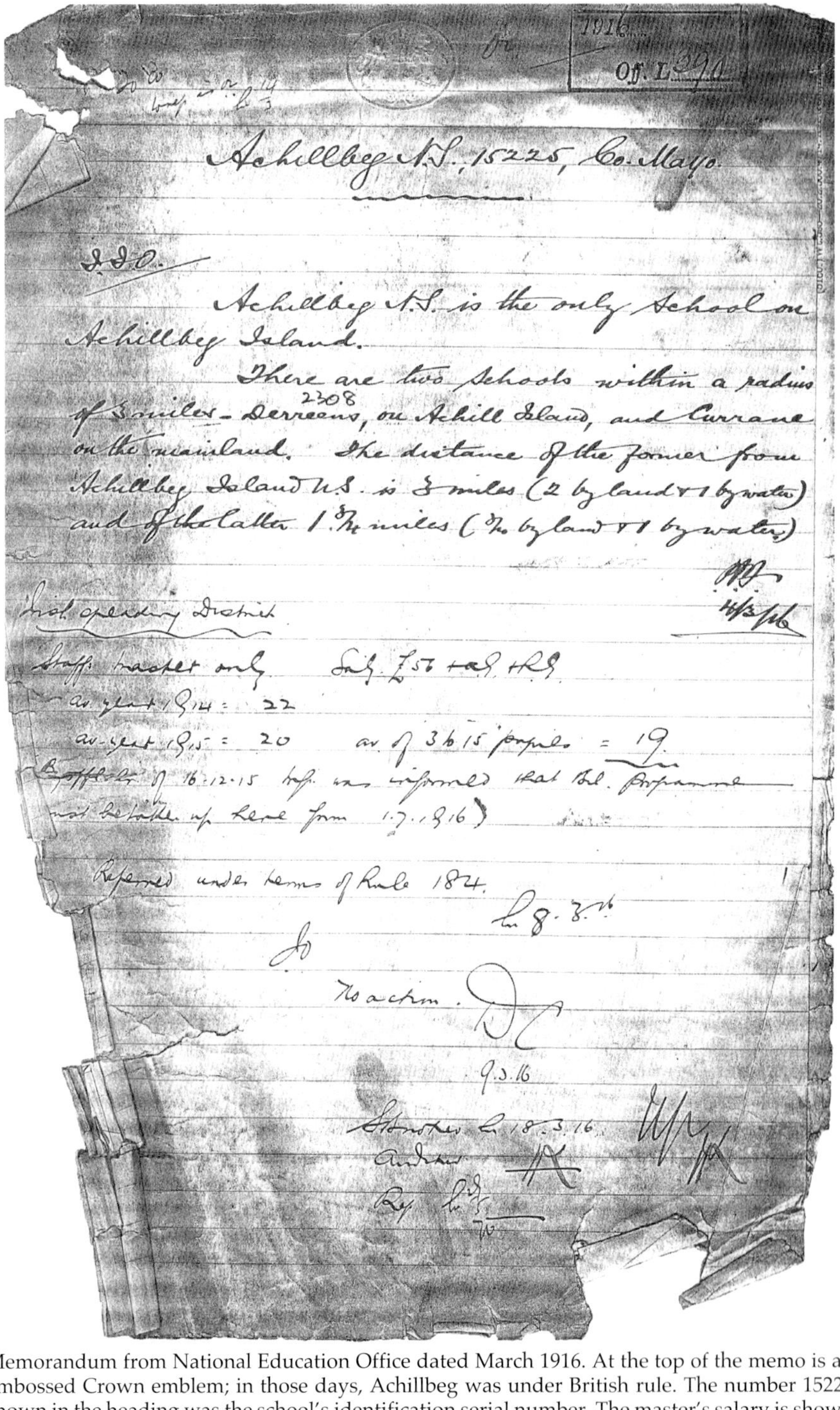

1916
Off. L 3291

Achillbeg N.S., 15225, Co. Mayo.

S.I.O.

Achillbeg N.S. is the only School on Achillbeg Island.

There are two Schools within a radius of 3 miles – Derreens, 2308 on Achill Island, and Currane on the mainland. The distance of the former from Achillbeg Island N.S. is 3 miles (2 by land & 1 by water) and of the latter 1 1/2 miles (1/2 by land & 1 by water)

[illegible]
14/3/16

Irish speaking District

Staff: master only. Sal. £56 + [illegible]

av. yearly 1914 = 22

av. yearly 1915 = 20 av. of 3 to 15 pupils = 19

B. [illegible] of 16.12.15 [illegible] was informed that [illegible] Programme not be taken up here from 1.7.1916)

Referred under terms of Rule 184.

[illegible] 8.3.16

No action.

9.3.16

[illegible] 18.3.16

Memorandum from National Education Office dated March 1916. At the top of the memo is an embossed Crown emblem; in those days, Achillbeg was under British rule. The number 15225 shown in the heading was the school's identification serial number. The master's salary is shown as £56 per annum. The master at the time was Francis Power, the *Paorach.*

As already mentioned, some clues exist as to the standard of education prior to 1900. Census records for 1901 and 1911 list the description of 'scholar' against the names of those who, presumably, were children who were being educated: 23 children were listed thus in 1901, from a total of 30 aged between 4 and 15. The oldest child described as a 'scholar' was 15, though the majority of children aged 13, 14 and 15 were not shown as attending school. The youngest children receiving education were aged 4, though it is known that well into the late 1920s (and maybe longer) some children did not start school until they were as old as seven.

A properly designed purpose-built school was built in 1903 and opened in 1904. Island folklore suggests that it may have been built with the assistance of coastguard staff. Unlike any other previous building, it was on the southern side of the central valley. The site was probably chosen in order to avoid using any of the small amount of agriculturally productive land. The old school was referred to in a Dept of Education memorandum as 'Achillbeg Non-Vested National School', and was said to have been 'struck off' in 1904. No details about its enrolment or operation have survived, though a 'snapshot' picture may be had, again from census records. In comparison with the enrolment figures quoted in the last paragraph, by 1911 27 pupils out of 32 aged between 4 and 15 were attending.

The new school was a scaled down version of a standard design - throughout Ireland many of this type (though bigger) were built and many are still to be seen in use. It was tall, single-storeyed, stone-built and slate-roofed with a small entrance hallway at one end, which led into the single school room. An open fire was provided, for which each child had to bring a sod or two of turf every morning. Little information has survived regarding the first nine years or so of the new school's operation, though it is believed that on or around the time of its opening it catered for about 50 pupils. If this is so, the little school room must have been packed, and the teacher would undoubtedly have had an assistant or junior teacher to help. It is possible that two classes were provided, as one elderly ex-pupil had a vague recollection of a partition across the middle of the school room. If such a partition was installed at one time, it had gone long before the 1930s.

Achillbeg National School was open for 63 years. Three teachers were in charge for a total of 30 years. The remaining 33 years saw a succession of partly qualified, and sometimes unqualified, teachers. Most were young, and while some had the reputation of being very good, and were later promoted and moved on, others were of poorer standard. Some islanders recalled their school days with pride, and spoke of enjoying school, whereas others recalled schooldays (and teachers!) with a less positive outlook. 'I never learned a thing in that school . . .' said one islander.

Perusal of Department of Education records does not reveal much about the pupils who attended the school, other than occasional references over the years to an average number of pupils for a term or a year. There is, however, a more detailed record of most of the teachers themselves, from 1913 onwards. Immediately prior to that, all that is known is that the teacher in charge was a mistress rather than a master.

Recollections of former teachers and islanders may be combined to paint a picture of the administrative side of the school, which was far from conventional!

With L2271/22 (I.O. 30.)

NATIONAL EDUCATION OFFICE.

SUBJECT	MINUTE.

15225. Achillbeg N.S.
(Island school)

Mgr Rev. M Calleran P.P.
Achill Sound.

Staff: Master: (resigned 30.1.22)

average attn. Qr. ended 31.3.21 = 24
30.6.21 = 20
30.9.21 = 18
31.12.21 = 21

year - 31.12.21 = 21.

Pupils on rolls on 31.12.21:—

ages	3–5	5–6	6–7	7–8	8–9	9–11	11–14	14–15	15–16	16 & over	Total
Boys	5	1	1	2	2	2	3	4	1	1	22
Girls	0	1	1	1	1	1	5	0	1	0	11

The Bil. Programme is in operation. School is the only one on Achill Beg Island. No action was taken in 1916 as to continuance of grants, & the circs. have not changed since.

Proposed Prin. Patk. McFadden Trd. D.L.S. 1919/21, holds the temp^y. [illegible] cert of Tourmakeady College 1921.

Please see memo. with G.K. 6/1912 sanctioning change from a Mistress to a Master. Papers relative to appt of out-going teacher, Mr Power also attached.

Referred as to sanctioning appt. of Mr. P McFadden. [illegible] 27.2.22

I.O. Explain requirement of rule 86(b) to Manager, and inquire why a Mistress was not appointed to the vacancy.

Say that should the circs warrant the recognition of a Master, as principal, it will be necessary under Section VIII (b) of the regulations concerning the new permanent scales of salaries for N.S. trs for him to appoint a junior assistant Mistress, who, as the average attendance is insufficient for the recognition of a Junior Assistant Mistress paid on the full scale must be guaranteed by him a salary of £110 per annum of which a fixed sum of £75 will be paid from this Office, and request his observations

B
28/2/22

T.43

W^m [illegible] 4/3/22

L3439-22

Memorandum from National Education Office dated 1922, in connection with replacement of *An Paorach* by Mr P. McFadden.

From 1913 to 1922, the master in charge of the school was Francis Power, the *Paorach*, who lived in a house he had built nearby. Power was a well educated, well travelled man with a deep commitment to the Irish language and culture, and the education and advancement of his young pupils. His success in this field was considerable, and his personality, drive and enthusiasm were legendary. A separate chapter has been devoted to this remarkable man - see page 165.

Those who attended the school after the mid-1920s had recollections of teachers sometimes being only there for a short period of time, and teaching of very varying standards. One resident told of one of one young female teacher who showed more interest in local boys than in her charges in the school; 'On sunny days, she'd go down to the strand with a boyfriend', she said. Upon being asked what the children in the school did while the teacher's wanderings were in progress, 'Oh, she'd dismiss the class. We used to go and play in the school yard or play football'.

After the *Paorach* left in 1922, the Department of Education corresponded with Fr Colleran, the Parish Priest, regarding a possible replacement. With all education being carried out through the medium of Irish, a native speaker was needed. The Department claimed that the proposed new teacher, a Mr Patrick McFadden, did not have a sufficient level of fluency. Fr Coleman, who had been responsible for sourcing and appointing a new teacher, stated that it was McFadden or nothing; though a temporary junior assistant mistress had been helping, possibly since the *Paorach* had left. Little did those concerned know it, but successive Parish Priests, in their roles as the school managers, would find the provision of a suitably qualified teacher to be almost impossible for much of the school's next 40 years of existence.

If the Department was lukewarm about McFadden's appointment, he was equally unimpressed with his new environment. The *Paorach* had had his own house, having arranged its construction himself, but after he had moved on it seems that the Department attempted to lay claim to the building as 'teacher's accommodation'. While the dispute over who owned the house continued, the new teacher found that he had nowhere to stay. He and most of his successors were to find that while teaching in Achillbeg they had to arrange for a local family to accommodate them. Generous as the islander's hospitality was, this arrangement was hardly likely to attract many applicants for teaching jobs in a place seen by mainlanders as remote and bleak. After just a few months, McFadden moved on, being replaced by Miss Biddy Hesler in October 1922. The new teacher is believed to have come from Co. Roscommon. Her salary was £160 per year. This was £50 more than a junior assistant mistress would be paid at the time, and she had charge of 21 pupils - nominally, at any rate.

The problem of teacher's accommodation remained. Correspondence between the Office of National Education and the Parish Priest in June 1922 referred to '. . . a valid reason why a mistress (as opposed to a master) should not be appointed . . .' The 'valid reason' was that there was no official place of residence for a teacher. The point was that it was assumed that a female teacher would require a better standard of comfort than a master. That said, the same correspondence made clear the Priest's preference for a schoolmistress as,

The new prin. came here 3.6.29. There
9 pupils on roll. 5th Std. is the highest
here are no Stds. 2 or 3.

The new tr. understands her work well.
She gave a good oral Irish lesson to Infants
& Std. I. She taught a good lesson in Irish
on St. Patrick. She also gave a good lesson
in English to 4th Std. on Compound Division
She does not understand the best method to
keep all the pupils occupied. I pointed
to her that a change in the Time Table
would bring this about.

She makes good preparation of work.
She has no schemes of work in Irish yet
but I showed her how to make these out.
She makes mistakes in Irish conversation
but she will improve. Irish & English
written work is satisfactory.

In 1929, the School Inspectors visited Achillbeg school. Their overall report was very satisfactory. Ever mindful of the high turnover of teachers, they devoted some time to analysing the performance of the current incumbent. Happily, this was satisfactory too. Here is an extract from the Inspector's report:

The new prin(cipal) came here on 3.6.29. There are 29 pupils on the roll. 5th Standard is the highest. There are no Stds. 2 or 3.

The new teacher understands her work well. She gave a good oral Irish lesson to Infants & Std. 1. She taught a good lesson in Irish on St. Patrick. She also gave a good lesson in English to 4th Std. on Compound Division. She does not understand the best method to keep all the pupils occupied. I pointed out to her that a change in the Time Table would bring this about.

She makes good preparation of work. She has no schemes of work in Irish yet but I showed her how to make these out. She makes mistakes in Irish conversation but she will improve. Irish and English written work is satisfactory.

Author's Collection

'There are only 27 pupils . . . and of those the majority are very small. Of the 27, 10 are girls and in the circumstances a mistress would be a more suitable teacher . . . '

An memorandum from the Examiner of Schools to the Office of National Education described the vacant house built by the *Paorach*, and the difficulty in a new teacher occupying it, in quaint and understated terms; '. . . I believe that there exists between the Manager of the School and Mr Power a discrepancy of view as to who is the legal owner of this house . . .'. A discrepancy of view was exactly what existed, though it was doubtless described in stronger terms by the *Paorach*! The Priest, as the school's manager, insisted the house belonged to the school, while the *Paorach*, who had built it, insisted it was his. It is not recorded what the outcome was of this, the final example of many disputes between the local Parish Priest and the *Paorach*.

Nevertheless, the problem was eventually solved when the *Paorach's* house was finally sold to the Kilbane family, and Miss Hesler was able to board there, with Joe 'Mhaggi' Kilbane and his mother Biddy Kilbane. She is believed to have been married outside the island to become a Mrs Kelly. By April 1926 she had secured another post and her place was taken that month by Miss Catherine Mahon. For many years after she had left she would return from time to time to visit her former pupils, now in their adult lives.

Catherine Mahon taught for three years until April 1929. She was then transferred to a school at Saula, Achill. Once again, her post was advertised, and once again there were few enthusiastic takers. Fr Colleran had been advertising in the *Daily Independent* but had had no answers from qualified people. One person who had applied did in fact have to be turned down. This was to become a tiresome and unrewarding task for Fr Colleran and his successors until the school's closure - in fact, at one stage he was so desperate to find a teacher that he had searched for prefects and monitors from other local schools who had recently completed their own education, in the hope that one of them might be suitable as a teacher for Achillbeg.

However, in June 1929 the next teacher, Miss Margaret Mary Tighe, was appointed in a temporary capacity to complete the term, as the school had been teacherless during the month of May. Miss Tighe was originally from Tuam, Co. Galway, and her teaching career on Achillbeg continued for two years. When Miss Tighe had been appointed to her post in Achillbeg, the appointment had been conditional on her improvement of her own spoken Irish. She may not have been able to do this, yet she remained in the post. The reality was that Irish or no Irish, she was too good to lose. In June 1931, after the summer term ended, she was appointed to a permanent post at Derreens National School on Achill.

With growing use of the English language elsewhere, and the difficulty in attracting teachers to Achillbeg, the exclusive use of Irish as the medium of the school began to lapse during the 1920s and early 1930s. Despite the *Paorach's* successful revival of the native tongue, a former pupil in the school at this time recalled that only a few of her lessons were conducted in Irish.

Recalling schooldays in the early 1930s one resident remembered his first day at school. All the children went barefoot, and despite the *Paorach's* efforts some years earlier, still had to bring two lumps of turf each day for the fireplace. As in all schools, some children took to the idea of daily school and others were

27 aḋ Deire-Foġṁair, 1936

Condae Muiġeó
Uiṁir 16379
Scoil Acaill Beag.

A Ċara,

I dtaoḃ na litre a scríoḃais ar an 13aḋ lá de'n ṁí seo, tá iarraiṫe ag an Aire Oideaċais orm a ċur i gcuiṁne duit gurab iad na bainisteóirí scoil a ḋeineann oidí do ṫoġaḋ. Is oċ leis a ráḋ leat naċ bfuil tú ion-toġṫa, fés na Rialaċa, mar ċongantóir i Scoil Náisiúnta, toisc ná fuil de ċáiliḋeaċt agat aċ cáiliḋeaċt Fó-ṁáiġistreasa amáin.

Is mise,

Rúnaí Aire.

Acaill Beag,
Acaill,
Co. Muiġeó.

C.nf Ċ.

This letter was sent from the Department of Education to a teacher who, not unreasonably, had requested that she be allocated a higher rate of pay as she was the only person in charge of the school. The letter is of interest in that it is typed using an old Gaelic font rather than the universally used standard typeface of the time.

It reads:

27th October 1936

County Mayo
Number 16379
Achillbeg School

Dear Madam

Regarding the letter you wrote on 13th of this month, the Minister for Education has asked me to remind you that it is the School Managers who appoint teachers. He regrets to tell you that you are not eligible, according to the rules, as an Assistant Teacher in a National School because you are qualified only as an Assistant Mistress.

Yours.
Secretary to the Minister
(Name blanked out)
Achillbeg,
Achill,
Co Mayo

National Archives, Dublin

reluctant to leave their homes - so the teacher used to bribe them with promises of bread and jam, or sweets. Jam was a luxury in the 1930s, of course! After school, or during break time, the children sometimes played on the strand. In the afternoon, when they went home, their feet were often covered in sand. One resident recalled the easiest way for a mother to clean her children's feet - in this household at least, she would keep the water the potatoes had been boiled in and wash the children's feet with that. The recollection of those who attended the school in the 1930s is that there were about 40 pupils, many coming across from Cloghmore. However, in the *Paorach's* time (1913-22) it is thought that there were about 30. The extra number in the 1930s would doubtless be accounted for by those from outside the island - the actual school enrolment figures show about 12 as an average for the time. In winter, the daily journey to school could be uncomfortable, as the low stretch of land which lies between the houses and the school would very occasionally be flooded. One islander remembered the sea almost crossing this place in the 1920s on one occasion. In effect this almost created two islands - the school and the teacher's house being on one side, the houses on the other. To go to school, he had to walk across in icy cold water, ankle deep. Like most children, his day's activities were conducted barefoot, including the journey to school. This low-lying area in the middle of the island was, and is, a natural wind tunnel. In winter, large pieces of foam are often whipped up by the wind, and blown off the raging sea at the west side of the island, and across the central valley. One islander remembered that during a particularly severe winter storm, whole waves could blow over the island at this point, icy sea water splashing down on the land in much the same manner (as he described it) as a helicopter dropping water on a forest fire.

In the 1930s the school taught English, Irish, Arithmetic (including long and short division, as one former pupil observed), Geography, History, Dictation and Catechism. The National Anthem (*Amrhán na bhFiann*/The Soldier's Song) was taught to all pupils, though during the 1920s one teacher refused to teach this on account of her political views. The school day started at 9.00 am, and finished at 3.00 pm, with a break for lunch. On arrival, the children would place their two lumps of turf in a bin in the hallway, and hang their coat up on one of the hooks nearby. Inside the single classroom the teacher was at the front (nearest the door), with a roaring turf fire beside him (or her) in cold weather. The blackboard was on an easel to the right of the fireplace, the door from the hallway on the left. Former pupils recall dark green paintwork on lower panels which were of vertical matchboard plank panelling. Examination of paint flakes, where they still survive on the remaining salt-bleached woodwork, indicate that at an earlier stage the interior woodwork was painted red. The desks were long benches, some of which held six children. The front desks were reserved for children aged 5-11, with those aged 12 and over at the back. One islander believes that for a time there was a partition or screen separating the two lots of desks. As children went back year after year, a move towards the back was seen as a sign of growing up. Two large cupboards and a table completed the furnishings. In the period in which the school operated, it was normal practice for boys and girls to be educated in separate schools, but the school in Achillbeg was too small for this. There were no separate boys and girls

Conndae ... Mayo

Uimhir na Scoile ... 15225

Scoil ... Achillbeg Island

ROINN OIDEACHAIS,
BRAINNSE AN BHUN-OIDEACHAIS,
SRÁID MAOILBHRIGHDE,

Iml. MR 1/42 BAILE ÁTHA CLIATH ... 11th March 1942

20 MÁR 1942 O.N.

I gCÓIR NA hOIFIGE.	FREAGRA.
Manager is requested to be so good as to furnish his observations in regard to the absence of Mrs Bridget Kilbane, principal teacher in the above-named school on 15th, 19th, 22nd, 27th and 30th January, 1942, for which the cause assigned on the school return was "storms."	Storms are the cause of her trouble She is living in Achilmore and has to teach in Achillbeg. The sea between both and over what she has to pass is sometimes dangerous.
	DF Referred 21/3/42 B9 Io Inspector on duty at present. 26/3/42
T. O'Muirie ~~Tomás Ó Muirgeasa,~~ Leas-rúnaí	
Rev. J. Campbell P.P. Achill Sound	Signiú ... James Campbell Dáta ... 18 : 3 : 42

(1228) T. 5551—Gp. 27—5,000—1/'42—M.P.W.

Correspondence between Revd Campbell and the Dept of Education relating to the closure of the school on several days in 1942 due to bad weather. The two columns read:

Manager is requested to be so good as to furnish his observations in regard to the absence of Mrs Bridget Kilbane, principal teacher in the above named school on 15th, 19th, 22nd, 27th and 30th January 1942, for which the cause assigned on the school return was 'storms'.

Storms are the cause of her trouble. She is living in Achilmore [*sic*] and has to teach in Achillbeg. The sea between both and over what she has to pass is sometimes dangerous.

Signed
18.3.42

National Archives, Dublin

entrances - but the playground was originally segregated, even to the extent of separate outdoor toilets, which may still be seen in the back of the schoolyard. In the school's last years, the segregation was discontinued due to low numbers, and the fact that for the last five or six years all the children were from the one family. The playground was level, well built and well drained, and was used for football matches, not only during break time but after school and at the weekends. On Sundays, young people from Corraun would come to Achillbeg to play against the islanders, who had a good reputation locally as footballers. Each year the playground drains were cleared to ensure continuing comfort to its users.

The school's next teacher was both the last fully qualified permanently appointed teacher, and also the longest serving on the island. Originally Miss Bridget English (from Achill Island), she married a local man, Michael Kilbane, during her stay on Achillbeg. On her appointment, the Revd James Campbell (the Parish Priest) wrote 'I think she knows the Irish Language . . . this is a small island . . .' Miss English was, however, a native Irish speaker, and was able to teach the children in their own language from the outset. This was of more importance than just keeping the national language alive. In order to encourage native speaking communities, especially rural ones, a Government grant of £2 was available for every child between the ages of 6 and 14 who was educated in Irish. According to Department of Education guidelines, each child had to speak Irish in the home 'fluently and naturally', and must have a satisfactory level of attendance in their school. While unqualified when she took the post, Miss English completed her qualifications with flying colours. In the 1930s, a School Inspector visited, reporting '. . . she (Miss English) has proved to be an excellent teacher. Her school reports can stand comparison with those of highly qualified schools . . . there was very little interest in (learning in) Irish until she awakened it . . .'. This reflects the position of the two languages at the time. Irish was the 'language of the hearth' but there would have been a perception in the minds of many that it belonged to the past, and was primitive; that 'educated' people spoke English. Clearly, between 1922, when the *Paorach* left, and the start of Miss English's time some nine years later, some teachers had reverted to the English tongue. The Inspector's report continued 'Every pupil of hers for the last two years has benefited from the Gaeltacht grant of £2'.

For 13 years Miss English/Mrs Kilbane taught the island's children, from May 1931 to July 1945, after which she was transferred to Bunnacurry, Achill. It appears that by 1941/2 she was living on Achill, and travelling across to Achillbeg in the mornings to teach. The school remained closed on days when weather prevented her from crossing - for example, during the school year 1940/1, the school did not open on one day in October, two in January, and one in April.

An interesting episode in the school's life was recorded in Mrs Kilbane's time. A memorandum in old Department of Education files suggests that she was taken to task by her superiors as a result of the fact that she brought Achill children across with her in the boat, and included them in her own class. It is unclear why she would have wanted to do this, but the school authorities took the view that these children would be better served by attending their own local

Achillbeg School, about 1946. *Back row, left to right:* Tommy Gallagher (conspicuous to his companions because 'he always wore shoes'), Tommy Lavelle, Martha Gallagher, Delia Gallagher, and Michael Joe Kilbane. *Middle row:* Elleen Geary (not an island native, but lived there for a short period with relatives), Mary Kilbane (now Gannon), Tommy Gallagher, Bridie Lavelle (born in Scotland). *Front row:* Joe Kilbane, Briege Kilbane, Paddy Kilbane. The picture was probably taken by the teacher at the time. A Miss Annie Cafferkey had been teaching temporarily, and this was about the time that Vera Joyce came to the school.

Peg Masterson

school at Derreens. One pupil of the time believes that combining the island children and those brought across, there were as many as 40 pupils at times. The school roll book, however, told the 'official' story - which was that the average enrolment varied from just over 30 in 1921, to 12 in 1945 - and the corresponding attendance figures for the same period were 20-12.

A school inspector's report from October 1945 has survived, which shows the enrolment for the school year 1945/6. These were as follows:

Name	*Age*
Tomás Ó Maolfhabhair	13.7
Tomás Ó Gallchobhair	12.1
Peig Ní Mhaolfhbhail *	13.7
Sean Mhaolfhbhail *	7.5
Micheal MacGiollabháin	12.4
Seosamh MacGiollabháin	5.6
Delia Ní Ghallchobhair	10.8
Marta Ní Ghallchobhair	13.2
Tomás Ó Ghallchobhair	4.5
Maire Ní Giollabháin	8.4
Padraig Ó Giollabháin	4.8
Eibhlín Ní Ghadraigh	5.4

* Mhaolfhbhail = Mulvihill, not an island name. Their parents were living in Scotland, and the children staying with their grandfather while their parents worked. Their mother was originally from Achillbeg.

The point was made that apart from the last three names on the list, the families of all the others already had their youngest children at school - in other words, the last three were the only families with younger children who would swell the school numbers in forthcoming years. With five children aged twelve or over, the numbers were expected to decline in the short term. The inspector did not expect that the two oldest would be back after the end of term. The last named child was living with her mother and grandfather, as her father had gone to England. It was expected that the child and her mother would leave Achillbeg 'any day now' to join him. The only children too young to attend school were the two younger siblings of the Ó Giollabháin (Galvin) family. It is assumed that this family were not on Achillbeg for long, as this surname does not appear elsewhere in any known surviving official records.

The report continued:

> There are a couple of empty houses on the island, and other houses with old people, or people of advanced years . . . there may be no more than 8 or 9 on the roll in a year's time. As I see it, it will be difficult to maintain an average of 7 (if the school is to continue) within a few years.
>
> But if the school was closed now, no education would be available for the students unless they go to Doirín where there is a school. There is a school in Corrán but the way over from Achill Beag is dangerous due to the strength of the current. A boat service could not be established between these two places. A boat service could be established between Achill Beag and Cloch Mór (on the way to Doirín) and the cost of the service would be less than the salary of the teacher in the school in Achill Beag. But if that was

Contae Mayo (8).

Uimhir na Scoile 15225

Scoil Achillbeg

12279-57

Roinn Oideachais,
Brainse an Bhun-Oideachais,
Sráid Mhaoilbhríde,

Iml. RR 12101 Fol Baile Átha Cliath 1/7/57

I gcóir na hOifige.	Freagra.
Manager is requested to be so good as to state whether he has yet secured the services of a suitable teacher for the principalship of the above-named school, to succeed Miss B. Henry, temporary principal teacher.	I have not even got an applicant for a better place & school. If this Achillbeg school is not to be soon without any teacher the Dept. should consider seriously appointing this Manager as permanent teacher otherwise she too will depart for some permanent position even in a factory in England.
~~Labhrás Ó Muirthe,~~ Rúnaí. Reverend J. Godfrey P.P., Achill Sound	Síniú ... Godfrey P.P. Dáta 2/7/57.

9240A.15,000.E.P.C.Ltd. G38. S

The trials of finding a teacher for the school in the 1950s: Memorandum from Dept of Education to Fr Godfrey, the parish priest, and his reply. *National Archives, Dublin*

> done the students would have to walk most of a mile on the island to the port - spend 20 minutes or so in a boat that is not suitable for children, and then walk 2 miles after that to the school in Doirín . . .
>
> The way from Cloch Mór and Achill Beag is often not calm. Sometimes it cannot be crossed at all. Occasionally you could cross in the morning, but you could not return in the afternoon . . .

The report summarised that it would be better to keep the school open, and added that in any case, the Archbishop of Tuam would not agree to its closure.

In 1945 Mrs Kilbane's place was taken temporarily by a Miss Annie Cafferkey from Achill, who had previously taught in Slievemore National School. Another temporary teacher followed for a couple of months - this was a Mr Paddy Henry. Mr Henry soon moved on elsewhere, while Fr McEllin, the current Parish Priest, placed the usual advertisements for a successor. In correspondence with the Department of Education, he stated that a female teacher would be preferred, as there were a number of very young children in the school at the time. However, of the three respondents to the advertisements, none were qualified. A recommendation was received that a lady from Mulrany, Miss Vera Joyce, would be suitable, even though she was not bilingual. She started teaching in January 1946, though her formal appointment did not take place until June. Miss Joyce was to hold the post until 1955. During this time she did not enjoy good health, and the journeys to and from the school from her native Mulrany cannot have made her working life easier. From 1950, although she was nominally in charge, two temporary teachers were drafted in to assist in running the school during her long periods of incapacity. Another Mulrany man, Mr Colm Moran, was joined by Miss Eveline Gallagher for this purpose. A report by the teacher's trade union, INTO, described the 'almost impossible conditions under which a teacher has to live . . .' By November 1955, Miss Joyce had to leave the teaching profession due to the state of her health and her replacement was Miss Bridget Henry, from Belfarsad, Corraun, who remained until the school closed for summer in mid-1959. Miss Henry had found the job difficult, as she was also studying herself, despite the fact that she was staying with relatives in Achillbeg. She emigrated to Britain at this stage. She is remembered by one former pupil for growing marrows in Garraí uí Shúilleabháin (Sullivan's Garden, near the school).

With the school's records not having survived, the only reliable information on individual 'roll-calls' is that collected from those who were pupils in the last 15 years of the school's life. In 1949, the school's 11 pupils were drawn from five families:

Maureen Gallagher
Peg, Paddy, Briege and Mary Kilbane
Michael and Joe Kilbane
Bridget and Eddie Lavelle
Tommy and Delia Gallagher

Despite the difficulty in appointing a teacher to the island, and pleas from successive Parish Priests for help, the Department of Education maintained its

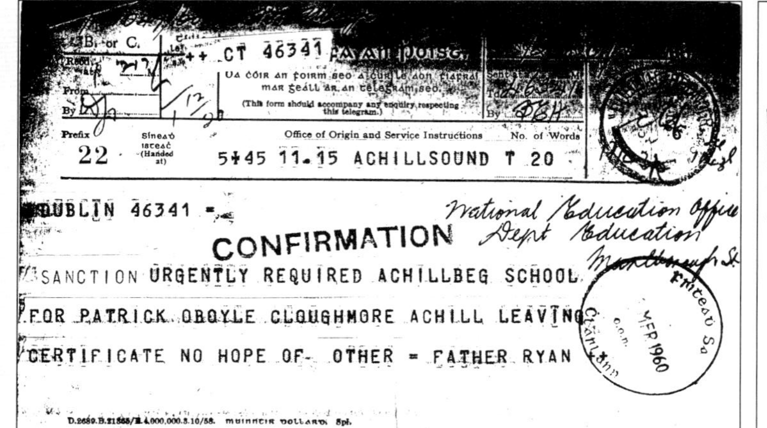

CT 46341

Prefix 22 · Office of Origin and Service Instructions 5445 11.15 ACHILLSOUND T 20

DUBLIN 46341 =

National Education Office Dept Education Marlborough St

CONFIRMATION

SANCTION URGENTLY REQUIRED ACHILLBEG SCHOOL

FOR PATRICK OBOYLE CLOUGHMORE ACHILL LEAVING

CERTIFICATE NO HOPE OF OTHER = FATHER RYAN

Above: Telegram sent to the Department of Education by the parish priest, asking them to confirm as a matter of urgency the appointment of a new teacher for Achillbeg school. 'No hope of other' refers to the fact that numerous requests and newspaper advertisements had failed to find any other applicant. The implication was that if the Department did not appoint the one applicant the priest had, then the school would close. The teacher concerned was appointed shortly afterwards. *National Archives, Dublin*

Right: A sign of the times, 1960. Father Ryan's communication to the Dept of Education.

19691/60

COPY – Orig. to RR

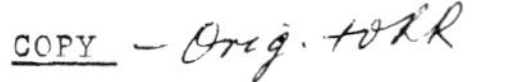

St. Columba's,
Achill sound,
Co. Mayo. R/15225

27. XII. 1960.

The Secretary,
Department of Education,
(Primary Branch),
Dublin.

A Chara,

As I have been unable to find fully qualified teachers for the Principalship of Tonragee and Achillbeg schools, I propose to extend the appointments of these teachers for a further period, from 1st January.

Is mise,
le meas,

(Sgd) T. J. Ryan P.P.

MF/

stand on pay and conditions. One temporary teacher at this time was told that she would not be paid for the summer months, as temporary teachers did not qualify for any summer pay. She challenged the decision, and on her behalf the Priest wrote '. . . no teacher is prepared to stay on the island without accommodation . . .' He went on to point out that they were happy enough to accept her as a teacher, even though she was not officially qualified, so why not pay her accordingly? In addition, he made the point that had it not been for his efforts in persuading islanders to allow teachers to stay in their houses, there would have been no teacher at all for the previous two years. The Department stuck to their guns, and the teacher concerned resigned the following year.

The Department did not neglect the school entirely though - in the late 1950s the building was given a complete facelift and was repainted - for the last time, as it would turn out.

The start of the autumn term in 1959 had to be delayed. A girl from Clare Island had been asked to take the job after Miss Henry had left, but after three weeks of persuasion she declined to do so, hardly surprisingly in the circumstances. Her place was taken by Mr Stephen Campbell, who finished the school year for her. The Parish Priest wrote to the Department asking them to appoint him permanently, as he had actually been planning to emigrate before he started teaching; and expressing his fear that the school would close should he leave. The Department did not refuse outright this time, as they had before, but they spent so long considering their decision that Mr Campbell left anyway at the end of the term - why stay if there was a strong possibility that he would receive no pay over the summer?

By September 1960, the school was struggling. One 24-year-old female teacher from Dublin applied for the post, but having seen what was involved, subsequently withdrew, especially after the Department of Education refused to pay her the full rate on account of her youth and incomplete qualifications. Fr Ryan, the Parish Priest, wrote to the Department to let them know that there was still no accommodation for teachers, and those that had agreed to serve in recent years had been able to do so only on account of the generous hospitality of the islanders, who had allowed successive incumbents to lodge with one of the island families. With Achillbeg seen as small and isolated, no qualified teacher seemed keen to make the daily journey there, let alone live on the island - even if there had been a house available.

In 1962, a Sean Gibbons was briefly appointed; he appears to have left almost immediately. The Parish Priest, by now at his wit's end, wrote in frustration that he had placed advertisements repeatedly in newspapers for a suitable teacher, and had not received one reply. He reported to the Education authorities, 'No girl would be interested, none offered, and I wouldn't ask anyone' - the point being that he wanted both they and the Government to give assistance to the islanders, or re-house them on Achill or the mainland.

The hard weather played its part in throwing obstacles at the island's educational system too. In January 1962 the island was cut off for the greater part of three weeks, while the severe winter in the early months of 1963 caused supply and transport difficulties. In both cases, teachers were unable to cross to the island and the school had to close temporarily. While the threat of closure

Teacher Patrick O'Boyle. *Author's Collection*

A poor quality picture but it is the only one surviving of the school's interior when in use. In the spring of 1962, the seven children of the Gallagher family are taught by Patrick O'Boyle. *Author's Collection*

was now very real, one young man was to save the day - for the moment, anyway. Patrick O'Boyle, aged 19, who had recently passed his Leaving Certificate, was appointed on a temporary basis. Patrick was to teach in the school for that year only, but by September 1961 there were still no takers for the post, so he remained another year. Again, the authorities made every effort to find a permanent teacher for that autumn term, and again they failed. O'Boyle was appointed for one more year, but he did not return to the school, opting for more permanent work elsewhere. His place was taken by Michael McNamara, who was to be the school's last teacher. Originally from Polranny, Corraun, Mr McNamara presided over the lessons of the last family of school-age children until the end of the summer term in June 1965. He boarded during the week on Achillbeg with a local family. His appointment, as often in recent years, had only just been made in time; in September 1961 and 1962 the school re-opened a few days late as the teacher in each case was not yet in place. Apart from the isolation, the teacher's pay on a rate for junior or unqualified staff was just £305 per year - even by the standards of the day, not a substantial level of remuneration. A note in a Department file from the period indicates that the annual cost of running the school in 1961/2 was £400: £305 for the teacher's salary, and the rest for what little upkeep was necessary to the building, and books, pencils and the like. One teacher actually wrote to the Department of Education around this time, outlining what was expected of anybody holding the position, and describing in detail the sacrifices of time, freedom and comfort that were necessary. He made the point that in these circumstances the pay and conditions were hardly fair. The letter fell on deaf ears, and a terse reply was sent back - the pay was determined according to the Department's standard rules, and that was that. Fr Ryan continued to write to the Department reminding them of the difficulties, saying that closure was a constant threat due to lack of a teacher, let alone a suitably qualified one.

It is possible to give a description of a typical day at school from this late period in the school's life, although for many years earlier the routine was probably much the same. As in earlier years the school day started at 9.00 am and ended at 3.00 pm, with a half-hour lunch break. At lunch time in the warmer months, when no fire had been lit in the classroom's fireplace, one teacher recalled boiling up spare rib soup he had made on a small portable 'primus' gas cooker which he brought with him.

The children sat at long bench-type desks of the type common at the time; former pupil's opinions vary as to how many they held, though they may have varied over the years. One teacher who was at the school in its twilight years estimated that there was seating capacity for perhaps 20 or more children, though in his time there were less than half that number in attendance. It is thought that at the time of the school's opening, there could have been as many as 50.

In the morning the teacher allocated work for the older children, and while they were thus engaged, the younger children were taught. Subjects were divided into half-hour lessons, and each child's progress recorded in a book. As well as the 'staples' of reading, writing, and mathematics, Irish and British history were taught as well as geography. An elderly map of Ireland adorned the wall, the ink beginning to flake off it; this was kept company by a large map

R.R. 12101

Very Reverend T. Ryan, P.P.,
Achill Sound,
CO. MAYO.

19 Deireadh Fómhair, 1965.

Mayo 15225 Achillbeg.

A Athair Oirmh.,

With reference to your letter dated 12th October, 1965, regarding the closing of the above-named school, I am to inform you that grants have now been withdrawn from the school. The Inspector will call on you in the near future to collect the school records.

Mise, le meas,

Letter from the Department of Education to Fr Ryan, the school's manager, in 1965. Two islanders subsequently recovered the school's records and delivered them to the parish priest, but it has not been possible to trace their whereabouts since. *National Archives, Dublin*

The school from the front. The neat wall enclosed the playground, though to a young islander the whole island was a playground. Sunday afternoon football matches took place here in the 1920s, with many crossing from Achill to take part - and they often returned home as the losing team! *Author*

The school room. The fireplace survives, hearth now choked with stones. Fallen rafters are strewn about, mingling with broken floor joists. The blackboard stood on an easel to the right of the fireplace. *Author*

The back of the school. The children's toilets can be seen to the right, as well as the wall dividing the girls and boys playground areas. In later years, with all pupils being from one or two families, no distinction was made between boys and girls in the playground. In the distance are some of the houses which constituted the main settlement. With a little imagination, it is easy to see how impressive the valley must have looked when all the fields were carefully tilled. *Author*

Above left: Achillbeg National School. This is the view on entering the building. The wood panels are now salt-bleached and hardened, and the remains of four coat hooks can still be seen. Where the panelling ends, there was once a cupboard across the hallway in which turf was kept. On entering the school each morning, each child had to throw two lumps of turf into it. To the right, the schoolroom is through the doorway. The walls of this were similarly panelled, though this has all disappeared now, as have the floor and roof. Traces of green paint are still to be seen inside the doorway. *Author*

Above right: View from schoolhouse window. How many young scholars longed for class to be finished, as they gazed through it on a day as sunny as this? *Author*

of Europe before World War I. 'Safety First' posters warned pupils of the dangers of overhead power lines and traffic on roads; by the 1960s these were a poignant reminder of the isolated state of the island community. The blackboard was on an easel in the corner.

As 1965 dawned it was clear that the school's time was up, as the remaining population were making plans to leave. At the end of the summer term the school closed as normal for the holidays. The last teacher, Michael McNamara, locked the school for the last time and gave the key to the Parish Priest, as was always done when the school was shut for the holidays. Michael emigrated to Britain; life moved on, and the school never re-opened. That September, the one remaining family of children who had attended it were temporarily accommodated in the Parochial Hall at Achill Sound while the Parish Priest secured places for them in a nearby school. Achillbeg's contribution to the local educational system was complete.

After the school closed, a letter was sent from the Department of Education to Fr Ryan, the Parish Priest at Achill Sound, informing him that an inspector would call to collect the school's records. According to the school's last teacher, the desk and some cupboards contained roll books and other paperwork which dated back to the early 1920s - around the time the *Paorach* had left, in fact. What happened next is hard to establish, as the school's papers do not appear to have survived, either among Parish records at Achill Sound, or within the Department of Education's archives. What can be ascertained is that at Fr Ryan's bidding, two islanders retrieved anything of importance, including some of the old desks and two large wall maps. These were delivered as instructed, but cannot be found since. At least two of the desks were subsequently re-used in the school at Achill Sound - a familiar sight, no doubt, to those final Achillbeg pupils who had transferred there. However, it is possible that at least some material was left in the schoolhouse as there is anecdotal evidence of some papers lying around the old school yard, exposed to the weather, in the early 1970s. The papers may, however, have been from another source - the lighthouse authorities had used the school for a time as a store just after the island was abandoned. By the mid 1970s, a visitor to the island noted that the school building was unlocked, but completely intact. It was empty of all furnishings and anything that might have contained papers - if anything had been left, it was by now long gone. This gentleman decided he would like to buy the school to convert into a holiday house, but both the Parish Priest and the Department of Education claimed that each other owned it, and both declined to be involved in any plans for the building. The newcomer purchased a nearby house from a former islander instead, and continues to maintain it as a holiday home.

The school building lay empty and unwanted, while weeds grew around it. As the years passed it deteriorated. During the 1970s a mainland businessman prepared plans to open an outdoor pursuit centre on Achillbeg, possibly using this building, but nothing came of this plan. By the early 1990s the roof was beginning to fall in and the floorboards had long given way. In the building's centenary year, 2003, the now roofless walls were still completely sound structurally, and fragments of wooden window frames and matchboarded panelling in the hallway remained, bleached and preserved by the salt-laden air and wind.

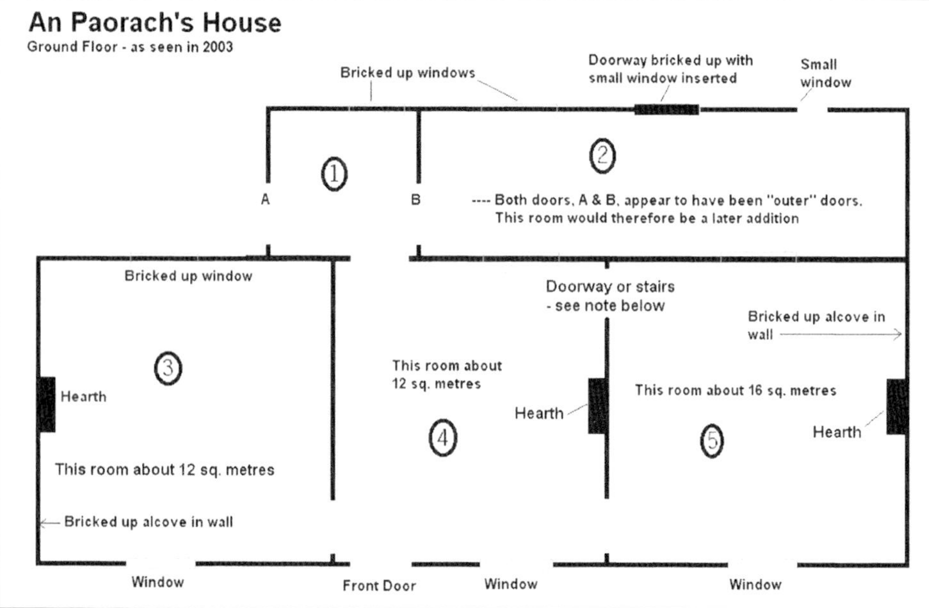

Notes

1. This is no more than a porch or lean-to at the back of the house. It was possibly a small kitchen at one time.
2. This room appears to have been built much later than the rest of the house. It is possible it dates from after the *Paorach's* time. This room may have been subdivided further, perhaps by wooden internal walls. It contains one bricked-up window, one bricked-up door with a small window inserted in its place, and another small window.

3 and 5. The main rooms of the house, each with fireplace. Above each of these rooms was a low ceiling, with a small room above. These two upstairs rooms were where the *Paorach* housed his occasional guests, including English composer Philip Heseltine and Nobel Peace Prize winner Sean MacBride. These upstairs rooms were very small indeed, and it would barely have been possible to stand upright in them. They each had two small windows in the gable ends of the house.

4. This was the main 'living room', where many a learned discussion must have taken place - in Irish. This room does not appear to have had an 'upstairs'.

Note re 'Doorway or Stairs' out of room 4.

This gap in the wall has no lintel above it, and the wall between 'W' and 'Y' is constructed in such a way that the presence of a staircase rather than a door is possible. There would not have been any need for two doorways from '4' to 'Y', so it is likely that a small staircase led from here up to the room above. It is not clear how the 'upstairs' room above 'Y' was accessed, but since it was little better than an attic, a ladder might have sufficed.

The narrow rooms at the back of the house were somewhat crudely built and of 'lean-to' construction. They did not have an upper level.

Examination of the few remaining pieces of woodwork in door and window frames show that these were painted in bright colours - blue, red and green at different times.

All but the front windows are bricked up, and look as if they have been for some time. It is not clear when this took place, nor is there any folk memory about the house being extended, which appears to have been done by first adding the back room '1', and later '2'. This may have happened long after the *Paorach* had left.

Outside the house, a neat wall surrounded the property, and a straight path edged with rocks from the sea shore led to the gate. The house was neat and tidy, and is believed to have had a well kept garden around it.

The plan and description given is based on observations of the ruin of the house as seen in 2003.

Chapter Eight

Francis Hugh Power, The *Paorach*

'He passionately instructed us in the idea that the Irish language, song, history, games and anything Irish was more worth while than anything else'. (A former pupil of *An Paorach*)

The earliest first hand account of a teacher still available at the time research was under way for this book was of Francis Hugh Power, who taught in Achillbeg from 1913 to 1922, after which he moved on promotion to Newport. The stories which abound in folklore and recollection about Power the man, Power the personality, Power the enthusiastic advocate of traditional Irish culture, and Power the schoolmaster, all have a remarkable consistency - that of a man revered by his fellow islanders, to whom he was invariably known as The *Paorach* - a translation of his surname 'Power'.

The *Paorach* was born in Tipperary in August 1879. His family origins were there, though there is some evidence to suggest that he may have spent some time in England in his youth. He is believed to have been educated at Oxford or Cambridge where, among other things, he appears to have excelled at learning languages. His mother encouraged him to join the priesthood, but he did not want to do this and instead he went to sea. While engaged on a long sea journey, he picked up an Irish grammar book and read it thoroughly - little knowing that it would change his life. He became deeply interested in Irish culture and the language in particular, which was in decline due to a number of factors, mostly political interference and the increasing number of Irish people emigrating to English-speaking countries.

When he returned to England, fired with an enthusiasm for learning Irish and playing a part in preserving and encouraging its use, he joined an English branch of the Gaelic League. This was primarily a cultural organisation, but was becoming more politicised as Ireland's destiny unfolded towards independence. These were days of political struggle and turmoil: Ireland had embarked on the road to nationhood, and a new national confidence filled the air. The *Paorach* wanted to help, to be part of it; and he duly arrived back in Ireland and enrolled at De La Salle Training College in Waterford to study teaching. He achieved results which were described as 'outstanding', and were among the best 12 results in the College.

He wanted to teach in a remote rural community in order to play his part in the preservation of the Irish language, and to improve his own growing fluency. In 1913 there seemed no more suitable place for this than Achillbeg. On his arrival, he found to his surprise that instead of a completely Irish-speaking community as he would have found in many adjacent mainland districts at the time, virtually everybody was completely bilingual. The establishment of a Coastguard presence in the 19th century had brought English speaking Irishmen, and Englishmen themselves, into Achillbeg. The island school's previous teachers had taught in English, and the custom of Achillbeg residents migrating to Scotland or elsewhere for summer work had resulted in the

The *Paorach's* house stands over the beautiful vista of the sea and the distant mountains of Connemara to which this part of the island is geologically related. The flat area in the foreground was known as Macalla. *Author*

The *Paraoch's* house., described as the island's only two-storey house. The nature of this upper storey is evident - it was no more than two unconnected attic-style rooms, one at each end of the house. When occupied by the famous teacher, the house had a neatly-tended front garden surrounded by the wall. In later days, the Kilbane family owned the house. *Author*

English language becoming widely known in the island (as well as Scottish Gaelic dialects). In addition, he discovered that the Parish Priest of the day was opposed to the use of Irish in the school, opposed to the playing of football, and opposed to Irish dancing! The *Paorach* was determined to halt what he saw as a growing trend towards speaking English, while ensuring that islanders enjoyed as high a standard of general education as they would get anywhere else. The bilingualism of islanders was born of necessity: while Irish was the language spoken in the houses, the fact that the majority of islanders had to travel each year to find seasonal work meant that fluency in English was essential. He taught in Irish and spoke it, and as a former pupil observed 'We were taught English in the school for an hour every day. I could never understand how they (mainland people) could speak that language, but I'm glad I learnt it, for we emigrated to England when I was about 15 . . .' The *Paorach* wrote '*An Ghaeilge Abú*' (Up with Irish) inside the covers of all the school books. His enthusiasm for the native tongue, and his insistence on reverting to teaching through this medium was not well received at first by either the islanders or the educational authorities who would not support him, but he persisted successfully. The *Paorach* had an unassuming appearance, stocky but short in stature and with receding hair, and a quiet gentle manner, but he was not a man to take 'no' for an answer! Some of the adult island population were more inclined to speak English than Irish, and he held night classes for those who wished to brush up on their native tongue.

Former pupils remember him arousing great enthusiasm in his pupils. He held their attention without ever having to resort to corporal punishment - a rare thing in the education system of the time. One pupil wrote, 'He passionately instructed us in the idea that the Irish language, song, history, games and anything Irish was more worth while than anything else'. This was no myopic nationalism or air-headed idealism: despite living in politically turbulent times, he would not tolerate any form of criticism of Britain, the British people, or anybody else for that matter. He rejoiced in, and enthusiastically and proudly communicated his sense of culture, patriotism, nationality and citizenship. He inspired his pupils with, as one described, 'a non-bigoted view of Irishness . . . which I still maintain'.

He was adamant that island children were entitled to as good an education as they would receive anywhere else, and he worked long and hard towards that end. If a pupil wanted to learn about something he did not already cover, he would tell them to bring in a book about it and he would teach them from that. Always conscious that his charges would almost all spend at least some of their adult life outside the island, he taught geography, shorthand, and many other subjects. A number of his former pupils became highly qualified teachers themselves elsewhere in their adult lives. He was a fluent speaker of several languages, an accomplished scholar of the Classics, and a keen and knowledgeable enthusiast of all aspects of Irish culture. He taught the children about life, about the sea and the land, and the world beyond their own shore. He showed his charges how to grow *garleog* (garlic) in a walled garden behind the school, and he told them that if they ate it they would never have cancer. Garlic was used by the islanders to ward off colds - by placing it in their shoes!

The walled garden was also used to grow other vegetables, flowers and plants. Watercress was grown in drains near the school, and residents in the 1930s and 1940s remember clumps of it still growing, long after the *Paorach* had moved on elsewhere.

Among his many other extracurricular activities were swimming, karate and music. He was an accomplished player of the bagpipes and violin, and taught many islanders to play them. Under his tutelage, despite the small size of the school, a school band was formed. Some years after his death (in the 1950s) his widow presented his pipes to the Guth na nÓg Pipe Band in Galway, with whom the *Paorach* had been associated some years after leaving Achillbeg. Accordions were a popular accompaniment to many a sing-song in the *Paorach's* time, but he did not like them, and try as he might, was not very good at playing them. Everybody has their limits!

As might be expected from his days at sea, he was a keen and expert sailor, and owned a yacht in which he taught many young people to sail. Sometimes he sailed to Westport and back. One former pupil recalled that on days that the Westport-Liverpool boat was passing the island, the *Paorach* took his class of young scholars up the hill behind the school to a place called Lár na Scoilte and taught them to signal to ships in Morse Code. He used a sword to reflect sunlight towards the boat. Another islander recalled that he also taught many of his pupils to swim, and to play backgammon and chess. Twenty years after he left, a chess board would still appear at many an island gathering. He would often undertake lengthy boat trips away from the island. Sometimes he took older boys out fishing, or to dances in Mulrany by boat. On one occasion he rescued a man from drowning off Achillbeg.

He is believed to have had a brother, who was a lawyer, and a sister in Co. Roscommon who may have visited him in Achillbeg occasionally. The *Paorach* was a man of wide experience and of good education, well known for his ability to converse articulately on almost any subject. For all this, he was not aloof or detached - he was very much what is nowadays known as a 'people person'.

As well as introducing a wide range of subjects not then common in country schools, he fought for outside support too. It had been the custom from an early stage for each child to bring a couple of sods of turf to school with them every morning for the fire. The *Paorach*, who in the words of one of his then pupils, 'would not let the parish priest away with anything', tackled Father Collins, the priest at Achill Sound, telling him that in other districts it was common for the Church to supply turf to the schools, so why not on Achillbeg? The stage was thus set for a stormy relationship, as the priest refused. It was customary at the time for the priest to visit the island twice a year for the Stations of the Cross, or occasionally at the time of a birth, and when he did the *Paorach* would inevitably end up arguing with him over some matter relating to the school. In those days when officialdom and the Church were often seen as absolute authority, not to be questioned in any circumstances, he frequently took issue with the local parish priest over a number of matters. Even after the *Paorach* had left Achillbeg, one dispute continued. The priest was attempting to locate suitable accommodation for a newly arrived teacher, and suggested she stay in the house the *Paorach* had occupied, as it was seen as the 'teacher's house'. The

Paorach insisted it was his house, as he had arranged to have it built, and maintained (probably correctly) that any rent would be due to him. The dispute was settled when an island family bought the house in the late 1920s and rented a room to the teacher who was in Achillbeg at that time.

In the mid-1910s he used to travel across to Cloghmore in order to listen to local children there talking among themselves (in Irish) and then he would go back to Achillbeg to pass the local dialect on to the island's English-speaking children in the school. He had a dog named *Bran* which followed him everywhere, and a former resident remembers meeting him on several occasions walking up the road towards Derreens with *Bran* following him. If he stopped to speak to somebody *en route*, he would say '*Ag mo chos*!' ('Heel!') to the dog.

One of the *Paorach's* friends used to visit him from Dublin occasionally, and would bring sweets with him, which were distributed to the island children. The identity of the visitor is not known, but islanders remember him as always being immaculately dressed. One Achillbeg man recalled that gifts of clothes 'from a big shop in Dublin' were made to his family after these visits.

The *Paorach's* stature in the educational world travelled far in the short period he lived on Achillbeg. Several of his former pupils later became teachers themselves, others became nuns, and others held a variety of professional jobs in later life. Several of his pupils became well-qualified teachers of Irish. As well as educating local people to a very high standard, he and a Mrs Waddell from Keel established the Scoil Ácla, the Achill Island Summer School. In early days, this took the form of day classes in his house on Achillbeg. In addition to Mrs Waddell, a Dr Kathleen Lynn was involved at times in the operation of the Summer School. Some local people attended, and many more made the daily boat trip over from Achill. Among these were Sean MacBride, later to become a Nobel Peace Prize winner, Philip Heseltine (later known as Peter Warlock, the composer) and Dr Douglas Hyde, future President of Ireland. The *Paorach* would not take payment from anybody for his summer school activities, even though his own personal income from regular teaching was poor: in 1916, he received a salary of £56, or just over £1 per week. The Summer School lapsed some years later, but was revived again (on Achill Island) in 1985, and still attracts large numbers of students in the summer months.

The *Paorach* was a single man when he arrived in Achillbeg, though judging by the number of people he seemed to have had staying with him, he was never lonely. He had the island's only two-storey house, and his visitors had an attic-type upper floor to sleep in. One night towards the end of his period on Achillbeg, he went on horseback from Achill Island to a dance some distance away on the mainland - a lengthy journey even by the standards of the day. He met a girl there (Maura) who was later to become his wife, after he had moved away from Achillbeg. He had at least one daughter. One former resident believed that he was married shortly before he left Achillbeg, but that his wife never came to the island.

In 1922, Francis Power, the *Paorach*, moved on. It is thought that he may have taught briefly in Mulrany, though in 1934 he was in Cuilmore National School, Lecarrow. Later in the 1930s he was the head teacher of a school in Newport, where he had settled with his wife and daughter. He retired in 1944 and moved to Galway, but his retirement was short lived, as he took up another post in the Jesuit's College there, teaching Irish. Between 1945 and 1954 he was in Coláiste Iognáid (St Ignatius College, Galway) where he taught everything but English and Religion through the medium of Irish, as he had done elsewhere. Day to day conversation was also in Irish. As in Achillbeg School, he had many unusual side activities for his pupils: physical education classes were recalled by a former pupil as 'marching and countermarching in the handball alley with the *Paorach* calling the commands in military fashion'! It seems that he finally retired in 1954, aged 75. He died shortly afterwards, having devoted his life to all that was best in nurturing and teaching those who would inherit his beloved land in future generations.

The *Paorach* was a strong critic of anybody who would see communities such as Achillbeg as remote or unimportant. He stoutly defended his island neighbours, pupils and friends, and their right to a good education. Sadly, while his successors included many very good teachers, his like was not to be seen again in Achillbeg National School.

Francis Hugh Power, *An Paorach*, pictured many years after had left Achillbeg. This picture is taken from a school photograph in Coláiste Iognáid (Jesuit College), Galway, where he spent the twilight years of his career. The picture is dated 1949.

Coláiste Iognáid, Galway

Chapter Nine

Famous Visitors

In early 1918, the *Paorach* took in a young Englishman as a guest and pupil. His name was Philip Heseltine, and he was interested in learning Celtic languages - Welsh, Breton, Manx and Cornish, as well as Irish. Heseltine seemed a private individual, not mixing socially to any great extent. The islanders respected his privacy, as he respected theirs. However, Heseltine was no mere tourist or casual scholar - unknown to either his host or his neighbours, he was later to become known as Peter Warlock, the composer. However, such was his sense of privacy, that not even the *Paorach* knew of his background or his compositions. One islander recalled him simply as a young man who let his beard grow . . .

Heseltine, or Warlock, was born in London in 1894, the son of a wealthy family with a background in the legal profession and the art world. From a young age, he showed a considerable musical talent, and after attending Eton College, he spent some time in Germany studying German and music. In 1913 he was admitted to Oxford, where he studied Classics, only to move on again to the University of London. He was appointed as a music critic by the *Daily Mail* in 1915, but decided that this life was not for him: after four months he left the job, and took up editing early music for the British Museum. He became friendly at this time with the author D.H. Lawrence, and between them they planned to publish Lawrence's literary output, having moved to Cornwall. This was not to last: the two fell out and Heseltine returned to London, where he married in 1917 after his girlfriend became pregnant. Britain was in the throes of World War I, and Heseltine was a conscientious objector to the military conscription then in force. Although Ireland was then under British rule, conscription had never been extended there - in the domestic political circumstances of the time such a policy would have been impossible to enforce, to say the least. Heseltine therefore moved to Dublin, where he pursued his interest in the occult to the extent that his reputation suffered unfavourably in London. As a result he adopted the name Peter Warlock which he used when sending a collection of his songs to his London publisher. He left his wife and son in London, though they visited him occasionally. Heseltine wanted solitude to write music and to study traditional Irish life and language, so he moved out to Achill where it seems that he stayed at first in Dugort, possibly with the local school teacher, who introduced him to the *Paorach*. He moved over to Achillbeg for some two months as the *Paorach's* house guest. While there, he wrote to friends in England, giving a rare outsider's view of life in Achillbeg at the time. It is worth looking through his writings for references to the island, for example in February 1918, possibly soon after arriving, he wrote:

> I received your letter which reached me on this desolate islet only this evening. Our posts are infrequent - three a week at most, unless - as happened today - someone* makes a special journey across the narrow strip of sea that separates us from the mainland . . .

* That 'someone' would have been Johnny Kilbane, who was the island postman.

Apart from anything else, the apparently erratic nature of the post is likely to be related to February weather. Heseltine had commented elsewhere to the effect that during his stay the weather was indeed very stormy. In addition, this was before the days of what we call 'unsolicited mail' nearly a century later, so the volume of mail to be taken to the island might not have been large enough for daily visits to Achill specially for the purpose.

Heseltine relaxed by walking around the island, and it is likely he made the short journey over to Achill for long walks there too.

Upon his return to Dublin, Heseltine wrote to his former music teacher:

> For over two months I was away upon an inconceivably desolate island in the West, studying the Celtic languages and Irish in particular - a hard study but one from which I have derived a great deal of profit: the subject is very much more comprehensive and illuminating than it would seem at first sight. Besides which - my visit afforded me a wonderful chance to observe a strange and absolutely foreign people, and their ways of life, which were vastly interesting.

Heseltine progressed well with his studies, as the *Paorach* remembered that he 'made good progress with the Irish language and was soon speaking and reading it with an ease . . .'

In fact, within two months Heseltine was able to converse freely in Irish and had also acquired a good working knowledge of Cornish - one of a number of languages which the *Paorach* was able to teach.

Of the island itself, Heseltine wrote:

> I have never known such barrenness, such utter desolation: it reflects into one's very soul till one becomes chill and numb - such desolate lives in such a desolate region - black wintry weather and the full force of the Atlantic beating, always beating, almost at one's very door. The island was not a mile square, all told: and the greater part of it consisted of bleak, weather-beaten rocks. Yet nearly a hundred souls live there - scratching the miserable ground here and there, to eke out a meagre living with a few potatoes . . .

This somewhat harsh view of the island and life there was doubtless shaped by the time of year, and the weather; but other contributory factors could have been Heseltine's periodic bouts of depression, and the fact that he chose not to mix with the local people to any significant extent. During research for this book, many former residents were interviewed - some with vivid memories of childhood in the late 1910s, others who recalled an equivalent childhood in the late 1950s, and many more in between. One common feature for all was the carefree idyllic nature of childhood in Achillbeg, the simple natural pleasures of growing up free of traffic, smoke, electronic games and fast food. This seems far removed from Heseltine's 'desolate lives' who were 'scratching the miserable ground here and there'. It is well to consider here, though, the difference between a child's innocent perceptions, and those of an adult - either native or visitor. Once a child had grown up in Achillbeg, he or she would sooner or later be faced with the issue of how to make a living. Life was undoubtedly hard for many adult residents.

Achillbeg was, as Heseltine described, a small place, and its community was closely knit. In such communities worldwide, little happens that is not common knowledge soon after. And yet, among those interviewed for this book who had detailed memories of the *Paorach* himself, and of life in the year 1918, nobody remembered this particular young English visitor. A measure, perhaps, of Heseltine's private nature. Nevertheless his observations are of interest as giving a view of an outsider's perception. His description of his host was much more positive. Of the *Paorach*, he said, 'My host - the schoolmaster, was a charming person, of great versatility and strange experiences - the very embodiment of enthusiasm - living only for the preservation of the Irish language. He is also a champion bag-piper, and almost taught me to play that wonderful instrument!'

Overall, Heseltine had a more positive view of the island and its effect on his soul than his initial description suggested. Reflecting on his two months there, he wrote in May 1918, 'It is wonderful how much more clearly one can think about music when one is right away from it than one possibly can do when in the whirl of a concert-season. I have done a great deal of work at the philosophy and history of music while I have been in this country. The wilderness is the best place for meditation - and I have spent a considerable time in the most desolate and solitary region of the West coast'. In Dublin later in the year, he wrote: 'As a result of this long period of exile I have come back to Dublin and to musical work with quite a new enthusiasm . . . '

After Heseltine left Achillbeg he returned to Dublin, remaining there until August 1918 when he moved back to Britain. He lived at different times in London and in Wales. Financial difficulties and depression afflicted him for some years, and he was found dead aged 36 in his London flat in December 1930. No clear evidence was found to show whether his death had been an accident or suicide. His musical compositions consisted mainly of solo songs with piano accompaniment, but he also wrote choral pieces and other works for piano or orchestra, and was a highly respected writer on musical matters.

The *Paorach*, interviewed some 25 years later, recalled Heseltine as an agreeable but somewhat eccentric character, who walked about his house in garish yellow and black striped pyjamas; 'I remember', he said 'one day he had to catch the train from Achill Sound to Westport. He delayed so long doing the astrological calculations to see whether the day was propitious for making the journey, that when he arrived within sight of the station the train was about to steam out.' Heseltine ran, the driver saw him, and the train waited. From Achill Sound the train took travellers to Westport and onward to Dublin.

Heseltine was one of three visitors who were later to become well known. Another was Sean MacBride, who occasionally visited for the same reasons that Heseltine did: to learn from the *Paorach*. If Heseltine became famous in the world of music, MacBride did so even more in the political world.

Sean MacBride was the son of Major John MacBride and Maud Gonne MacBride, the famous advocate of Irish nationalism. MacBride was born in 1904, and was just 12 when his father was executed in Kilmainham Jail for his part in the 1916 Easter Rising in Dublin. Sean had been brought up in France with his mother, but moved to Ireland in 1918, at which time it is likely that he attended the *Paorach's* summer school in Achillbeg. It is unclear whether he actually stayed in Achillbeg, though with no other relatives to stay with in the area, it is likely that he did. With his father's execution still fresh in his mind, he joined the struggle against British rule in Ireland, and was one of those present at negotiations for the Anglo-Irish Treaty in 1921. By now a leading member of the Irish Republican Army, he fought against the Free State forces in the Civil War in the early 1920s, and was eventually captured and imprisoned after the Four Courts Battle in Dublin. He later became the Chief of Staff of the IRA, but was soon to change his direction altogether: he studied law, and became a Senior Barrister in Dublin in 1943. Five years later, having risen through the ranks and become the Irish Government's Minister for Foreign Affairs, he was the man who following constitutional change was to declare Ireland a Republic (as opposed to a 'Free State').

MacBride became highly respected internationally for his tireless work on behalf of oppressed peoples. He took part in many court cases of this nature in Ireland, and internationally, occasionally acting as legal advisor to foreign Governments, as in Greece in 1958. He was one of the founders of Amnesty International. In 1974, he was awarded the Nobel Peace Prize. He carried out valuable work for the United Nations in the 1970s, and was a UN Commissioner for several years. Following much other work in the field of peace negotiations and human rights, he was the author of the *MacBride Principles* which acted as the basis for fair employment legislation in Northern Ireland, and which have been widely consulted internationally since.

However, one elderly Achillbeg resident remembered his visits some 80 years later thus - 'he often would fight with the young lads . . .' (on Achillbeg)!

MacBride died in 1988 - how much of his life, one wonders, was influenced by *An Paorach's* teaching?

The *Paorach* had one other visitor of note who was also a leading figure in Irish cultural studies and politics. He was Dr Douglas Hyde, who later became the first President of the newly formed Irish Free State. Hyde was born in Sligo in 1860, the son of the Church of Ireland Canon of Elphin. In 1880 he commenced studies in Trinity College, Dublin, where he excelled in literature and studied law. Like the *Paorach,* Hyde was determined to do all he could to stem the decline of the Irish language, and in 1893 he became one of the founders of the Gaelic League, dedicated to encourage the use of Irish in all walks of life. Hyde published plays and poems in Irish, and his work *Casadh an tSugain* was the first Irish language play to be produced professionally on stage. Again, in common with the *Paorach,* Hyde was a fluent speaker of a number of languages - among them French, German, Greek, Hebrew and Latin. He served as Professor of Modern Irish and Dean of Celtic Studies at University College, Dublin until 1932. In 1915 he stepped down as President of the Gaelic League, as he was unhappy about its increasingly political tone, despite being an ardent nationalist himself. In 1937 he became the unanimous choice of all parties to take his place as the first President of the Republic of Ireland, a position he held until 1945, by which time he was 85. He retired to Co. Sligo, where he died peacefully in 1949.

As a highly respected Irish scholar, he doubtless had much in common with the *Paorach's* views on the revival of the language. No details survive of his visits, but they are likely to have taken place at about the same time as those mentioned above - did the three ever meet? To what extent were the ultimate careers of these three of the *Paorach's* many house guests influenced by him?

Chapter Ten

Doing 'The Stations'

As mentioned before, Catechism was taught in the school to prepare the children for making their First Communion. With Achillbeg having no church (since medieval times, at any rate) the islanders travelled across to Cloghmore on Sundays and walked or cycled up the road to Derreens church for Mass. When a death occurred the local priest would go to Achillbeg, and the remains were then brought to Cloghmore. When a birth was in progress both he and a nurse from Cloghmore would travel across. In addition, the priest travelled to the island twice a year for the Stations of the Cross. At Easter, islanders would go to the Holy Well, walk around it three times and face Croagh Patrick while praying. Croagh Patrick (or 'The Reek'), a mountain on the mainland, is visible in all directions from a great distance on account of its height and distinctive peak. St Patrick, Ireland's patron saint, is said to have climbed it, and each year it is a centre of pilgrimage for the devout from all over the country and beyond.

The 'Stations' was a major event in Achillbeg. Different households took it in turns to host the event. The host family would be up from a very early hour in the morning, or perhaps all of the previous night, cooking and preparing a feast for virtually all the island population, plus, of course, the visiting priest. Some families would give their house a new coat of paint in advance. Walls were whitewashed, and door and window frames were painted. Inside, the house was cleaned thoroughly and perhaps repainted, and an altar would be made from a table or two chairs covered with a new white tablecloth.

One girl spoke of her regular job when the 'Stations' took place in her house - she always made the *rollacins* - long rolls of butter scraped off a block with a special knife. The priest apparently liked butter set out like this. On one occasion in the 1950s, she and her sister set out the night before to travel over to Cloghmore to go to the dance at Mulligan's. The sea was choppy, so they tied their boat up well with a thick rope on reaching the pier. Friends were waiting with a car to give them a lift. On their return at 3 am, a bad storm had sprung up, and the girls fell asleep in the car on the pier. When they awoke it was daylight, and the first thing they saw was the priest out in his boat, crossing towards Achillbeg! They quickly retrieved their boat, noticing that the rope was frayed so badly that it would hardly have held it much longer - and they set off as quickly as they could. After frantic preparation, all was well!

After the 'Stations', it was time to celebrate. A big dinner was served to all in the house chosen for the occasion. One priest, Fr Prendergast, always asked for fish. On one occasion, the household hosting him had very little left, so an alternative was offered. He asked if there was any fish, whereupon the youngest child in the house went off and found the small remaining pieces - to the delight of the priest, but not the child's mother! The catering effort was made easier in the latter years of the island's occupation, as one house had a coal range, and many others had gas cookers, cylinders being brought across by boat. Prior to these developments of the late 1950s, all cooking was done over open fires. An islander with memories of the 1910s recalled: 'We went into the different houses and we always got a big feed, a roast or whatever. The priest had to be looked after well. We didn't go to school, anyway . . .' Some years later 'we'd go to Danny Ned's (a neighbour's house) for a bit of music and dancing - there were a few good singers in those days . . .' The house referred to in this instance had been the *Paorach's* house, by this time owned by members of the Kilbane family,

The priest would be taken back to Achill when he had eaten his fill, and festivities would begin. Dancing and singing, accompanied by an accordion player, would go on into the small hours of the next morning.

The rear of the *Paorach's* house, showing a lean-to, a later addition. *Author*

Chapter Eleven

Folklore

Achillbeg is rich in folklore and local stories, or *piseógs*. As in most parts of Ireland, many are unrecorded and undoubtedly many more have been lost in the mists of time. What follows represents the memories of the a number of former residents, and what can be gleaned from the records of Folklore Commission. The Irish Government established this body in the 1930s to record various facets of Irish culture and life which even then were disappearing fast. In a remarkably far-sighted move, it was arranged that every school in the State would ask children in their junior classes to seek out elderly relatives and neighbours, and ask them about life in their own youth. The stories thus recorded were first-hand accounts of beliefs and events which dated back as early as the 1850s. In some parts of Ireland, first-hand accounts of life in the immediate aftermath of the Famine were recorded.

Each school collected the relevant information and once the teacher had checked over it, the children's essays were sent to Dublin for storage. The records of the Folklore Commission can therefore be viewed on microfilm in several libraries and archives throughout the country.

Unfortunately, Achillbeg's records did not survive, if indeed they were ever recorded. While the intention was that all schools did so, there were a small number of schools across the country that did not participate. It is possible that an occasional teacher would have less interest in the project than others, though there seems no obviously clear and consistent reason. Microfilm records for Co. Mayo include Achill Island itself, and Corraun. However, many of the stories collected from children are common to Achill and Achillbeg, and are therefore repeated here.

Achillbeg held one ace card, though. As stated elsewhere, the *Paorach* had moved on from Achillbeg to Newport, where he was a head teacher in a local school by the time the Folklore Commission was undertaking this survey. The records from his own school have survived - along with a neat handwritten note attached to them pointing out that while in Achillbeg he collected several stories himself. Some 15 years after leaving Achillbeg, he still had the island's interests at heart. Among the stories thus attributed specifically to Achillbeg were the beliefs that it was unlucky to spit over the side of a boat or throw refuse overboard. In addition, if a man fell overboard it was 'not right' to lift him back into the boat. Instead, he should be towed ashore.

Many stories surrounded the old Iron Age fort at Dún Chill Mhór. An old legend told of two giants who lived here - one on the Daingean and one on the Dún. One guarded the area while the other was away, but when the first was approaching on his return the giant on guard mistook him for a stranger and threw a rock at him, and he fell to the ground. In one version of the tale, the first giant was so grief-stricken at having killed his brother by accident that he killed himself. In another version, the stone thrower approached his fatally wounded brother as he gasped his last breath. The wounded giant asked him to bend

Burial mound, Dún Chill Mhór, and remains of upright cross to the left. The low mound here is said to be one of the two giant's graves. *Author*

Stony beach near Maimín na Croisc, looking towards Dún Mhór. A mermaid was reputed to sit on the rocks here, singing. *Author*

down over him, and as he did so, he leaned up and fatally stabbed him - either way, the two giants are reputed to be buried in the Dún under two *leachta* (altars). One former resident, on recounting this tale, remarked that the mounds under which the giants are buried are not very big, 'they must have been pretty small giants!', she said.

Above a cove to the north-west of the island, a pot of gold was said to be buried. A snake or large worm guarded it by wrapping itself around the pot. The finder would throw a lump of beef to the snake, and while it disentangled itself from the pot in order to eat it, there was just enough time to take the pot away from it. If the finder was not quick enough, the snake would eat them instead. In another version of the story, the snake had two heads, and instead of throwing a lump of beef, you had to throw two old people to it - and be quick retrieving the gold, as the snake would waste no time in eating them.

Occasionally, Achillbeg children might find themselves on the Achill side of the water, perhaps when accompanying their parents elsewhere. One Achillbeg man remembered playing, as a boy, in the Cloghmore and Derreens area of Achill, where there was a house near the graveyard which was said to be haunted. Generally, he and his companions did not dare enter the grounds of it, though on one occasion they did. While they did not encounter a ghost, the occupant of the house appeared and sent them away! The house is no longer in existence.

Not far from Dún Chill Mhór was a well, variously known as the Holy Well, Blessed Well, or Sacred Well, and dedicated to St Patrick. The water of this well was said to have healing qualities, and many stories are told of a fish that lived in it. The fish was brown, and its behaviour could be used to foretell good or ill luck. If the fish jumped out and fell on its back, somebody would die. If it bumped into the side of the well, those who saw it, or a relative, might become blind, while it was a good omen if it swam round and round. In the 1980s, some 20 years after the last residents left Achillbeg, a visitor to the island reported having ulcers cured by the water in the well, despite the failure of many years of medical treatment elsewhere

Fish were not the only creatures subject to folklore: hares were considered to be lucky, as were otters. It was bad luck to kill one.

Weasels were the subject of further stories: one account told of a man who was walking up the pier and saw a rat attacking a weasel. He kicked the rat, which released the weasel, bit his attacker's toe and ran away. That night, the man's toe became infected and swelled up. He went to bed feeling sick, to be awoken in the middle of the night by the weasel sucking the poison from his toe. Weasels were seen as good; it was said that when one died, others would appear from over a wide area to burrow a hole to bury their dead colleague. One story told of a time when weasels from the island flocked to the pier to board the next boat across to Cloghmore to attend one of these 'funerals' on Achill! In the days when most of Achillbeg's young people went to Scotland for seasonal farm work, they were often horrified to see how the Scots treated weasels - there, they were seen as pests and Scottish folklore suggested that if one was killed and hung on the fence, others would be frightened away by the sight of the corpse.

One folklore-related prediction at least did come true: an old saying held that when badgers came, people went. In the 1950s badgers did make it to Achillbeg. They dug up potato fields, and what was left of the crop was not fit for human consumption, and had to be fed to the cows. A few years later, both badgers and people had left the island.

Each house made its own butter. The churning process was often shared between family members, but if a visitor called to the house while churning was in progress, he or she had to take a turn at it - bad luck would follow if this did not happen. When making a new churn, it had to be done in daylight. Should a churn be out at night, the fairies would be watching, and they would take the churn away. While churning butter, if a man left the house smoking a pipe, no butter would be made in the churn. It was considered 'not right' to throw out water while churning, or 'you would throw out the butter with the water'.

Achillbeg had its own ghost. Above Leargán, a woman was said to have been seen, and heard, as she sheltered under a rock feeding her child. There were various versions of this tale - in one, she wore rags, and in another she did not have a child. While several people claimed to have seen or heard her, no ill seems to have befallen them, though bad luck was meant to follow a sighting. One former resident remembered her aunt being told by a relative that the ghost had been seen one night in the 1920s above their house. Those who heard the story were genuinely frightened, and warned the children in their household not to go near the place she was supposed to have been seen.

It was said that if a noise like squelching water-logged boots walking along the shore was heard, it foretold a death. In order to exorcise this, one had to put salt on one's tongue. In the late 1800s, a man was supposed to have heard the mysterious footsteps while walking on the shore searching for driftwood, and when advised to put salt on his tongue he laughed and refused. He later drowned at Uaich Dhilisc Mhilis.

It was bad luck to hear, or worse still, see, the fairies or 'little people'. Again, a pinch of salt on the tongue was the remedy. Perhaps related to the ghost of the woman with the child, but common throughout Ireland, was the belief that if a banshee was heard, death of somebody close was imminent. A banshee was a supernatural female figure who was encountered, typically, in remote places, and could be heard wailing. In Ireland today, if a person is crying loudly they are said to be 'wailing like a banshee'. To see a banshee was if anything a worse omen than hearing one.

The 'little people', or leprechauns, required care when dealing with them. Leprechauns generally guarded pots of gold, sometimes under the end of a rainbow. They were small men, wizened up and very old, with suits of red or green. Those who met them were supposed to ask them for the pot of gold. If they would not say where it was, it was bad luck to let them go, and best to kill them by throwing them into a fire. A story which was current in Achill and Achillbeg in years past was of a boy who heard a hammering noise in his garden. When he went to investigate, he found a leprechaun. When he asked him for the treasure, the leprechaun gave him a stick and told him to dig in a particular place, where he would find a reed which would always bring him luck. The boy dug, found the reed, and brought it to his mother. His mother was angry and broke the reed, and the boy went back to the leprechaun, caught him, and threw him into the fire. Only then did he find the leprechaun's pot of gold.

Another story concerns a man who caught a leprechaun and put him in a cage, and kept him in his house. The leprechaun said nothing until the man refused a meal of potatoes that his wife had prepared, saying he was not hungry. As he left his house he fell and broke his leg. The leprechaun told him that if he ate the potatoes, his leg would not be broken any more. The man did so, and released the leprechaun. The next day he found the pot of gold and was rich thereafter. In this story, there is no mention of any necessity to kill the leprechaun!

On New Year's Day, it was said that those who brought water in from the well would be bringing it in all year. This much was probably true! Bringing water from a well after dark was bad luck - it was said that the water would turn to blood.

Once a man had set the date for his wedding, it was bad luck for him to go to sea. In a similar vein, a red-haired girl was a bad omen for seafarers - if a boat was setting out on a fishing trip, and a red-haired girl was anywhere about the pier, or waved to the boat crew, then they would catch no fish. The red-haired girl surfaced elsewhere among a litany of bad omens - a local child wrote in 1938 'If you meet a red-haired woman when you are going to the fair with a cow you will not sell her'.

The birth of a child had its own share of folklore. If a person was asked to sponsor a child at its baptism, it would be very bad luck to refuse to do so - the child, it was said, would die. If the child died, no other child borne by the same mother should carry the same name - or that child would die too. A dead child's clothes were not to be worn by any other child, or that child would die of the same illness.

During childbirth, it was good luck for the expectant mother to wear something belonging to her husband. After a child had been born, the fairies knew. However, the child's forthcoming baptism would render it impervious to the mischief of the fairies - so a new born baby had to be watched over prior to baptism to avoid being stolen by them. This belief was taken very seriously at one time.

Some illnesses were curable by old folk remedies. It was said at one time that a cure for toothache was obtained by chewing a frog's leg, but this had to be done while the frog was alive. Presumably this activity would take the sufferer's mind off the toothache! Warts could be cured by rubbing a live snail on the wart, and then putting it on a hawthorn bush - not a useful one in Achillbeg, as there were no hawthorns!

A story collected by the Folklore Commission research from a girl in Achill Island told of an old man who believed that if a worm was placed in the hand of a new born baby by a man who was a seventh son, and the worm died, then the child would have the power of healing as he or she grew up.

If one tossed a coin or a button, much could be read into whether it landed as 'heads' or 'tails'. 'Heads' with a button was good luck, 'tails' unlucky. Other ill luck would follow the killing of a spider, losing a half-crown coin, or seeing a weasel looking out of a hole. If a robin flew into a house, that also was bad luck as it foretold a death.

The discovery of a bird's nest containing eggs was bad luck, as was collecting 13 eggs from the hens. A double-yolked egg, or two chickens hatching from one egg was unlucky, as was owning 15 chickens. If a black cat broke its leg, this also was an ill omen.

After all this negativity, it is reassuring to know that as many things were seen as good omens. Among the signs of impending good luck were meeting a black cat at night, meeting a strange man at the start of a journey, and seeing two magpies. During a journey, it was good luck to meet a man on a white horse - it meant that you would not encounter any trouble. Once a journey had been commenced, it was bad luck to return for something forgotten. While going to Mass, it was good luck to meet a black sheep turned towards you (but bad luck to meet a grey-haired man). At night a meeting with a white cat was unlucky, but a hare meant good luck, as this would provide protection overnight. However, a daytime meeting with a hare crossing the road ahead was unlucky! If a farmer was taking a cow to a bull, and he met another man *en route*, the cow would produce a heifer.

One obscure story gathered from an elderly Achill Island man in the 1930s, and which may have carried some authority in Achillbeg was that it was good luck to meet a red cow in daylight, or a black dog between two rivers at night.

As if the demands of approaching or avoiding these omens was not enough to contend with during the day, there were a few to be aware of while sleeping! It was good luck to dream of pigs, as it meant good news was to come, but bad luck to dream of horses. Dreaming of the dead meant news for the living, possibly of a marriage or birth, while a dream about marriage foretold a death. A dream on a Friday night was said to come true on Saturday night. A stranger would call to the house of those who dreamt of being away from home. Relevant to Achillbeg people was the belief that to dream of money meant that the dreamer would cross the water - to Britain or the USA for work, no doubt.

Dreaming of a fair-haired girl meant marrying a good wife, while dreaming of a black-haired girl meant the opposite!

Some apparently bizarre superstitions have a sound basis in common sense. For example, the one quoted above about ill luck befalling a child who was given a dead child's clothes would be valid if the dead child had had a disease. In times past, with little knowledge of germs, sterilisation and sanitation, the clothes could conceivably carry an infection.

The impression may be given here that the people of Achillbeg, and for that matter all of Ireland, were obsessed with superstitious beliefs. However, many European countries had, and still have, their own versions of banshees, fairies, good and bad omens and the like. Scandinavian folklore abounds with bloodthirsty tales of what awaits those who fall under the spell of trolls. The Austrian and Swiss Alps have their equivalents too: in Ireland the 'Little people' or leprechauns were widely believed in. One of the writer's ancestors told of seeing a leprechaun walking along the road in front of her in Co. Kildare in the 1920s - after she momentarily turned away, he vanished. She claimed to have had a good look at him - he was just over a metre tall, and wore old fashioned clothes. The same type of story existed with minor variations all over the country, Achillbeg included.

These stories may be seen in context as part of a national store of a rich folklore - which is precisely why the Folklore Commission was established in the 1930s to record it.

Chapter Twelve

Place Names

Throughout Ireland, there exists a rich and comprehensive tradition of localised place names. Much of this tradition was, and is, oral; frequently it can be seen in rural districts to this day, where many names are given by local people to features of the landscape which would be overlooked by a traveller through the area. These names may have their origins in geographical features, or may commemorate people who formerly lived there or for some reason were famous (or notorious!) locally. They may not be recorded on maps routinely, if at all. If we look into the origins of these names, we can often uncover a fascinating new panorama of local history, of cultural features, obscure or subtle folklore otherwise unrecorded and often long forgotten. In these days, with increasing personal mobility and instability of rural populations, a rich vein of our culture is becoming invisible, forgotten.

Such is the case with Achillbeg. During research for this book, it was found that the only island place name commonly recorded was what was variously spelt as 'Tra bo Dearg' or 'Traboderig' - in English, the 'beach of the red cow'. This is the name given to the sandy beach, or strand, on the island. 'Tra' or 'Traw' in place names is Irish for 'strand'. The name is well known to islanders, and its pronunciation is best described in English as 'TRAW-bo-Jarrig'. The correct Irish form is Trá Bó Deirge. It will be seen from the several maps reproduced in the book that the only other names mentioned, and only then on one single map, are names given to the two hills on the island. The northern one is described as Cregoah on William Bald's map of 1855, while the southern one is described as Knockillanaskra. Other early maps describe 'Cregoah' as 'Cregalomen'. The best general consensus obtained during research for this book* suggests that the most likely original form of this may be 'Creig an Lomáin', denoting a rocky outcrop or a rock near a hole or recess. Given the physical characteristics of this place, it would be accurate enough.

It must be remembered that the earliest accurate map makers of the island were English, and they would have reproduced Irish place names spelt in a manner that was recognisable to English speakers and writers. Thus, a place name could be reproduced in a form which when read subsequently by an Irish speaker, would be unrecognisable. 'Knockillanaskra' is a good example of this. To an English speaker, as spelt on Bald's map, it looks like 'KNOCK-ILL-AN-ASKRA'.

* To date, Achillbeg's place names have existed only in oral tradition. Any attempt to record them accurately is fraught with uncertainty. In addition to grammatically correct descriptions in Irish, with accurate translation into English, some place names may be based on nicknames, local colloquialisms (in either language), and it is possible that some now appear to have a meaning which would not have been the original one, due to misunderstandings and mis-pronunciations during translation over the years. For this work, the author gathered the names orally from former residents, along with meanings where possible. For spelling, grammar, and cross-checking of translations, as well as research into other possible meanings, three separate sources were consulted, with an emphasis on the Irish language itself, place name history, and local tradition and folklore.

The intricacies of Achillbeg's local place names are evident in this picture. Here, we are looking across at Aill Taghnach (Taghnach's cliff) from Uaich na Sionnach, the 'cove of the foxes'. For a start, there are three coves - Uaich na Sionnach Mhór, (the big fox's cove), Ualch na Sionnach Láir (the middle, or central, fox's cove), and Uaich na Sionnach Beag (the small fox's cove). The holy well is just to the left, out of the picture and up the hill behind the photographer. What we see on the other side of this natural bay is the southernmost hill, faced by a cliff, with a small flat area in front of it, which has almost become a small islet itself. The hill is Oileán an Sciorta, the 'land of the ticks', and the area in front is Athoire, the meaning of which is uncertain. Along the top of the cliff is Cosán na nGabhar, the 'goat's path'. The small grassy outcrop in front is Gob an Bhioráin. This probably means 'the end of the point' though 'Bioráin' means a stack or pinnacle of rock (in the sea); an appropriate description in the circumstances. The narrow strip connecting Gob an Bhioráin with the rest of the island is An tSiorán, the 'pinnacle of rock'. The area to the left of the picture just above the small stony beach is Athoire, which possibly means a ford across tidal rocks. *Author*

Garraí an Tuair Mhóir, the 'Garden of the Big Fruit', according to former islanders, though the place name may refer to the garden of the tower, or big cattle field. No trace of any tower exists, nor is there any archaeological evidence or folk history to suggest the presence of any structure here. In view of the exposed location, it seems unlikely that 'big fruit' grew here in abundance, though the islanders were adept at cultivating the land very efficiently. Cattle may well have grazed here, but the presence of overgrown ridges indicate that in recent times at least, these fields were full of potatoes. The electricity poles to the lighthouse cross the field. *Author*

If pronounced in this way, Achillbeg residents will say there was no such place, and they are right - the place was pronounced completely differently. The initial 'Knock' indicating a hill in Irish, was dropped altogether from the name, though it could conceivably have been in use in the 1850s and abbreviated later. 'Ill . . .' was also dropped colloquially, and the '. . . askra' part sounds in the local accent more like '. . . gurta'. The place, representing the top part of the southernmost hill, is actually pronounced in a way that to an English speaker sounds like 'Lawn - iss - gurta'. The Irish name is Oileán an Sciorta, the 'island of the ticks'. The northern hill's name of Cregoah is even more obscure. The area shown as such on Bald's map was identified by several former residents as 'Camiligh', though other islanders were unaware of any name for it, but had names for areas on its slopes, such as Gort Breac Ard on one side and Criogán Tommy on the other. Cregoah does indeed sound like a name with some sort of Irish origin, but in current folk memory at the time of research, which included three former residents in their 90s, nobody had ever heard of it or anything like it. There is a small rocky outcrop on this hill which may give a clue as to the origin of 'Cregoah' - in Irish, 'creg' can mean a mound. The nearby name recorded by islanders as Criogán Tommy would mean 'Tommy's rock'.

As elsewhere in Ireland, the study of place name origins is a fascinating subject in its own right. Since the vast majority of places were originally named in Irish, but later anglicised by the (British) Ordnance Survey, there are often inaccuracies and inconsistencies in these translations. Loss of subtlety or inference in translation from Irish to English by Ordnance Survey mappers in the early 1800s was common. These early recorders of place names spoke a different language and had different accents to those from whom they collected the names. Many place names (as on Achillbeg) were orally handed down rather than in written form, therefore no ready comparison could be made with written records.

However, the dropping of 'Knockillaun . . .' from the start of the place name of the southern hill could have another explanation. If a place name is long, or has many syllables, locals will often call it by a shortened name - in the Ireland of today, Carrickfergus, Carrick-on-Shannon and Carrick-on-Suir are all known as 'Carrick' to the local people. Thus, what may have been pronounced as 'Knock ill lawn iss gurta' became 'Lawn iss gurta'.

Hence the importance of recording such information, which is what this chapter sets out to do.

So, at this stage, with only oral tradition to go by, we start with a clean slate to record the names by which places were known from the late 19th century to date. The map overleaf shows names collected from residents with personal memories going back to the 1910s. One of the main contributors, however, was born nearly half a century later, and her own memories date from the 1950s - and, of course, correspond with the earlier ones.

Since the place names come from an oral background, and to the writer's knowledge are reproduced here in written form for the first time, the Irish form is given as the places were named in Irish by an Irish speaking community. The dialect spoken by the islanders was, and is, that spoken by native speakers from the mid and south Achill, and Achillbeg areas. This is known locally as the

Achillbeg
Map showing place names
Carrowgarve
H.W.M.
Doonnaglass
Belnaglass
Belnaglea
Gubnacliffamore
ACHILLBEG ISLAND
Achillbeg School
Trawboderg
A R P
0 2 26
360

'Upper Achill' dialect, as distinct from that in 'Lower Achill' - the western end of Achill Island. Therefore, I have recorded the pronunciation of the names based on that given by local Irish speakers - in all cases either former residents or recent descendants of them. Capital letters denote an emphasis on that syllable. However, there are varying local opinions on the meanings, and spellings, of some names: where relevant, a note to this effect is added. Finally, a description of the meaning of the name, where available - this has also been recorded according to the understanding of those who lived on Achillbeg, but with notes added where this appears to differ from other possible translations.

Several English language place names were recorded by British officialdom at various times. The Admiralty, in their records of coastal navigational information, describe an anchorage for their gunboat, the *Orwell*, as being 'off the coast guard station . . . locally known as the Pool'. The archaeologist T.J. Westropp who surveyed Dún Chill Mhór in 1911 and 1914 describes the central valley of the island as being known locally as the Scalp. He may have confused this with the name given by locals to the cliff above the southern side of the valley, as local people referred to this central valley as Baileamuigh.

There were three place names in Achillbeg which referred to whole areas of the island - like districts, or 'provinces' - as one islander described it, with a smile! The north-west corner of the island was known as the Tail, while the area to the east of it, and stretching round the eastern side of the northern hill, towards the central valley, was known to some as Baileamuigh. The entire southern hill of the island was known as Oileán an Sciorta. Within these areas were the place names listed below, which could refer to very small and localised features, such as individual fields, rocks or wells. The naming of features in as detailed a form as this was important for accurate location of livestock grazing away from the houses. This raises an issue: in the eyes of one islander a place name might refer to a specifically defined patch of land, whereas to another it might be a more general term for a slightly wider area. A degree of overlap is therefore occasionally understandable.

Key To Map Showing Place Names

The following names have been collected from former Achillbeg residents. Since no previous written record of these has been found to date, translations and spellings may have several possible origins. Where there is some doubt, other possible versions are given. Pronunciations (shown in brackets) are described as they sound in English.

Map Ref.

1 An Baile Amuigh or Baileamuigh (BAL-ya-mike). *Meaning:* The outside village, or outside the village. *Note:* Name given to housing area in central valley, or to the general area of the valley. (1).*

2 An Fraoch (An FREE-a). *Meaning:* The heather. *Note:* Flat area in valley floor.

3 Aill Taghnach (or Taighnigh) (Al-TY-na). *Meaning:* Taghnach's cliff (or derived from Tamhnach - a grassy upland or arable place above a mountain). *Note:* Aill, or Allt, is a locally used name for a cliff. Taghnach's identity uncertain (2).

* Notes can be found on pages 191 and 192.

4 An Mhalaidh (Wallie/Mollie). *Meaning:* The incline.
5 An tSiorán (An CHEER-awn). *Meaning:* The pinnacle of rock.
6 Árd De Valera (Ard De Valera). *Meaning:* De Valera's height. *Note:* Peak thus named after a bonfire was lit to give news of Eamonn De Valera's electoral success in 1917.
7 Ardán Leathan (ARD-an LA-hann). *Meaning:* High ground under rocky outcrop.
8 Athoire (a-HOAR-a). *Meaning:* Possibly a ford, or passageway across tidal rocks.
9 Bearna Ghort Breach Ard (BER-nee gort sprach ard). *Meaning:* Gap/way out of the high speckled field - see Nos. 63 and 64 on this list.
10 Bearna Glaise (BAR-na Glash-a). *Meaning:* Gap of the fairy cow. *Note:* Near Dún Beag (3).
11 Bóthar na Páirce (Bore na parka). *Meaning:* Road of the field or park. *Note:* Known as a 'look out place' on the island.
12 Breacaill na Gaibhnaigh/Brough Gaibhiga (BROCK-al-GOW-iga - sometimes pronounced BROCK-al-DOWN-iga). *Meaning:* Speckled cliff of the kids (young goats) (Breac / aill = speckled cliff). *Note:* Broughil or Brough may be a distorted form of bruach = a bank (of a stream/river).
13 Bruaigh Dhubha (Brewi WOO-a). *Meaning:* Black ledges/banks of the dark colouring. Bruacha = banks. *Note:* Poor quality turf (*breithdn*) was once dug here, hence the dark colour in the ground. 'Dúch' was a black colouring substance found in turf bogs.
14 Caladh an Rí (Collan Ree). *Meaning:* The king's landing place/port/harbour. *Note:* Near the pier (4).
15 Caladh Peat Pheadair (Calla Pat Paddar). *Meaning:* Pat's cave. *Note:* On north shoreline.
16 Cam leac (lic?) Camallaigh (CAM-el-igh). *Meaning:* The crooked flat rock. *Note:* May refer to nearby rock outcrop. Possible origin in 'cam' = crooked, and 'lic' ('leac') = a stone, flagstone, or rock.
17 Carraig a Choiscéim (Carrig a Coshkeem). *Meaning:* Footstep Rock. Islanders knew this as a good place to fish.
18 Carraig na Loinge (Carrig na LONN-ya). *Meaning:* Rock of the ship.
19 Ceap an Éisc (Cap an EEsk). *Meaning:* Ceap = plot of land. Iasc/Éisc = fish. *Note:* A small field where fish may have been landed at one time. Above north shore line - narrow field.
20 Céibh an Rí (Cave an Ree). *Meaning:* The king's cave (4).
21 Cill Aill Taghnaigh (Killen al-TY-na). *Meaning:* Church of Taghna's cliff. *Note:* Taghna's identity uncertain (2).
22 Cill Mhór (KILL more). *Meaning:* Big Church.
23 Cladach an Riobaill (CLADD-a-Rubble). *Meaning:* Shore area of 'The Tail'.
24 Cosán na nGabhar (COOS-awn an-GOW-a). *Meaning:* The goat's path.
25 Creig an Lomáin (Creg-OH-a/Creg-a-loamen). *Meaning:* Outcropping rock/rock of hole or recess. *Note:* One old map shows 'Cregalomen' (5).
26 Creig an Aifrinn (CREG an AFF-ran). *Meaning:* Mass rock. *Note:* Used as an altar (6).
27 Creig Éaminn Bháin (CREG Eamonn Bawn). *Meaning:* White Eamonn's hillock (5).
28 Creig Mhór (Creg (na) WORE). *Meaning:* Large Rock.
29 Creigh na Cille (Creg na Killa). *Meaning:* The rock of the Church. *Note:* Near Mass Rock and above Holy Well.
30 Criogán Tommy (CREG an TOE-mee). *Meaning:* Tommy's rock.
31 Cúl an Garraí (COOL a Garry). *Meaning:* Back of the garden. *Note:* Also known as 'Bernaglasha', or round garden, where hayricks were made.
32 Daingean (The DANG-an). *Meaning:* Fortress. *Note:* Promontory adjacent to the 'Dun' - Dún Chill Mhór.
33 Duirling (DUR-ling). *Meaning:* Flat stony beach area.
34 Dún (The Dun). *Meaning:* The Fort. *Note:* Name loosely given to the narrow piece of land on which Dún Chill Mhór is situated.
35 Dún Beag (Dun b'YUG). *Meaning:* The small fort. *Note:* Iron Age remains. See Bearna Glaise.
36 Dún Mór (or Dún Chill Mhór/Kilmore)/Dún (Dun More/KILL-more). *Meaning:* The big fort. *Note:* Iron Age remains - see *Appendix One*. This area is also known as the Dún.
37 Dún na gCurrach (Dunna Curra/Gurra). *Note:* Meaning not certain. Dún = fort. Believed to be the remains of Iron Age fort, near Dún Chill Mhór.
38 Dún na Glaise (DUNN-a Glass) . *Meaning:* Fort of the Grey Fairy Cow. *Note:* Small islet off Achillbeg (3).
39 Faiche (FA-ha). *Meaning:* The name means a lawn, green or field. This describes the area of the Giant's Grave. *Note:* Where the two legendary giants are buried.
40 Feorainn (FOOR-een). *Meaning:* Rocky sandy headland/grassy shore. *Note:* Near the pier.

41 Garraí Bhilly (Garry Villy). *Meaning:* Billy's garden. *Note:* Arrow field on north side
42 Garraí bhogaigh (Garry boggy). *Meaning:* The boggy garden. *Note:* Probably a 'colloquial' name. Situated near the 'Tail'.
43 Garraí an Choirce (Garry an CORK-ya). *Meaning:* The oat garden. *Note:* Kilbane's garden.
44 Garraí an Dúna (GARR-een DOON-a/GARR-een Doon). *Meaning:* Garden of the fort. *Note:* Near Dún Mór (Iron Age fort).
45 Garraí Éamiann (Garry Ay-mon). *Meaning:* Eamonn's garden. *Note:* Adjacent to Trá Bó Deirge beach.
46 Garraí an RR (Garry an Ree). *Meaning:* The King's garden (4).
47 Garraí an Seoighe (Garry an SHOW-ya). *Meaning:* Joyce's garden. *Note:* Identity of Joyce unknown
48 Garraí an Tuair Mhóir - or túir mor (Garry an TUR-more). *Meaning:* Known to islanders as 'Garden of the big fruit' May mean garden of the big cattle field (or big tower). *Note:* There is no evidence of any tower here or nearby (7).
49 Garraí Cruaidh (Garry CROO-ee). *Meaning:* The hard garden.
50 Garraí Gainimh (Garry GAWN-ee. *Meaning:* The sandy garden.
51 Garraí na Feorainne (GARR-een a FORN-a). *Meaning:* From 'feorainn' - grassy place or grassy shore.
52 Garraí na Loinge (Garry na LUNN-ya). *Meaning:* Garden of the ships (8).
53 Garraí uí Shúilleabháin (Garry SOOL-a-vawn). *Meaning:* Sullivan's garden (9).
54 Garraí Uachtair (Garry ook-tha). *Meaning:* Upper or high garden. *Note:* Could possibly mean garden for cream (dairying?). Uncertain translation.
55 Garraí Úr (Garry OOR). *Meaning:* New garden.
56 Garraí Waltie (Garry WALL tee. *Meaning:* Walter's garden. *Note:* Possibly a coastguard name, or a derivation of a local nickname
57 Garraí na Sméara Dubh (Garry na Smair-a DOO-ah). *Meaning:* Garden of ditches with blackberries. *Note:* field on north side of island.
58 Garraín Tuaidh (GARR-een TOO-ee). *Meaning:* The little northern garden. *Note:* This is the most likely meaning, though it is uncertain. It is possible that 'TOO-ee' relates to a nickname of some sort.
59 Gob an Bhioráin (GUBB-a VEER-awn). *Meaning:* End of the point/mouth. *Note:* 'Biorán' = stack or pinnacle of rock (in the sea).
60 Gob an Oileáin (GUBB-an ILL-yawn). *Meaning:* The point of the island.
61 Gob Leice Buí (GUBB-ar LECK-a BOO-ee). *Meaning:* The point of the yellow flat stone.
62 Gob (?) (GUB a Va-ha)
63 Goram Glas (spelling uncertain) (GURR-um glass). *Meaning:* Area near the Blessed well. *Note:* Exact origin of name unknown. 'Glas' = green. (10)
64 Gort Breac (?) (Gort Sprach). *Meaning:* Speckled field. *Note:* Probably derived from 'breac' = speckled. See Bearna Ghort Breach Ard. The origin of 's' sound in name as pronounced is uncertain.
65 Gort Breac Ard (Gort Sprach Ard). *Meaning:* The high speckled field. *Note:* As above. See Bearna Ghort Breach Ard.
66 Idir Dhá Chlaí (Ijor a DAW clee). *Meaning:* Between two ditches.
67 Lár na Scoilte (Lor na skol-cha) (?). *Meaning:* Centre(?) of crack fissure. *Note:* Where *An Paorach* signalled to emigrant ships.
68 Leargán (LARRA gawn). *Meaning:* Big area of rising ground. *Note:* From 'leargán' = a height, the slope of a hill.
69 Leargacha Buí (LARR-acka BOO-ee). *Meaning:* Yellow tracts of rising ground. *Note:* Could also (possibly) be derived from 'leargacha' = plural of 'learg' = tract of rising ground, slope.
70 Log na bhFhaoileán (LOCH na WAIL-an). *Meaning:* Hollow of the seagulls. *Note:* Sometimes pronounced loch-na-welligh, which may have a different origin.
71 Macalla (Mac ALLA). *Meaning:* Echo. *Note:* Flat area on inland side of *Paroach's* house, where an echo may sometimes be heard.
72 Máimín na Croise (MAW-meen a Crusha). *Meaning:* The mountain pass of the cross. *Note:* Where the two giants clashed. The place name suggests early Christian origins - it is not far from where the ancient church is reputed to have been.
73 Maolán na mBan (MWEE-lin na Mon). *Meaning:* 'Maolán' = bare coastal rock. 'na mBan' = of the women. Possibly also from 'maoileann' = ridge/low rounded hill. *Note:* Place where girls and women bathed. This small beach is surrounded by 'bare coastal rocks'. Above this place is a 'low rounded hill' - the island's northern hill.

74 Oileán na nÉan (ILL-awn A Nane/n'yane). *Meaning:* Island of the birds. *Note:* Small islet off the west coast of Achillbeg.
75 Oileán an Sciorta (ILL-awn a SKIRT-a). *Meaning:* Known to islanders as the 'land of ticks' but could mean 'the marginal portions' denoting this more remote area of the island (1, 11).
76 Páirc (Park). *Meaning.* The park or field.
77 Poll an Leathaigh (Pool a LAGH-ee). *Meaning:* The hole of the muddy area - OR - hollow of the rack of seaweed (?) *Note:* Pol = poll = the hole. 'a leitheaigh' = of the mud, slush, slime. 'an leathaigh'= broad seaweed, wrack.
78 Robail/An Rioball (Rubble). *Meaning:* Stony 'rubble' ground near shore. *Note:* Near the 'Tail'.
79 Sceilp (Scalp). *Meaning:* Cleft or fissure (in rock); cave. *Note:* One elderly resident referred to it as Sceilp Inallach, possibly meaning a prominent rock or outcrop.
80 Sceilp an Chapall (ShKELP a KAP-al). *Meaning:* Fissure of the horse. *Note:* Could be a description of a geographical feature as no folk memory survives of any horses on Achillbeg.
81 Sceig Mhór (SHKEG More). *Meaning:* The big rock (or large area of stony ground?).
82 Scailp (an Eala?) (SHKELP in allah). *Meaning:* scailp = cleft, fissure, cave.
83 Srath Mór (Shra More). *Meaning:* sragh = sraith = a scraw (as used in roof) or swathe of grass. Mór = large. *Note:* Near Máimín na Croise.
84 Tail (Tail). *Meaning:* The 'Tail' of the island (north-west corner) (1).
85 Teach na bPaorach (Toch na PWEER-och). *Meaning:* The house of the Powers. *Note:* The *Paorach's* house.
86 Tobar Biddy (TUBB-ar Biddy). *Meaning:* Biddy's (Bridget's) well.
87 Tobar an Chuirdín (TUBB-ar a Cur Jeen). *Meaning:* The well of the hag - OR - if derived from 'an chorragáin', = the well of the heap of stones. *Note:* A 'cuirdín' in this form is believed to have meant a hag, a hostile and unfriendly elderly female (or worse!) This is a term still used in the area (12).
88 Tobar Frank (TUBB-ar Frank). *Meaning:* Frank's well.
89 (TUBB-ar LA-hawn). *Meaning:* Well of the ducks. *Note:* Near north shoreline.
90 Tobar Leathaigh (TUBB-ar LA-hee). *Meaning:* Well of the seaweed.
91 Tobar Mhic Suibhne/Tobar Uainín (TUBB-ar OON-een). *Meaning:* Sweeney's well. *Note:* Sweeney's identity unknown.
92 Tobar na bhFrogannaí (TUBB-ar na FROG-anee). *Meaning:* The well of the frogs.
93 Tobar na hAille (TUBB-ar na HAL-ya). *Meaning:* Well of cold drinks - OR - well of the cliff.
94 Tonn Scardeoige/Scairdeach (Tunn SCORE-jug). *Meaning:* 'Scáird' = a splash, squirt or cascade. May mean 'where waves gush'.
95 Trá Bó Deirge (TRAW-bo JARR-ig). *Meaning:* The strand of the red cow (13).
96 Tulscán na Tairbh (TULSK-awn na Tarriv). *Meaning:* The cove of the Bull. *Note:* Possibly related: 'tul scán': an outburst, a fall away of rock, fissure in cliff face, or 'tolscán' = a place of a flurry of water. 'Toll' = hole, cavity or hollow.
97 Uaich Bhuí (Eye-a wee). *Meaning:* Yellow cove.
98 Uaich Dhilisc Mhilis (Eye-a Jillis Villis). *Meaning:* Cove of sweet dilsk (or dulse). *Note:* May be Uaimh Duilisc Milis. Dilsk/dulse is an edible seaweed.
99 Uaich Dhuine Mhairbh. (Eye-a DUNNA warra). *Meaning:* Cove of the dead person. *Note:* Identity of any possible casualty unknown.
100 Uaich Dhoirlinge (Eye-a Durling). *Meaning:* Cove of the flat area/pebbly area/stony beach.
101 Uaich a Dún (Eye-a Doon). *Meaning:* Cove of the fort. *Note:* Near Dún Chill Mhór.
102 Uaich (?) (Eye-a Frugida). *Meaning:* Not known.
103 Uaich Úi Mháille (Oh WALL-ya). *Meaning:* O'Malley's Cove (14).
104 Uaich na Gabhair -or- Uaich an Ghabha (Och-na GAW-a/Augh-a Gow-a). *Meaning:* Cove of the goats/cove of the smith.
105 Uaich Phádraig (Eye-a Paw-rig). *Meaning.* Patrick's Cove. *Note:* Also known as Cuan Padraig.
106 Uaich na bPréachán (oh FREY-awn). *Meaning:* Cove of crows or birds nests.
107 Uaich Reille. *Meaning:* Reilly's Grave - OR - could relate to 'raoile' = a roll of wool; therefore 'the grave of the roll of wool'. *Note:* Identity of Reilly uncertain.
108 Uaich na Sionnach (OWN-a SHIN-na). *Meaning:* The coves of the foxes (15).
109 Uaich Tabac (Eye-a TOE bac). *Meaning:* Cove of tobacco. *Note:* Maybe washed ashore after a shipwreck.

These places were known by the English language names given:

110 The Coastguard's House(s). *Note:* Also known as the Watch House.
111 Watch House Road. *Note:* Path built by coastguards from beach to their premises (16).
112 The pier. *Note:* (not known by a specific name).
113 The well. *Note:* The 'Blessed Well' or 'Holy Well' (dedicated to St Patrick).

Notes:

(1) The 'Tail', Oileán an Sciorta, and Baileamuigh were names given to three loosely defined areas of the island, and can be taken as 'regional' names, rather than localised place names. Some older islanders used the name Baileamuigh to refer specifically to the area in the middle of the island where the majority of the houses were. This is in fact where the original settlement of houses was confined, according to old maps.

(2) Taghna - one theory is that this may be a very approximate translation of St Dympna, commemorated in the nearby Achill place name of Kildownet/Kildavnet. Achillbeg had clear connections with this area, as shown by several early maps which show the island named as 'Kil-danat' or 'Kil-da-mat' Island. Another theory is that the name is derived from a nickname, or localised colloquial term, long lost in history.

(3) There are several possible interpretations of this. 'Bearna na Glaise' means the gap of the fairy cow. However, the pronunciation of this is 'BAR-na na Glasha', with two distinct '..na..' syllables. It is possible that if this is the meaning of the name, it could have been shortened in everyday speech, as is commonplace with place names elsewhere in any language. Off Achillbeg's northern-western corner, the sea channel between the island and Achill is marked on maps as 'Belnaglass', an anglicised version of 'Beal na Glaise' (pronounced 'BELL na Glasha'). This means 'the sea mouth of the fairy cow'. Close to 'Belnaglass' is the islet of 'Dunnaglass', already referred to as containing some of the Iron Age remains in the area. This name comes from Dún na Glaise, or 'the fort of the grey fairy cow'. Throughout Ireland, there are several instances of 'fairy cows' appearing in old folklore and legend. These can manifest themselves in place names from time to time. The origin of this particular example is unknown.

(4) It was commonplace in years gone by for many Irish islands to have a 'king'. The 'king' would be a senior member of a prominent family, and would generally be elected by general consensus. The title was somewhat casually used, and successors could be appointed as frequently as each year. The tradition does not seem to have assumed as great an importance in Achillbeg as in other places, but this is one of several place names which shows that at one time at least, this tradition was in place.

(5) 'Cregalomen' was recorded on Bald's Map, but the name is unknown to islanders whose personal memories span the period 1910 onwards. However, one former resident knew this place as 'Cregoagh', pronounced CREG -oh -ah. Her memories dated from the late 1920s. Other former islanders had never heard of this name, or any obvious variation of it. The name may be a very rough translation of Creig Iaminn Bháin which has been identified by islanders as being nearby. 'Cregalomen' was used on an early map, but this is likely to be only a very rough approximation as a result of an English-speaking surveyor crudely attempting to anglicise an Irish place name. 'Cregalomen' is one of only three place names recorded on *any* map of the island, including all Ordnance Survey issues. The only one regularly quoted at all was that of the strand, Trá Bó Deirge, usually anglicised as 'Traboderg'.

(6) In the 'penal times' of the 18th century, when severe impediments were placed in the way of Catholic worship by the laws of the day, religious services used to be held in the open, usually where a flat rock could be used as an altar. 'Mass rocks' are to be found all over Ireland.

(7) The origin of this place name is uncertain. Of all the places on Achillbeg where fields or gardens were maintained, this was among the most exposed. It is hard to imagine any kind of sensitive crop thriving here. It is possible the name may translate as the garden of the tower, or the garden of the cattle. There is no trace of any tower, nor is there any folk memory or historical record to substantiate this version, however cattle would have been grazed here.

(8) A good view of boats approaching the island towards Trá Bó Deirge was to be had from here.

(9) Sullivan's identity is not known. He/she may have been a member of the coastguard staff, or possibly a visiting teacher.

(10) The 'Blessed Well', or 'Holy Well' was reputed to have had supernatural powers. Signs of good or ill luck could be foretold from sightings of a fish in the well - this is referred to elsewhere. The well was dedicated to St Patrick.

(11) Oileán an Sciorta was also known as Knockillaun na Sciorta. 'Knock', meaning 'hill', referred to the southernmost hill on the island, to which this name was given. Since 'oileán' means island', and this area is not actually a separate island, a more accurate translation of the place name may therefore be 'the hill of the ticks'. This referred to the small burrowing insects known as ticks, which would live on the islander's cattle given the chance. In recent times, at least one islander who grazed sheep had to rotate them periodically to other areas of the island in case they became infested by these insects. The heather growing on this side of the island doubtless provides a haven for these insects. This area is, and was, also well known for midges - no visitor escapes

their attention on summer evenings! Another place name which probably relates to this area is Lár na Scoilte.

(12) A 'Cuirdín' is something that no lady would wish to be described as one islander believes that the well was so named because at one time in the distant past it was owned by a bad tempered woman who would not let anyone else take water from it!

(13) The only place name recorded generally on maps from 18th century onwards. The name was anglicised as Traboderig, Traboderg or Trabodearg on Ordnance Survey maps. The origin of the name is not known for certain, but nearby is Tulscán na Tairbh, the 'cave of the bull'. One former islander believes that both these names may be related to a rock formation seen at low tide which resembles several cows or bulls heads. In the distant past before the pier was built, it is likely that cattle were loaded on and off boats here.

(14) May refer to Grainne Ní Mháille (Grace O'Malley), the 16th century pirate queen who ruled large coastal areas of the West of Ireland. Her presence was very much felt in the area, and the castle nearby at Kildownet on Achill Island is said to have been used by her. (Some evidence also exists to suggest that this castle long pre-dated Grainne.) O'Malley is, however, a common name in the general area, and it is possible that people of this name lived on the island at one time.

(15) There were several adjacent coves, named Uaich na Sionnach Mór (the big fox's cove) Uaich na Sionnach Láir (the middle fox's cove) and Uaich na Sionnach Beag (the small fox's cove). Pronounced OWN-a SHIN-na generally, but one former resident pronounced it as OWN-a SHA.

(16) The Watch House Road was apparently built by the coastguards in the 19th century for transport of supplies from the beach to the house they occupied. While it is well documented, and its location fits in with what little is known of the coastguard presence on the island, some islanders had never heard it referred to by this name.

Oileán an Sciorta, the land, or island, of the ticks. The name may also be interpreted as meaning the 'marginal portion'. Both descriptions would be accurate. The author can confirm the accuracy of the first; never in my life did I receive such a merciless attack by biting insects as I did the day I took this photograph - all in the space of time it took me to sit on a rock to change the film in my camera. One former islander had commented that while living on the island, his relatives were reluctant to keep livestock grazing in this area for too long, as they would be bitten by insects. Regarding the second possible meaning of the name, this area is indeed the more marginal part of the island. As the southernmost hill, it is further away from the mainland than the other, and more exposed, bearing the full brunt of whatever the Atlantic Ocean throws at it. Consequently, there are no houses, roads or fields here, in fact this area contains nothing man-made but the lighthouse. In this view, we are looking north. Trá Bó Deirge beach may be seen in the centre of the picture, and the northern hill beyond. The cultivated area above the beach, and sloping down to the coast on the right is the 'Páirc'. Beyond this, mainland Corraun is on the right, and the southern end of Achill Island on the left. The bridge across the narrow channel separating them may just be seen on the horizon.

Appendix One

Description of Antiquities at Dún Kilmore on Achillbeg

From *Larger Cliff Forts of West Coast of Co. Mayo*, by T.J. Westropp, 1910.
(Proceedings of the Irish Academy)

Dun Kilmore (OS75) (1)

The most complex of the Irish promontory forts, save Doon-Eask Fort near Dingle, is 'Dun Kiluole' or Dun Kilmore, on Achillbeg Island. (2) It is most remarkable that such a work escaped the notice of the Surveyors; neither it nor the name appears on the Ordnance Maps. It shows how unfavourably the determination to dispense with antiquarian aid has affected the Survey from a national point of view, when such forts as Dunroe, Porth, Dun Fiachra, Poon Castle, and Doonaunmore promontory forts are absent from 'authoritative maps', and others like Dunabrattin, Ferriter's Castle, Meenacuroge, Brumore, Dundahlin and Doonegall have only recently been marked; but the surveyors are hardly blameable.

The fort, or senes of fortifications, stands on three low headlands westward from the Scalp or low valley through the Islet. (3)

At the landward end we first find a fosse 10 feet wide and rarely over 4 feet deep, with a stone-faced earthwork inside, convex to the land. The mound is about 20 feet thick and 9 feet high; much of it only retains the facing for about 4 feet up from the fosse, but near the northern bend is a reach 8 to 10 feet high, well built and carefully laid slabs, with a regular batter of 1 in 4 to 1 in 5 - a rather unusual slope. This rampart is 138 feet long, and has fallen with the cliff at the southern side, but runs along the northern cliff (a steep, grassy slope) and meets the ring-fort. The gateway faces the east, and is 6 feet wide, lined with set slabs like those in the evidently very early forts of Moghane and Turlough Hill.

Entering the forecourt we find, at 36 feet from the inner piers of the gate, a kerb-like row of blocks running NNW and SSE; its object is not apparent.

At 65 feet from the outer gate we find a ring-fort. (4) There is no trace of an outer mound; and the fosse is nearly filled, to the cast. A gate-way faces the outer gate, which it exactly resembles in design and width. The mound is earthen, and was once stone-faced all round, though little of the masonry remains. It is 20 feet thick and rises 4 feet to 6 feet over the garth; and to the west it is 18 feet thick and 9 feet high above the ditch. It measures 259 feet over all, east and west, and 220 feet inside, the northern part having fallen with the cliff; the garth is only 150 feet across, north and south. The western fosse is 6 feet wide below, 10 feet at the field-level, and 3 to 5 feet deep. It still holds water in wet weather, as we had every opportunity of observing in the late August, so destructive, by its endless storms and rain, in Co. Mayo. There is a gangway 3 feet wide, 45 feet from

Notes:

(1) OS75 refers to reference number of the Ordnance Survey map which shows the area. Throughout the report, the 'fada' is omitted from 'Dún' - it is spelt 'Dun' throughout.

(2) Islanders living today are unaware of the name 'Dun Kiluole'.

(3) Islanders did not refer to this area as 'The Scalp'. The area around the low valley was known as Bailemuigh.

(4) A footnote to the original text read: 'The occurrence of a ring inside a promontory fort is not unprecedented. Besides Dunnamoe in Ireland the two promontory forts at Appenay sur Belleme (Orne), France, have each a low ring-fort or mote, 6 feet high, the earthworks rising nearly 11 feet over the fosse; they yielded worked flints and fragments of vases. The fosse is nearly 56 feet deep.' (*Bulletin Soc. Préhist. de France,* 1910, p.325).

the northern cliff, opening westward; thence there is for 18 feet a deep cutting into the ring, with set slabs, and long since grassed over. The ditch is 4 feet 6 inches deep for 96 feet, and more shallow for 114 feet to the edge of the south cliff which is uninjured, and forms a steep, grassy slope.

In the garth is an early burial-ground, called Kilmore; no trace of a church remains, but there are numerous graves lying east and west in a low rectangular mound, hardly a foot high, measuring 43 feet east and west, and 25 feet north and south. There are also some small cist-like enclosures of slabs, and a round, low slab pier or altar, 3 feet high and 6 feet across at 16 feet from the east gateway. A similar 'altar' lies outside the mound at 54 feet to the west of the last, and 100 feet from the north cliff. Each is heaped with rounded stones from the shore, nearly all of pure white quartz, which frequently are laid *ex voto* on undoubted altars and on holy wells elsewhere. On my asking one of the bystanders if such was the case, there was some hesitation in the reply; and at last we were told that it was children put them there, and that the place was not a Christian burial-ground. A basin, or 'bullaun', 16 inches across in a block of brown gritstone, lies near the north-west corner of the mound, as is common in old graveyards. There are hut-enclosures against the rampart to the north-west.

At 167 feet from the ring-fort we reach a creek between the two outer headlands. The neck of each is fortified. The southern, called the Dún, has two fosses, with three mounds running straight across it, at 30 feet from the head of the creek. The outer mound is barely traceable and 8 feet wide; the outer fosse is 9 feet to 10 feet wide and 4 to 5 feet deep. The central mound is 16 feet wide, and appears to have had a strong fence to its landward face, leaving a banquette behind. This feature occurs in better preservation at Ferriter's Castle in Kerry, and the inner west mound of Cahermurphy Castle in Clare. Traces also occur in Doonagappul on Clare Island, which bears considerable likeness to the inner Dun of Kilmore. Inside is another fosse, 16 feet wide above, and in parts 7 feet deep. It has a levelled inner mound, 7 feet to 12 feet thick.

The middle of the fosse is filled up from 42 to 71 feet from the northern cliff by a hut nearly levelled, and measuring 27 feet north and south by 32 east and west over all, with walls 6 to 10 feet thick. The whole works are 123 feet long, and the ends seem uninjured by the sea. There are no hut-sites on the headland, off the end of which is a detached rock of equal height with the Dun.

The northern headland is called 'Dangan', we were told that last year (1909) the side-wall of a mortar-built structure of that name, with several 'loop-holes' in it, slipped down the north cliff. There is faint trace of a wall across the neck; then, at 138 feet from the end of the creek, is a fosse, 28 feet wide at the ground-level, 9 feet deep, and 36 feet long, to the south of the gangway, which follows the fine of the ridge of the neck. All to the south has perished in the landslip which, with masses of stones of the overthrown building, hangs about 12 feet down, needing but little to start it again on its journey into the sea below.

Inside the fosse is the wall, below of dry stone (or rather, perhaps, a stone-faced mound), on which rests the base of the mortar-built wall 10 feet thick, and barely 4 feet high. It was probably a mediaeval guardhouse, built across the older works, utilising the northern half of the fosse for a basement story.

Appendix Two

Census Statistics 1901 and 1911

1901 Census

Condensed information from House and Building Return as on 11th April, 1901.

Houses				*Particulars of Inhabited Houses*				***Families, etc.***			
House No.	*Type of building P - Private House*	*No. of out buildings, sheds, etc.*	*Is house inhabited ?*	*Walls 1 - stone 0- mud, other*	*Roof 1 - slate or similar 0 - thatch*	*No. of rooms*	*Windows in front*	*No. of distinct families in each house*	*Name of family head*	*No. of rooms occupied by each family*	*No. of people in each room*
1	P		Yes	1	0	2	2	1	James Kilbane (Pat)	2	9
2	P	1	Yes	1	0	1	1	1	John Kilbane (Pat)	1	1
3	P		Yes	1	0	2	2	1	Mary Bourke	2	4
4	P	1	Yes	1	0	2	2	1	Edward Kilbane (Jas)	2	9
5	P		Yes	1	0	2	2	1	Bridget Corrigan	3	5
6	P		Yes	1	0	2	2	1	Pat Gallagher (Michl.)	2	2
7	P		Yes	1	0	2	2	1	Michl. Gallagher (Grace)	2	5
8	P		Yes	1	0	2	2	1	John Gallagher (Red)	2	7
9	P		Yes	1	0	1	1	1	James Kilbane (Jas)	1	6
10	P		Yes	1	0	2	2	1	John Gallagher (Anthony)	2	5
11	P		Yes	1	0	2	2	1	Michael Gallagher (Pat)	2	9
12	P		Yes	1	0	2	2	1	Joseph Gallagher	2	5
13	P		Yes	1	0	1	1	1	John Gallagher (Pat)	1	6
14	P		Yes	1	0	2	2	1	Peter Gallagher	2	3
15	P	1	Yes	1	0	2	2	2	Edward Kilbane (Ned) *	1	3
									John Gallagher	1	2
16	P		Yes	1	0	2	2	1	John Kilbane (James)	2	6
17	P		Yes	1	0	2	2	1	Pat Gallagher (Grace)	2	7
18	P		Yes	1	0	2	2	1	Bridget Gallagher	2	6
19	P		Yes	1	0	1	1	1	Michael Corrigan	1	4
20	National School		No	-	-	-	-	1	-	-	-

* House No. 15 contained two families, those of Edward 'Ned' Kilbane and John Gallagher. Edward Kilbane was listed as the property owner. No information was recorded about the school. This was not the existing school building, but its predecessor - see Chapter Seven.

Inhabitants of Achillbeg (from form A details)

House No. (a)	*Christian Name*	*Surname*	*Relation to head of family*	*Education (b) RW=Can read and write*	*Age last birthday*	*Occupation*	*Marital status S-single M-married*	*Language (c) I-Irish E-English*
1	James	Kilbane	Head	RW	55	Farmer	M	I E
	Grace	Kilbane	Wife	Cannot read	32		M	I E
	Patrick	Kilbane	Son	RW	10	Scholar	S	I E
	John	Kilbane	Son	RW	9	Scholar	S	I E
	Farrell/Hariet*	Kilbane	Son	RW	8	Scholar	S	I E
	Thomas	Kilbane	Son	RW	6	Scholar	S	I E
	Maude	Kilbane	Daughter	RW	4	Scholar	S	I E
	James	Kilbane	Son	RW	3	Scholar	S	I E
	Bridget	Kilbane	Daughter		1		S	I E

* Farrell/Hariet: described as 'Hariet' in 1901 census, Farrell in 1911. Noted as male in both.

House No. (a)	*Christian Name*	*Surname*	*Relation to head of family*	*Education (b) RW=Can read and write*	*Age last birthday*	*Occupation*	*Marital status S-single M-married*	*Language (c) I-Irish E-English*
2	John 'Pat'	Kilbane	Head	RW	35	Farmer	S	I E
3	Mary	Bourke	Head	Cannot read	60	Farmer	Widow	I E
	James	Bourke	Son	RW	23	Boat builder	S	I E
	Martha	Bourke	Daughter	RW	24	Farmer's daughter	S	I E
	Maude	Bourke	Daughter	RW	20	Farmer's daughter	S	I E
4	Edward	Kilbane	Head	RW	50	Farmer	M	I E
	Anne	Kilbane	Wife	Cannot read	40	Wife	M	I E
	James	Kilbane	Son	RW	15	Farmer's son	S	I E
	Pat	Kilbane	Son	RW	13	Scholar	S	I E
	Mary	Kilbane	Daughter	RW	11	Scholar	S	I E
	John	Kilbane	Son	RW	9	Scholar	S	I E
	Michael	Kilbane	Son	RW	6	Scholar	S	I E
	Anne	Kilbane	Daughter	RW	4	Scholar	S	I E
	Edward	Kilbane	Son	Cannot read	5 months		S	
5	Bridget	Corrigan	Head	Cannot read	50	Farmer	Widow	I E
	Hugh	Corrigan	Son	RW	27	Farmer's son	S	I E
	Bridget	Corrigan	Daughter	RW	17	Daughter	S	I E
	Catherine	Corrigan	Daughter	RW	13	Daughter	S	I E
	Anne	Corrigan	Daughter	RW	10	Daughter	S	I E
6	Pat	Gallagher	Head	Cannot read	78	Farmer	M	I E
	Margaret	Gallagher	Wife	Cannot read	73		M	I E
7	Michael	Gallagher	Head	Cannot read	46	Farmer	M	I E
	Mary	Gallagher	Wife	Cannot read	40		M	I E
	Pat	Gallagher	Son	Cannot read	28	Farmer's son	S	I E
	Anthony	Gallagher	Son	RW	25	Farmer's son	S	I E
	Hugh	Gallagher	Son	RW	20	Farmer's son	S	I E

8	John	Gallagher	Head	RW	50	Farmer	M	I E
	Catherine	Gallagher	Wife	Cannot read	42		M	I E
	Catherine	Gallagher	Daughter	RW	14	Daughter	S	I E
	John	Gallagher	Son	RW	11	Scholar	S	I E
	Rose	Gallagher	Daughter	RW	8	Scholar	S	I E
	Peter	Gallagher	Son	RW	6	Scholar	S	I E
	Michael	Gallagher	Son	Cannot read	2		S	I E
9	James	Kilbane	Head	Cannot read	39	Farmer	M	I E
	Margaret	Kilbane	Wife	Cannot read	32		M	I E
	Mary	Kilbane	Daughter	RW	8	Scholar	S	
	James	Kilbane	Son	RW	6	Scholar		
	Bridget	Kilbane	Daughter	Cannot read	4	Scholar	S	
	Michael	Kilbane	Son	Cannot read	1			
10	John	Gallagher	Head	Cannot read	63	Farmer	M	I E
	Mary	Gallagher	Wife	Cannot read	60		M	I E
	Sarah	Gallagher	Daughter	Cannot read	23	Daughter	S	I E
	Bridget	Gallagher	Daughter	RW	22	Daughter	S	I E
	Mary	Gallagher	Daughter	RW	20	Daughter	S	I E
11	Michael	Gallagher	Head	Cannot read	60	Farmer	M	I E
	Mary	Gallagher	Wife	Cannot read	60		M	I E
	James	Gallagher	Son	Cannot read	20	Farmer's son	S	I E
	Mary	Gallagher	Daughter	Cannot read	23	Daughter	S	I E
	Hugh	Gallagher	Son	RW	15	Scholar	S	I E
	Sarah	Gallagher	Daughter	RW	18	Daughter	S	I E
	Maude	Gallagher	Daughter	RW	12	Scholar	S	I E
	Michael	Gallagher	Son	RW	8	Scholar	S	I E
	Bridget	Gallagher	Sister	Cannot read	50		S	I
12	Joseph	Gallagher	Head	RW	40	Farmer	M	I E
	Mary	Gallagher	Wife	Cannot read	40		M	I E
	Martha	Gallagher	Daughter	RW	6	Scholar	S	I E
	Mary	Gallagher	Daughter	RW	4	Scholar	S	I E
	Thomas	Gallagher	Son	Cannot read	2		S	I E
13	John	Gallagher	Head	RW	35	Farmer	M	I E
	Margaret	Gallagher	Wife	Cannot read	37		M	I E
	Hugh	Gallagher	Son	RW	21	Farmer's son	S	I E
	John	Gallagher	Son	RW	14	Farmer's son	S	I E
	Peter	Gallagher	Son	RW	11	Scholar	S	I E
	Margaret	Gallagher	Daughter	RW	9	Scholar	S	I E
14	Peter	Gallagher	Head	Cannot read	60	Farmer	M	I E
	Sarah	Gallagher	Wife	Cannot read	60	Farmer	M	I E
	Pat	Gallagher	Son	RW	18	Farmer's son	S	I E

House No. (a)	Christian Name	Surname	Relation to head of family	Education (b) RW=Can read and write	Age last birthday	Occupation	Marital status S-single M-married	Language (c) I-Irish E-English
15	Edward	Kilbane	Head	RW	30	Farmer	S	I E
	Sibby	Kilbane	Mother	Cannot read	69		Widow	I E
	Margaret	Doogan	Niece	RW	20	Farm labourer	S	I E
	John	Gallagher	Head	Cannot read	30		M	
	Mary	Gallagher	Wife	Cannot read	26		M	I E
16	John	Kilbane	Head	RW	32	Farmer	M	I E
	Sarah	Kilbane	Wife	Cannot read	30		M	I E
	James	Kilbane	Son	Cannot read	3		S	I E
	Pat	Kilbane	Son	Cannot read	3 months		S	I E
	Pat		Servant	RW	12	Farm servant	S	I E
	Mary		Mother	Cannot read	75		Widow	I E
17	Pat	Gallagher	Head	Cannot read	60	Farmer	M	I E
	Mary	Gallagher	Wife	Cannot read	55		M	I E
	Michael	Gallagher	Son	RW	28	Farmer's son	S	I E
	Thomas	Gallagher	Son	RW	25	Farmer's son	S	I E
	Pat	Gallagher	Son	RW	18	Farmer's son	S	I E
	Mary	Gallagher	Daughter	RW	4	Daughter	S	I E
	Anthony	Gallagher	Son	RW	8	Scholar	S	I E
18	Bridget	Gallagher	Head	Cannot read	60	Farmer	Widow	I
	John	Gallagher	Son	RW	26	Farmer's son	S	I E
	Pat	Gallagher	Son	RW	22	Farmer's son	S	I E
	Catherine	Gallagher	Daughter	RW	19	Farmer's daughter	S	I E
	Maggie	Gallagher	Daughter	RW	17	Farmer's daughter	S	I E
	Norah (d)	McHugh	Boarder	RW	33	National Teacher	S	E
19	Michael	Corrigan	Head	RW	29	Farmer	M	I E
	Mary	Corrigan	Wife	Cannot read	29	Wife	M	I E
20	(None)	(School)						

(a) House numbers were allocated for census reference purposes only. They were not numbers in the sense of those forming part of a postal address.
(b) Those described as 'cannot read' would equally have been unable to write.
(c) It is thought that where a description was given as 'Irish and English', that the first named language was the person's main (or first) language.
(d) In House No. 18 the teacher, Norah McHugh (who was not a native of Achillbeg) boarded with the Gallagher family. Alone amongst the island population, Miss McHugh could only speak English. Under British rule in those days, education policy was that all children were educated in English only. The use of Irish was actively discouraged for several generations, this being a major factor in the national decline of the native tongue as 'the language of the hearth'. Miss McHugh's landlady was one of two islanders who could only speak Irish; but all her grown up family were bilingual.

1911 Census

Condensed information from House and Building Return as on 2nd April, 1911.

Houses / ***Families, etc.***

House No.	Type of building	No. of out buildings, sheds, etc.	Is house inhabited ?	Particulars of Inhabited Houses: Walls 1 - stone 0- mud, other	Roof 1 - slate or similar 0 - thatch	No. of rooms	Windows in front	No. of distinct families in each house	Name of family head	No. of rooms occupied by each family	No. of people in each room
1	P		Yes	1	0	2	2	1	Michael Corrigan	2	8
2	P		Yes	1	0	2	2	1	John Gallagher (Red)	2	7
3	P		Yes	1	0	2	2	1	James Gallagher	2	5
4	P	1	Yes	1	0	2	2	1	Jm Gallagher (Anty)	2	4
5	P		Yes	1	0	2	2	1	John Gallagher (Molly)	2	6
6	P	1	Yes	1	0	2	2	1	Joe Gallagher	2	6
7	P	1	Yes	1	0	2	2	1	Jms Kilbane	2	1
8	P		Yes	1	0	2	2	1	James Kilbane (Jas)	2	7
9	P		Yes	1	0	2	2	1	Ml. Gallagher (Grace)	2	3
10	P		Yes	1	0	2	2	1	Pat Gallagher (Ml.)	2	4
11	P		Yes	1	0	2	2	1	Bridget Corrigan	2	3
12	P		Yes	1	0	2	2	1	Jas. Kilbane (Pat)	2	12
13	P		Yes	1	0	2	2	1	Michael Gallagher	2	7
14	P		Yes	1	0	2	2	1	Edward Kilbane (Jas.)	2	7
15	P		Yes	1	0	2	2	1	Hugh Gallagher	2	4
16	P		Yes	1	0	2	2	1	Edward Kilbane (Ml.)	2	5
17	P		Yes	1	0	2	2	1			
18	P		Yes	1	0	2	2	1	Sarah Gallagher	2	5
19	P		Yes	1	0	2	2	1	Pat Gallagher (Grace)	2	7
20	P		Yes	1	0	2	2	1	Bridget Gallagher	2	8
21	P		Yes	1	0	2	2	1	John Kilbane (Jas.)	2	4
22	National School		No	-	-	-	-				

Inhabitants of Achillbeg (from form A details)

House No. (a)	Christian Name	Surname	Relation to head of family	Education (b) RW=Can read and write	Age last birthday (b)	Occupation	Marital status S-single M-married	No. of years married	Total children born alive	Children still living	Language I-Irish E-English
1	Michael	Corrigan	Head	RW	45	Farmer & seaman	M				I E
	Mary	Corrigan	Wife	Cannot read	47		M	11	6	6	I E
	Patrick	Corrigan	Son	RW	9	Scholar					I E
	Bridget	Corrigan	Daughter	RW	8	Scholar					I E
	Mary	Corrigan	Daughter	RW	7	Scholar					I E
	John	Corrigan	Son	RW	6	Scholar					I E
	Sarah	Corrigan	Daughter	RW	4	Scholar					I E
	Michael	Corrigan	Son	Cannot read	2						

House No. (a)	Christian Name	Surname	Relation to head of family	Education (b) RW=Can read and write	Age last birthday (b)	Occupation	Marital status S-single M-married	No. of years married	Total children born alive	Children still living	Language I-Irish E-English
2	John 'Red'	Gallagher	Head	RW	69	Farmer	M				I E
	Catherine	Gallagher	Wife	Cannot read	53		M	30	9	8	I E
	Anne	Gallagher	Daughter	RW	24		S				I E
	John	Gallagher	Son	RW	23	Farmer's son	S				I E
	Rose	Gallagher	Daughter	RW	19		S				I E
	Peter	Gallagher	Son	RW	17	Farmer's son	S				I E
	Michael	Gallagher	Son	RW	12	Scholar	S				I E
3	James	Gallagher	Head	RW	57	Farmer	M	12			I E
	Nancy	Gallagher	Wife	RW	44		M	12	3	3	I E
	Pat	Gallagher	Son	RW	11	Scholar	S				I E
	Owen	Gallagher	Son	RW	9	Scholar					I E
	Maggie	Gallagher	Daughter	RW	6	Scholar	S				I E
4	John 'Anty'	Gallagher	Head	Cannot read	80	Farmer	Widower				I E
	Bridget	Gallagher	Daughter	RW	30		S				I E
	Mary	Gallagher	Daughter	RW	28		S				I E
	Peter	Gallagher	Boarder	RW	74		S				I E
5	John 'Molly'	Gallagher	Head	RW	48	Farmer & butcher	M				I E
	Margaret	Gallagher	Wife	Cannot read	67		M	33	8	5	I E
	Pat	Gallagher	Son	RW	27	Farmer's son	S				I E
	John	Gallagher	Son	RW	24	Farmer's son	S				I E
	Peter	Gallagher	Son	RW	2	Farmer's son	S				I E
	Maggie	Gallagher	Daughter	RW	16		S				I E
6	Joe	Gallagher	Head	RW	48	Farmer	M				I E
	Mary	Gallagher	Wife	Cannot read	50		M	17	4	4	I E
	Martha	Gallagher	Daughter	Cannot read	16		S				I E
	Mary/May*	Gallagher	Daughter	RW	14	Scholar	S	* handwritng unclear			I E
	Thomas	Gallagher	Son	RW	13	Scholar	S				I E
	Pat	Gallagher	Son	RW	9	Scholar	S				I E
7	John 'Pat'	Kilbane	Head	RW	60 (b)	Farmer	S	-	-	-	I E
8	James 'Jas'	Kilbane	Head	Cannot read	48	Farmer	M				I E
	Margaret	Kilbane	Wife	Cannot read	45		M	19	6	5	I E
	Mary	Kilbane	Daughter	RW	18		S				I E
	James	Kilbane	Son	RW	17	Farmer's son	S				I E
	Bridget	Kilbane	Daughter	RW	11	Scholar	S				I E
	Michael	Kilbane	Son	RW	9	Scholar	S				I E
	John	Kilbane	Son	RW	7	Scholar	S				I E

9	Michael ‘Grace’	Gallagher	Head	Cannot read	85	Farmer	M				I E
	Mary	Gallagher	Wife	Cannot read	68		M	50	5	5	I E
	Hugh	Gallagher	Son	RW	30	Farmer’s son	S				I E
10	Pat (Ml)*	Gallagher	Head	Cannot read	40	Farmer	M		* probably Michael		I E
	Bridget	Gallagher	Wife	Cannot read	25		M	5	2	2	I E
	Catherine	Gallagher	Daughter	Cannot read	3		S				I E
	Mary	Gallagher	Daughter	RW	8 months		S				I E
11	Bridget	Corrigan	Head	Cannot read	65		Widow				I E
	Hugh	Corrigan	Son	RW	29	Farmer	M	1	-	-	I E
	Mary	Corrigan	Daughter in law	RW	24		M	1			I E
12	James ‘Pat’	Kilbane	Head	RW	69	Farmer	M				I E
	Grace	Kilbane	Wife	Cannot read	44		M		Not available		I E
	Pat	Kilbane	Son	RW	21	Farmer’s son	S				I E
	Farrell	Kilbane	Son	RW	18	Farmer’s son	S				I E
	Thonas	Kilbane	Son	RW	17	Farmer’s son	S				I E
	Matilda	Kilbane	Daughter	RW	15		S				I E
	James	Kilbane	Son	RW	13	Scholar	S				I E
	Bridget	Kilbane	Daughter	RW	12	Scholar	S				I E
	Margeret	Kilbane	Daughter	RW	8	Scholar	S				I E
	Annie	Kilbane	Daughter	RW	6	Scholar	S				I E
	Anthony	Kilbane	Son	Read	4	Scholar	S				I E
	John	Kilbane	Son	RW	19*	Farmer’s son	S				I E

* Note re ages of members of this family: It is not known why a 19-year-old son was at the end of the list - entries were almost always in order of age, starting with the eldest. Lodgers or cousins, grandchildren, etc., were normally left to the end - but John is described as ‘Son’.

13	Michael	Gallagher	Head	Cannot read	68	Farmer	M				I E
	Mary	Gallagher	Wife	Cannot read	60		M				I E
	James	Gallagher	Son	RW	32	Farmer’s son	S				I E
	Hugh	Gallagher	Son	RW	29	Farmer’s son	S		not available		I E
	Maud	Gallagher	Daughter	RW	21		S				I E
	Michael	Gallagher	Son	RW	17	Farmer’s son	S				I E
	Maggie	Corrigan	Granddaughter	RW	10		S				I E
14*	Edward ‘Jas’	Kilbane	Head								I E
	Other details unkown but house held seven people.*										
15	Hugh	Gallagher	Head	RW	33	Farmer	M				I E
	Catherine	Gallagher	Wife	RW	27		M	3	2	2	I E
	Mary	Gallagher	Daughter	Cannot read	7/2*		S		* illegible probably	7	I E
	Phelim	Gallagher	Son	Cannot read	4		S				I E
16	Edward ‘Neil’	Kilbane	Head	RW	50	Farmer	M				I E
	Sarah	Kilbane	Wife	RW	37		M	6	3	3	I E
	Mary	Kilbane	Daughter	Read	4	Scholar	S				I E
	Michael	Kilbane	Son	-	3	Scholar	S				I E
	Sarah	Kilbane	Daughter		1		S				I E

House No. (a)	Christian Name	Surname	Relation to head of family	Education (b) RW=Can read and write	Age last birthday (b)	Occupation	Marital status S-single M-married	No. of years married	Total children born alive	Children still living	Language I-Irish E-English
17	John 'Pat'	Gallagher	Head	Cannot read	50	Farmer	M				I E
	Mary	Gallagher	Wife	Cannot read	52		M	11	2	2	I E
	Mary	Gallagher	Daughter	RW	9	Scholar	S				I E
	Maggie	Gallagher	Daughter	RW	4	Scholar	S				I E
18	Sarah	Gallagher	Head	Cannot read	72		Widow				I E
	Pat 'Peter'	Gallagher	Son	RW	30	Farmer	M				I E
	Mary	Gallagher	Daughter in law	RW	27		M	6			I E
	Pat	Gallagher	Grandson	RW	5	Scholar	S				I E
	Peter	Gallagher	Grandson	Cannot read	9 months		S				I E

Although Pat & Mary are shown as married 6 yrs, nothing is entered in these columns to indicate how many children Mary had. The two shown, as grandsons of the householder Sarah, are presumably Mary's sons, and it must be assumed they have been omitted in error.

House No. (a)	Christian Name	Surname	Relation to head of family	Education (b) RW=Can read and write	Age last birthday (b)	Occupation	Marital status S-single M-married	No. of years married	Total children born alive	Children still living	Language I-Irish E-English
19	Pat 'Grace'	Gallagher	Head	Cannot read	73	Farmer	M				I E
	Mary	Gallagher	Wife	Cannot read	60		M		not available		I E
	Michael	Gallagher	Son	Cannot read	34	Farmer's son	S				I E
	Thomas	Gallagher	Son	RW	30	Farmer's son	S				I E
	Pat	Gallagher	Son	RW	28	Farmer's son	S				I E
	Anthony	Gallagher	Son	RW	22	Farmer's son	S				I E
	Pat Henry	Henry (?)	Grandson	Cannot read	3		S				I E
20	Bridget	Gallagher	Head	Cannot read	69		Widow				I E
	John	Gallagher	Son	Cannot read	40	Farmer	S				I E
	Pat	Gallagher	Son	RW	33	Farmer	S		These columns all		I E
	Catherine	Gallagher	RW	RW	27	Farmer's daughter	S		blank for this		I E
	Maggie	Gallagher	Daughter	RW	22		S		family group		I E
	Bridget	Corrigan	Granddaughter	Cannot read	4		S				I E
	Thomas	Corrigan	Grandson	Cannot read	2		S				I E
	Mary	Corrigan	Granddaughter	Cannot read	3		S				I E
21	John 'Jas'	Kilbane	Head	RW	60	farmer	M				I E
	Sarah	Kilbane	Wife	Cannot read	50		M	16	3	2	I E
	James	Kilbane	Son	RW	13	Scholar	S				I E
	Patrick	Kilbane	Son	RW	10*	Scholar	S	* Number on original document unclear			I E
22	National School										

(a) House numbers were allocated for census reference purposes only. They were not house numbers in the sense of those forming part of a postal address.
(b) Ages of people recorded in the census show a surprising amount of inaccuracy. Comparison of families shown in census result of both 1901 and 1911 will illustrate this. For example, one lady is shown as being 60 years of age in both years. Comparison of house residents in both years is fraught with uncertainty, as many names are similar, and there was a degree of intermingling with relatives on Achill and Corraun. Thus, a person living in one of the houses in one year could conceivably have moved, being replaced by a relative with the same name, and a similar age. The number allocated to a particular house in one census often differ from those in the other.

As a footnote, it may be pointed out in addition to the information contained above, there were other categories of information recorded which are not included in the tables. Among these were 'Religious Profession' - all inhabitants in both years census returns were listed as Roman Catholic. Another column recorded place of birth - in all cases this was given as County Mayo. The final column was headed, 'If Deaf and Dumb; Dumb only; Blind; Imbecile or Idiot; or Lunatic. Write the respective infirmities opposite the name of the afflicted person.' Happily, nobody from Achillbeg was described thus in either census. One wonders what public reaction would result from such a question being asked today!

Appendix Three

Teachers and pupil numbers in Achillbeg National School 1913 to 1965

Name of Teacher	*Arrived*	*Departed*	*Notes*	*Year*	*Average Attendance*	*No. of pupils Officially enrolled*
Pre - 1913			Unknown - though a Norah McHugh was recorded as boarding in the island in 1901, at which time education was conducted in one household or another. With a possible enrolment of 50 pupils, more than one teacher may have been present in the early 20th century. Immediately prior to 1913, a mistress was in charge.			50 (1903?)
Mr Francis Hugh Power	1913	30.1.1922	*'An Paorach'* - see Chapter Eight	1914 1915 1921	22 20 Mar.-Jun 20-24 Sep. 18 Dec. 21	33
Mr Patrick McFadden	27.2.1922	?	Appears to have commenced teaching in April 1922, and had moved on by that autumn. Probably a temporary post. A former pupil described him as a 'savage'!	1922		27
Miss Biddy Hesler	Oct. 1922	21.3.1926	Salary £160 per annum. Originally from Co. Roscommon, became a Mrs Kelly when married.	1923 1924 1925	23 19 Mar. 23 Jun.21 Sep. 19 Dec. 22	29
Miss Catherine Mahon	Apr. 1926	Apr. 1929	Transferred to Saula school, April 1929.	1926	21	
Miss Margaret Mary Tighe	3.6.1929	22.5.1931	Originally from Tuam, Co. Galway. Transferred to Derreens National School June 1931.	1929		29
Miss Bridget English (later Mrs Kilbane)	May 1931	July 1945	Married Michael Kilbane while in Achillbeg. To Bunnacurry 1945. Last teacher in Achillbeg with permanent contract. Native Irish speaker. Took children by boat from Achill to Achillbeg school.	1939 1940 1945	16.1 17	12
Miss Annie Cafferkey	?.1945	?.1945	Taught briefly - previously in Slievemore National School, Achill.	1945		12
Mr Paddy Henry	?	?	Taught for two months in 1940s only. Retired to Inishbiggle Island.		*c.* 15	
Miss Vera Joyce	Jun. 1946	4.11.1955	Originally from Mulrany. Suffered from poor health and had substitute teachers from 1950 - Colm Moran (from Mulrany) and Eveline Gallagher.	1955		9

Miss Bridget 'Briege' Henry	23.11.1955	Jun. 1959	Originally from Belfarsad. Emigrated to Britain, Summer 1959.	1958	All from one fanily	8
				1959	from now on	8
Mr J. Stephen Campbell	Sep. 1959	Jun. 1960	Originally from Currane.	1960		8
Mr Patrick O'Boyle	7.9.1960	Jun. 1962	Did not return in September despite being appointed.	1961	7.75	8
				1962	7.7	8
Mr Michael McNamara	1961	Jun. 1965	Originally from Polranny, Currane. Emigrated to Britain 1965. There was also a Jackie Gibbons, temporarily from February to October 1962.	1963	5.9	6.1
				1964	6.8	7
				1965	6.4	6.6

The school commenced operation in 1904, but records for the first nine years have not survived.

Actual and average attendance could differ considerably, especially in autumn months when some older children would have been away from Achillbeg working in the potato fields of Scotland or elsewhere.

In what survives of the school records, enrolment figures and attendance figures are indiscriminately and randomly quoted, leading to some confusion over the number of children in the school at any one time. It is still possible, however, to piece together the pattern of gradually declining school-age population through the 50 years or so up to 1965.

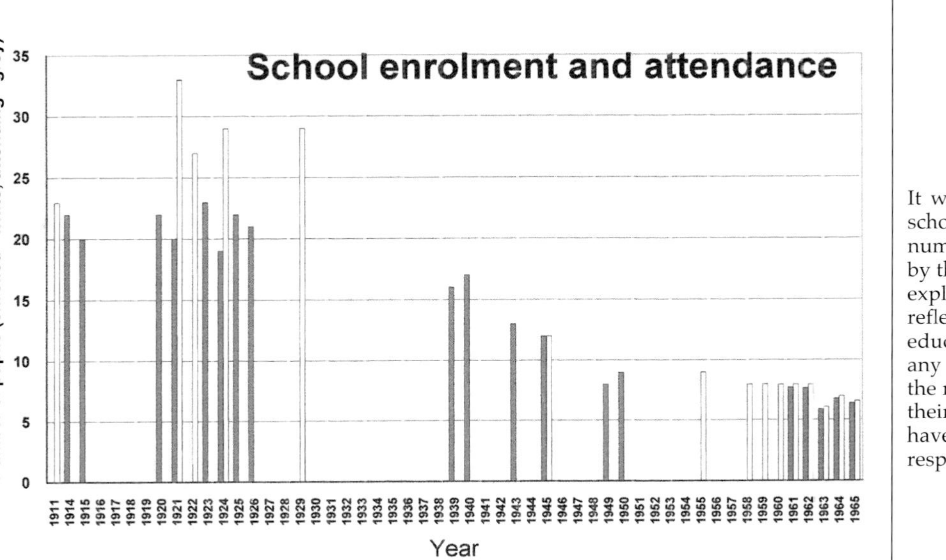

It will be noted that in the 1920s, the average actual school attendance (grey) was well below the average number of pupils officially enrolled (white), whereas by the 1960s what little discrepancy there was could be explained by natural occasional illnesses of pupils. This reflects the fact that in the earlier period children's education would not have been as big a priority, and in any event children were more likely to be absent due to the necessity of having to go away for work or to help their parents in the home or fields. Achillbeg would have reflected a nationwide trend for rural areas in this respect.

Acknowledgements and Sources

A project of this nature can only be completed with a wide range of assistance. Research included the historical and the anecdotal, as physical descriptions of the island blended with historical information and personal stories of life and culture there. Nothing specific has been published about Achillbeg before, apart from passing references in other publications, therefore almost all research was first-hand.

For historical material, Castlebar Library provided much information, and I am grateful to Ivor Hamrock and his staff for their untiring assistance. From the Library I obtained census statistics, articles in various old publications which mentioned the island or some aspect of it, maps and information on Griffith's Valuation of 1855, the Congested Districts Board, and the Folklore Commission in the 1930s. Details of Griffith's Valuation and other surveys are available here, and reference to conditions in neighbouring areas including Achill were taken from the *Report of the Distribution of the Seed Potato Fund* (James Hack Tuke, 1886). Various copies of *Muintir Acla*, the local Achill journal, were also useful. Other historical data was obtained from a number of other books, in particular *Achill* by Kenneth McNally (David & Charles, 1970), and *Achill: 5000 BC to 1900 AD* by Theresa McDonald (IAS Publications, 1992).

The National Archive (Bishop Street, Dublin) holds what records remain of the National School, as well as comprehensive microfilmed records of newspapers. They also contain the records of the Dept of the Taoiseach, within which occasional references are made to matters relating to piers, harbours and plans for rehousing the islanders on the mainland. Some maps are also here, as well as census details.

Other material may be viewed in The National Library of Ireland (Kildare Street, Dublin). Most Irish newspapers, going back many years, may be viewed here on microfilm. The famous photographic collection of William Lawrence is held here and may also be viewed on microfilm. Other photographic collections are held in the National Photographic Archive, Temple Bar. I am grateful to the staff of these institutions for their freely given help and patience. Also in Dublin, the staff of the Commissioners of Irish Lights (Lower Pembroke Street) were of great help in sourcing a number of the illustrations in the book, and providing comprehensive details about the construction and life of the lighthouse. I would mention George Ball and David Bedlow in particular in this regard. The staff of the Royal Irish Society were also most helpful in obtaining copies of old maps.

The most valuable and rewarding part of this research was the collection of personal accounts of life on Achillbeg - the recollections and memories of former inhabitants. I was fortunate to have met a number of people, mostly in the Achill area, but also further afield, who helped me in many ways. In no particular order, my thanks to the following: Tommy Johnston (Cloghmore) for initial moral support; and his son Edward who first introduced me to Achillbeg one sunny summer day in the early 1990s. Annie Corrigan (Achill Sound), Danny Kilbane (Dooniver), the late Anthony Kilbane (Ascaill) and Anthony Kilbane (Cloghmore) provided me with much detailed insight into past times in Achillbeg. Annie was the source of much information on old beliefs and customs and place names, and kindly gave permission for me to reproduce her painting of the area round the island school. Danny Kilbane told me a number of anecdotes and provided a vivid picture of what day to day life was like there. Danny was also of assistance in recording place names. The two Anthony Kilbanes provided details of life on the island and the general area as long ago as the 1920s - both gentlemen were in their 90s when interviewed. I am also grateful to Maureen Kilbane for arranging a meeting with Anthony Kilbane (Ascaill), who was able to give an account of life in the island school when Francis Power, the *Paorach*, was teaching there.

In several years' of research, I was unable to find any written reference to the island's old place names at all, as they had survived only in oral tradition. Consequently, the recording of these became a particularly important goal in itself. In this regard, I must single out Peg Masterson (Bunnacurry) who was of immeasurable help in locating and translating most of the more obscure place names on the island, and who allowed me access to much research that she has carried out on the subject, as well as lending photographs for inclusion, and providing further personal anecdotes. Peg also helped me to put together the jigsaw of which families were related.

Photographs of life in Achillbeg while inhabited are very rare. Peg Masterson and Joe Kilbane of Achill Sound were able to provide me with photographs of people in an island house and many anecdotes.

I would like to thank Maura Ryan of Achill Field School, Nick Pollard of Co. Wexford, and Mick Gibbons (Co. Galway) for their assistance in securing several photographs - in particular Mick's excellent aerial photograph of the western side of Achillbeg.

Michael McNamara, the last schoolteacher on the island, gave me an interesting insight into how life in the island was seen by an outsider in the 1960s - the last period when a permanent population lived there.

I would like to thank Nessa Kennedy, Maria Kilbane and the staff of St Finnians Home at Achill Sound for accommodating my visits to interview residents; Annie Corrigan in particular.

Judge Sean Gallagher (Cleveland, Ohio), the son of a former resident, provided details of his family history, and a film of islanders taken just after the final evacuation in 1967. I would also like to thank a number of members of the Corrigan, Gallagher and Kilbane families, now resident in the USA, Britain, and Australia, who took the time to correspond with me via email regarding aspects of their family history.

Theresa McDonald (Tullamore), and James Kilbane (Achill Sound) were the source of much interesting archaeological data, and information on the island's antiquities. James's comprehensive study (2001) of the Achill yawl (traditional design of local boat) was also of use; and is very interesting in its own right. His dissertation on local land use (*The Heritage of Mountain Grazing in Achill - The Booley, Land Use and Commonage*) was also very helpful. Barry Long, of the Geological Survey of Ireland, supplied me with details of geological surveys that have been conducted in the area in recent years.

Peter Mullowney of Newport Historical Society was able to provide me with some biographical details on Francis Power, the *Paorach*. I am grateful also to Adrian J. Ryder and Donagh O'Donaghue of Cólaiste Iónaid, Galway, and staff in De La Salle College, Waterford, who helped fill in several gaps in his biography.

John O'Shea (Dooagh), as always a source of much information relating to Achill, put me in touch with a number of sources of information. Many a night I left 'Marty Mac's' (The Annexe, Keel) in John's company with a beermat with somebody's phone number scribbled down on it! One of my pleasures in visiting Achill is always a visit to *Johnny's* - the Patten family bar in Derreens. Michael and Kathleen have been welcoming myself and my family for some years now, and Michael is very knowledgeable on the history of the area - more phone numbers on beer mats have left his premises in my pockets. I am also grateful to Michael for the loan of a map which is reproduced in the book, and also for the loan of a number of books (referred to in the text) which added various details of important information. Patten's bar is of interest within the story of Achillbeg, as it is here that the islanders did much of their socialising, and those former residents living in the area still do. I am grateful to a number of people I have met there, who have added to the rich litany of personal anecdotes - Johnny Gallagher, Paddy Kilbane and his wife Maria in particular. Paddy told me a number of tales of farming practices and social life in the 1950s, and provided me with transport to Achillbeg. I would also like to thank Tommy Gallagher (Cloghmore), Bernie Gallagher (Sraheens), Tommy Johnston, Jimmy Corrigan and Tom Corrigan for their suggestions on further sources of information. My thanks also to John Sweeney (Achill Sound) for assistance in tracing details of shipwrecks around the island's coast, aerial photos of the area, and matters relating to the island school.

Tony Daly (Dublin) and James Cahill (Castlebar) provided me with original information relating to the Coastguard Station. Without their help, I would have been unable to include any description of it whatsoever, as no official records are known to have survived. Brett Cunninghan of Belfast Coastguard introduced me to two colleagues who had carried out some research into the history of coastguard operations. I am grateful to Paul Lane, retired coastguard, Clyde, Scotland for further information.

Michael Patten (Derreens) and Noírín Gannon (Cloghmore) were of great help in proof-reading a first-draft manuscript. Noírín is a keen historian and well known local writer of poetry about Achill and life there, and she kindly gave me permission to reproduce her poetry from her book *Words from an Island*.

Donal Billings (Belfast), Maírtín McNicholas (Dublin), Fiachra Mac Gabhann (Partraí) and Noírín Gannon were of invaluable help in translating place names and narratives between Irish and English, and analysing their meanings.

I must also mention Mick and Nancy Golding of Dooagh, Ann Sweeney of Derreens, and Micheal and Una McLoughlin of the 'Ostán Óilean Ácla' (Achill Sound) who put up with my irregular appearances at short notice seeking bed and breakfast while on research trips. Their hospitality was greatly welcome; typical of Achill; and I will be back . . . !

To all mentioned above, and anyone else I have inadvertently forgotten, I am grateful for your contributions - but more so, your friendship.

To do justice to a project like this, lengthy research is necessary. Apart from being time consuming, it is costly. I am grateful to Kate Campbell (Northern Ireland Voluntary Trust), Selwyn Johnston (Enniskillen) and Deborah McArthur (Linenhall Library, Belfast) for assistance in seeking part funding for the project. The funding obtained was made possible by the Millennium Commission through a Millennium Award made by the Community Foundation Northern Ireland. This funding enabled the foregoing to be produced in this format.

Photographs are acknowledged in their captions: my thanks to all who gave permission for their photographs to be published.

My publisher, Oakwood Press, showed faith in the project from the outset, despite the fact that their main business is in books relating to transport history.

Last but not least, I must thank my wife Maureen for her tolerance while I was away on research trips - leaving her to cope on her own with our ever chaotic household. You see Maureen, I *did* get it finished, which means that all those brown envelopes full of papers in the study can now go permanently into the attic along with all the other stuff . . .

Go raibh mile maith agat!

Index

Trá Bó Deirge strand, 1993. When sea conditions permit, Achillbeg is a pleasant place for a day trip. This picture was taken on the author's first trip to Achillbeg. *Author*